PROFITS AND MORALITY

PROFITS
AND
MORALITY

Edited by Robin Cowan and Mario J. Rizzo

THE UNIVERSITY OF CHICAGO PRESS
Chicago and London

ROBIN COWAN is assistant professor of economics at the University of Western Ontario. MARIO J. RIZZO is associate professor of economics at New York University.

THE UNIVERSITY OF CHICAGO PRESS, CHICAGO 60637
THE UNIVERSITY OF CHICAGO PRESS, LTD., LONDON

© 1995 by The University of Chicago
All rights reserved. Published 1995
Printed in the United States of America

04 03 02 01 00 99 98 97 96 95   1 2 3 4 5
ISBN: 0-226-11632-8 (cloth)

A version of Chapter 5 appeared as Eric Mack, "Gauthier on Rights and Economic Rent," *Social Philosophy and Policy* 9, no. 1 (Autumn 1992): 171–200. Reprinted with the permission of Cambridge University Press.

Library of Congress Cataloging-in-Publication Data

Profits and morality / edited by Robin Cowan and Mario J. Rizzo.
   p.   cm.
   Includes bibliographical references and index.
   1. Profit—Moral and ethical aspects. I. Cowan, Robin.
II. Rizzo, Mario J.
HB601.P8854   1995
174'.4—dc20   94-21331
                                                                      CIP

Contents

Preface

In December 1990 Liberty Fund of Indianapolis, Indiana, sponsored a symposium on profits and morality in Montreal. Earlier versions of each of the papers in this volume, except the paper by Eric Mack, were presented at that symposium. We are indebted to Liberty Fund for its generosity, and to Charles King and David Lips (both of the Fund) for their expert guidance in organizing this conference. We are also grateful to the small group of other participants whose rigorous discussion and criticism at the symposium contributed immeasurably to the quality of the papers. In this regard we thank Jess Benhabib, Michael Bratman, Jules Coleman, Russell Hardin, David Kennedy, Loren Lomasky, Donald McCloskey, and Dan Usher. We are particularly indebted to Douglas Den Uyl for his masterful facilitation of the discussion as the symposium chairman. We would also like to acknowledge our gratitude to Geoffrey Huck of the University of Chicago Press for seeing this volume through many stages of review and revision.

Robin Cowan
Mario J. Rizzo

1 Fundamental Issues in the Justification of Profits

Robin Cowan and Mario J. Rizzo

On August 1, 1990, the day before Iraq invaded Kuwait, the benchmark price for crude oil, West Texas Intermediate, was $21; on August 6, five days later, the price was $28. Quarterly profits for the big oil companies rose dramatically in the third quarter of 1990, and shortly after the profit statements were released there was a public outcry. This outcry represents a not-uncommon feeling that somehow large profits, especially those of big business, are immoral or undeserved. Deciding whether this is in fact the case is a difficult task, for it involves not only theoretical investigation into the nature of morality as it relates to profits and profit making but also an empirical investigation of the nature of actual profits, such as those of oil companies, and how those profits relate to the moral theory. This essay provides an overview of issues related to profits and morality, more in the spirit of raising questions and problems than providing answers or solutions.

At the outset, it is important to distinguish between the notions of immoral, moral, and morally supererogatory. The distinction between moral and immoral exists in that morality forbids some actions and requires others, while simply allowing yet others. This is a distinction that is common, and, as a distinction, is well understood. An action is considered morally supererogatory if it is "above and beyond the call of duty." Morally supererogatory actions are not required by the strict application of moral rules, but are nonetheless considered morally good. The soldier who jumps on the grenade to save his fellows, or the pilot of a crashed airplane who gives his parka to one of the passengers, both perform supererogatory actions—they are not required by morality but are considered to be morally good things to do. This relates to the issue of profits in the following way. If beneficence, for example, is a supererogatory virtue, then walking past the beggar on the street may not violate the moral code, but it may not be the kind of action that deserves praise. It is not the sort of behavior that we would encourage, or that, perhaps, we would look for in our friends. Similarly, it may be that while declining to make profits out of the invasion of Kuwait is morally supererogatory, making profits instead does not break any moral strictures. If this is the case, we might not like the fact that the oil companies have made large profits, and we may think that beneficence or generosity would require that they did not, but at the same time we would find ourselves unable to apply moral censure on the basis of those profits. Absence of moral supererogation on the part of particular companies may be good reason for taking our business elsewhere, but it does not justify condemnation of their actions or profits as immoral.

The central focus of the papers in this book is not whether profits are supererogatory, even though this may be the issue that drives public sentiment. The focus here is, rather, on the other distinction, namely, whether profits and profit making are moral or immoral.

It is also important to note that arguments for or against the morality of profits can be overruled by other moral arguments. Even if profits are in general morally acceptable, there will be some profits, for example those due to theft, that we may wish to rule out immediately. Arguments for the morality of profits in general are likely to be overruled in cases where profits are obtained through activities that violate other parts of the moral code. Furthermore, it may be that profits in general are not immoral and thus that the makers of them are, prima facie, entitled to keep them, but that in order to right some grievous moral harm some profits must be confiscated. Exxon was forced to pay damages for spilling oil into Prince William Sound; some argue that taxes on profits are morally justified when used to alleviate extremes of poverty and degradation.

In cases like these, particularly the latter, what we observe is the conflict of two or more moral principles. This type of conflict is relatively common and can only be resolved by appeal to higher principles. We often find ourselves bound both by the duty to tell the truth and by the duty not to hurt peoples' feelings unnecessarily. Resolving that conflict in any particular case does not involve denying the existence of one of the prima facie duties. Whatever the resolution of such conflicts in the case of profits—either to leave the profits in the hands of their holders, or to right the other wrong—the first level case for the morality of profits is not affected. It would remain true that prima facie, making and keeping profits is acceptable. It is simply also true that not all prima facie duties or obligations are duties or obligations, all things considered.[1]

The subject that deals most explicitly with profits is economics. And for neoclassical economics, pursuit of profits, self-interested behavior, and use of the market to allocate goods are all tightly linked. The usual criterion by which economists judge outcomes of markets is Pareto optimality. An outcome is said to be Pareto optimal if no one's utility can be increased without decreasing someone else's; suboptimality implies that it is possible to increase one per-

1. See Ross (1930) on the distinction between prima facie duties and duties all things considered.

son's utility and not decrease another's.[2] Pareto optimality emerges as a criterion through concern with one aspect of utilitarianism, namely, the need to compare (in order to add up) the utilities of different individuals. Economists are generally uncomfortable with interpersonal utility comparisons, but tend to believe that utilities of individuals are nonetheless central to the rankings of various social outcomes. Economics shares with utilitarianism the view that, all else equal, increasing the welfare of one individual is morally desirable. This is the Pareto criterion. Economics tends to be unwilling to take the next step, however, which demands the maximization of the (weighted) sum of utilities.[3]

Using the Pareto criterion, economists believe the market to be a very good mechanism for allocating goods and services. Indeed, under certain conditions, any market allocation is Pareto optimal. A common concern with this criterion, though, has to do with rights. While a market system presupposes certain "rights," such as property rights, for a Paretian, these rights are purely instrumental. If there were a way to get to Pareto optimality without them (or without markets), these rights would not exist. These are not the sort of rights that a rights theorist thinks of. Traditional economics, then, insofar as it treats and defends the morality of profits, presupposes a particular moral view, a weakened utilitarianism, to which many moral philosophers have objected. (See text below.) Because the moral theory underlying the Pareto criterion is often found lacking, a discussion of the moral status of profits must look beyond traditional economics. Economics will, however, give important insights into the nature of profits themselves, and to this we now turn.

TYPES OF PROFITS

Economists usually identify several different types of profits.

Normal Profits

Normal profits are the return to the owner of a firm that operates in a perfectly competitive market, in long-run equilibrium. In a perfectly competitive market, when a firm maximizes profits, each factor of production will receive a per unit payment exactly equal to what it produces at the margin. The market price, or the cost of a factor, is equal to the value of its marginal

---

2. When goods are infinitely divisible this is sometimes stated as there being opportunity to make everyone better off, hurting no one. To see the equivalence of making one person better off and making all better off, simply take the winnings of the winner and divide it among all those who did not win. Infinite divisibility ensures that all can gain.

3. This paragraph contains many generalizations which obviously do not apply to all economists. Nevertheless, it is probably a fair description of the prevailing view, especially as presented in the textbooks.

product. Thus the return to capital, what it produces, is exactly equal to its opportunity cost, what its owner could receive in the next most profitable use, that is, in investing it at the market rate. When firms are earning normal profits, net *economic* return is zero, since revenues exactly equal costs, where costs include the cost of capital, which is the market rental rate of capital.

Supernormal Profits

These are profits in excess of normal profits and occur when revenues exceed costs, again including the cost of capital. In principle, supernormal profits cannot exist in perfectly competitive markets. If some firm were making supernormal profits, new firms would enter the market, thus bidding down the price of the output and bidding up the cost of capital until there was no incentive to enter. There is no incentive to enter when profits in this market are equal to those in other markets, that is, when profits are normal. Supernormal profits are often identified with monopoly profits.

Rents

Rents are the returns to ownership and accrue when an agent owns a good that has a special characteristic which, through no effort of the agent, is valuable.[4] Professional athletes or musicians are often given as examples of recipients of rents, but the owner of a quota to import a good or a quota to produce a quantity of milk, for example, may also be receiving rents. Typically in these cases, the quota or skill is not enough to generate income; it must be accompanied, in the musician's case, with a considerable amount of practice. It is true, though, that for most people no amount of practice will produce piano playing of the quality produced by Alfred Brendel. Some of Brendel's income is a return on the investment he has made through practice, but some of it, the part due to his special physical and mental abilities which most of us are incapable of supplying, is rent.

While this list exhausts the types of profits that economists usually define and discuss formally, there are two other types (which may be normal, supernormal, or rents) which it is appropriate to distinguish in a discussion of profits and morality.

Profits from Immoral Activities

There are members of our societies who have made considerable profits from extortion, selling what is euphemistically known as protection. On the

---

4. In discussions of rents in the context of ethics, examples of rent-producing goods are typically of the type given here, but it may be simply that the ''special characteristic'' is that the good has a vertical supply or demand curve.

face of it, it seems clear that profits from immoral activities must themselves be immoral. Any justification of the morality of profits that uses a deontological ethical starting point almost certainly rules out these sorts of activities.[5] A teleological, or consequentialist, ethics, though, may open the door for these sorts of profits (see Cooter and Gordley, this vol.). In principle, if the profits are used for sufficiently good works, or if the social system that encourages profit seeking has sufficiently good long-run effects, profits may thereby become morally acceptable. A railroad, perhaps, steals land from farmers. One result of this action is that costs of construction of the line are low and, consequently, costs of moving freight on this railroad are also low. This clearly will have a benefit to many actors in the economy. If these benefits are large enough, a purely consequentialist theory will judge the profits to be morally acceptable, since they were the result of an action that itself had overall good effects. Allowing profits from apparently immoral activities in by the back door, so to speak, is intuitively unappealing perhaps, but it is a possibility that arises when the underlying moral theory is consequentialist in nature.

Windfall Profits

Windfall profits arise purely from changes in external circumstances. The OPEC oil embargo of 1974 presents an example. Immediately following this event, the value of oil held by oil companies increased dramatically, through no efforts of their own, and presumably to their complete surprise. Had the oil companies made no changes in their oil-selling plans, with a pricing strategy described as charging what the market will bear, they still would have made large profits that were directly attributable to OPEC's actions. It is true that the profits that were made followed some decisions to sell the oil, but it seems completely unreasonable to ascribe *all* those profits to the entrepreneurial acumen involved in selling oil at higher prices.[6] It is important to notice that windfall profits are different from speculative profits. Speculative profits are made when a gamble pays off; in this case, the profit maker performed an action precisely in order to make profits if some specified event occurs. That

5. In a deontological ethical theory acts are good or bad in and of themselves, due to some characteristic they have or fail to have. Contrary to the view of consequentialist theories, the goodness of an action is not entirely dependent on the nonmoral goodness or badness it produces. Kirzner and Narveson are explicit that their theories rule out profits from immoral activities.

6. This may be a case of an event with two causes. The higher profits were caused both by OPEC's actions and by the decision of the oil company to sell its oil at a new, higher price. The claim here is that while the decision maker's actions are clearly responsible for determining exactly how much more profit the company makes, it is also true that the action of OPEC "sets the ball in motion" and so deserves to be considered a major cause of the higher profits.

it comes about is expected, though the expectation is generally probabilistic. Not so with windfall profits—the event causing the profits is a complete surprise to the profit maker.

PROFITS FOR AND AGAINST

Arguments about the morality of profits are often not explicit but are rather part of larger arguments for or against economic or political systems (especially the decentralized market system), or for or against particular ethical structures. This is true especially of arguments against the morality of profits, which tend to be couched in terms of attacks on arguments for profits or free markets.

Efficiency

For economists, arguments about profits are tied up in arguments about economic efficiency. The ethical criterion used in modern welfare economics is a weakened form of utilitarianism, namely, Pareto efficiency. Pareto efficient allocations are considered to be good, and the closer to Pareto efficiency, the better. Pareto improvements are morally desirable, and, until Pareto efficiency is reached, the outcome is not considered morally acceptable. Pareto efficiency is thought to be necessary for moral acceptability, since in an inefficient allocation, as mentioned earlier, at least one person's utility could be increased without decreasing anyone else's. Economists, therefore, have been concerned with the conditions under which Pareto efficiency will obtain.

A common argument, often referred to as an efficiency argument, is that the pursuit of profits regulates an economy in such a way that it can never stray far from efficient allocations. When an inefficiency exists (for example, a shortage of some good), a reallocation of productive resources (to produce less of a good in surplus and more of the good in shortage) will be a Pareto improvement. In a market economy the existence of such an inefficiency typically indicates a profit opportunity. The alert entrepreneur, seeing the opportunity, performs the needed reallocation of resources, which not only makes profits for him but also generates an ethically superior final outcome, assuming all agents consume both goods. Profits, then, are central to the process whereby Pareto efficient outcomes are achieved.

Sufficient versus Necessary Conditions for Moral Acceptability

This line of argument is attacked in several ways. First, while Pareto efficiency may be necessary, it is not sufficient for a morally acceptable outcome. There are many possible Pareto efficient outcomes in which an economy can find itself. An allocation in which one person owns everything, assuming that he is not sated, is Pareto efficient. Pareto efficiency is consistent with extremes of destitution, and thus the criterion is not enough. Economists are aware of this and have shown that, with the appropriate initial redistribution of resources, any particular Pareto efficient outcome that is desired on moral grounds can be supported as the outcome of a market economy. They can then argue that pursuit of profits, perhaps with some initial redistribution of resources, will generate ethically good outcomes. This raises another objection though. The technical assumptions about production technology and people's preferences required to get these results are very strict and are unlikely to be met in the world. Furthermore, deciding how much each agent should contribute or receive in the redistribution demands considerable knowledge about people's preferences, but it is likely to be impossible to entice people to provide this information truthfully. This is an issue of incentive compatibility in the transfer mechanism. Thus, it is unclear exactly what force these arguments about the merits of markets and the pursuit of profits have (see Hammond, this vol.).

Pareto Optimality and Utilitarianism

A second type of attack on the efficiency argument sketched above focuses on the moral criterion. As a moral theory, utilitarianism, which underlies the Pareto criterion, is often thought to have failings that simply cannot be ignored. Because of the consequentialist nature of the criterion, the theory has extreme difficulty coping with rights as generally understood. It could be, for example, that by confiscating some property from which a person gets no utility, and redistributing it to another, we can generate a Pareto improvement.[7] Such a confiscation, though, would be a violation of property rights and would violate any rights against coercion in general. On the other hand, some argue, leaving the good in the possession of the original owner may be the source of a violation of (positive) basic rights to food and shelter. Though an allocation may be Pareto optimal, it can involve a morally unacceptable amount of destitution. Redistribution to alleviate this suffering would not in general be a Pareto improvement and, therefore, is not justifiable under the Pareto criterion.[8] Utilitarianism, and thus the Pareto criterion, fail to consider aspects of morality that many feel are very important.

7. It is more difficult to create examples of this sort that argue against the Pareto criterion than against utilitarianism, since if the original owner gets any utility, however small, from the good, redistribution (without side payments) will not be Pareto improving, even though it may have an enormous positive impact on total utility.

8. This principle appears in Rawls as his difference principle applied to primary goods. See also Dworkin (1978), Goodin (1985), and Sen (1985b).

Only in special cases will the efficiency argument hold, which raises questions about its moral relevance. But even when the argument is relevant, problems arise from the consequentialist nature of the underlying moral theory.[9] The arguments given by standard economics in defense of profits are thus weak at best.

Evolutionary Arguments

A related, though distinct, type of consequentialist argument for profits takes place at a different level. It concerns the ability of a moral system to adapt to changes in the world. New technologies for human reproduction have generated a significant amount of ethical debate in the last decade or so. How our moral system will eventually respond is unknown, but it will have to respond somehow. Given that we live in a world in which this sort of "external" change takes place, it is important that our moral system be able to respond without completely breaking down. Thus an important criterion by which we must judge a moral system is its adaptability.

Some argue that the market system is very flexible and allows a maximum freedom of choice of action, at least in the economic realm. Experimentation with new types of behavior (new types of production, or new types of contracts, for example) is relatively easy. Ease of experimentation encourages a fluidity in the structure of the economy and so in the social structures surrounding it. Profits, then, are valuable not in that they maximize total utility or wealth, though they may do so, but rather in that profit seeking is the type of behavior that will cause the evolution of the moral system. On the other hand, the logical extreme of flexibility in the moral system is moral anarchy. If evolution comes about through experimentation, then having many different moral standards in a society is a good thing. The existence of any moral code can, in principle at least, be justified as a contributor to the future good of society because it challenges ingrained, and possibly pernicious, behavior, thereby contributing to moral evolution. If moral anarchy would not be a good thing, this type of argument for profits must argue that profit-seeking behavior does not lead to it.[10] Finally, the strongest possible version of this argument would also have to show that economic systems that do not encourage profit-

9. See Hammond, this volume, for a more detailed and thorough development of these arguments.

10. See R. C. O. Matthews (1981) for an argument that for efficient operation of the market system, the prevailing moral code must contain strictures against some particular types of behavior and encouragement of others. Spencer argues (1978, p. 76) that for this sort of evolution to be effective in improving moral codes, consequences of actions must be felt by the actors.

seeking behavior lack precisely the flexibility that it provides, and have no other way of encouraging moral evolution.

Both of the arguments just considered have been embedded in a consequentialist moral view. The argument to which we turn now, the free exchange justification of profits, is explicitly nonconsequentialist, employing a deontological moral theory.

Rights and Free Exchange

Concern with rights, while a source of argument against standard efficiency defenses of profits, is itself a source of a different defense. Property rights, sometimes seen as a necessary extension of rights against coercion, will almost certainly include the right to transfer (see Nozick 1974). When property rights exist, then, there seems to be a strong case for the moral acceptability of profits arising from free exchange. If two parties agree to an exchange in which there is no coercion (which implies that they both expect to be better off after the transaction), and in which there are no third-party effects, why should anyone object to it on moral grounds? On what grounds could it be forbidden? One response is that some such transfers could be forbidden in order ''to induce a pattern of exchanges that is better on the whole'' (Gibbard 1985, p. 25). Here we see a conflict between consequentialism and deontology. If consequences matter at all, it may be that by preventing some voluntary transactions we can produce another set of transactions that generates an outcome that is superior (on non-Paretian grounds). Certainly the law tries to prevent some transactions—indentured servitude, or voluntary slavery, for example.[11]

The Nature of Property Rights

Gibbard also argues that property rights, on which the free exchange justification rests heavily, are a complex social institution under which an allocation of resources is, in essence, a set of restrictions on members of society. My owning something places restrictions on what you can do to, or with, it. When two agents trade goods, they are simply changing to a new set of restrictions on who can do what to the goods they trade. Since the essence of property rights, on Gibbard's analysis, is to prohibit certain ways of changing these restrictions (for example, theft or extortion are not acceptable ways to change

---

11. Blackorby and Donaldson (1988) argue that in a world in which individuals and the government all have incomplete information, it may be possible to achieve ethically desirable outcomes only by bypassing the market mechanism. They argue further that rationing can be preferable to taxes and subsidies in maximizing utility subject to the constraint of, for example, an ethically acceptable distribution of medical care. (See also Hammond 1987.)

restrictions on who can do what to the good), why not prohibit others? Gibbard suggests that the reason we restrict certain exchanges of labor—those that take place for wages less than the minimum wages—is to generate more exchanges that take place above the minimum wage. The moral acceptability of profits from free exchange is predicated upon a certain institution of property rights. Other institutions could exist, though, so this one must be justified. How else but by appeal to consequences?[12]

What Is Free Exchange?

If Gibbard's charge can be parried, there is another attack that is sometimes leveled, this one on a more procedural level. What, exactly, does "free exchange" mean, and how prevalent is it? This line of attack has several branches. First, free exchange is often thought to include full knowledge and absence of coercion. But how much must a buyer or a seller disclose before being guilty of fraud? With full disclosure, would any exchanges take place? If the buyer is buying to take advantage of a profit opportunity, if that is disclosed, the seller will not sell but rather make the profits himself. Demanding full disclosure removes much of the incentive to trade, not to mention making most contracts impossible to write. Something short of full disclosure is necessary. But just how short is far from obvious.[13] Second, what counts as coercion? If a landlord offers to rent a piece of land only on the condition that the tenant buy seed from him (at inflated prices), does this count as coercion in the seed transaction? Does it matter if the tenant has no other source of livelihood, but perhaps another source of seed? Finally, to what extent are transactions free of third-party effects. Technological externalities, such as the production of pollution, are acknowledged as violating free exchange. When two parties trade, and in doing so create pollution, a third party involuntarily becomes party to the transaction. This is not denied, and the free exchange justification would rule out profits from such transactions. It may be, though, that pecuniary externalities constitute third-party effects from a moral point of view.[14] If my buying a particular house prevents you from buying it, is that a third-party effect? Concerns about pecuniary externalities lead procedural (free exchange) theories of justice, and some contractarian theories, to demand provisos on original acquisition. There may be no technological externalities involved, but when one shipwrecked sailor appropriates

12. See Nozick (1974), for example, for an attempted justification.
13. See Kronman (1978) for a discussion of this problem.
14. See Hausman (1992) for an argument that pecuniary externalities are pervasive and morally significant.

the only can opener, the other, can-holding sailors suffer fairly severe pecuniary externalities. (This can be seen as a pecuniary externality in that the holder of the can opener is able to drive down the "price" of the resources held by the other sailors by threatening to refuse to let them use the can opener.) This is the sort of situation that many of the provisos seek to rule out.[15]

Provisos on Initial Acquisition

The free exchange justification is strongest when both parties to a transaction have just title to the goods being traded. Intuitions are strong that the profits made by selling stolen goods are morally unacceptable. Thus, it is important that we ground the exchange process on just beginnings. Provisos added to prevent illegitimate beginnings to the free exchange process cannot be justified on procedural grounds though. They rule out certain starting points a priori. But if reasons exist for ruling out original allocations a priori, why cannot similar reasons be applied to intermediate or even final allocations? The response that later positions are arrived at through free exchange has been accused of circularity (see Reiman 1981).

Original acquisition, we should note, can take place at any time: economies are privatized, new goods are invented, and new ways of assigning property rights are discovered. We tend to think of physical goods as the things being acquired, but in fact the class at issue is the class of economically valuable things. This may include relatively abstract things like monopoly power. There can obviously be original acquisition of monopoly power, and this, by definition, will not leave as good and as much for the rest.[16] If acquisition of monopoly power is ruled out, then it seems that acquisition of market power should be ruled out as well. Transactions having pecuniary externalities are now in trouble. What this line of argument suggests is that if restrictions on original acquisitions are necessary to make the free exchange justification work, we may have to treat pecuniary externalities the same way as technological externalities. The upshot would seem to be that only normal profits can be justified by free exchange.

If the arguments above are correct, then the free exchange justification,

15. See, for example, Locke (1980) or Gauthier (1986). Locke's proviso states that an initial acquisition is acceptable, provided that in the acquisition of the good the acquirer leaves for his neighbor "as good, and as large a possession (after the other had taken out his) as before it was appropriated" (p. 22). Put another way, there must be "still enough, and as good left; and more than the yet unprovided for could use" (p. 21).

16. Nozick (1974) states that cornering the market for life necessities (like insulin), even through free exchange, is ruled out by his version of the proviso. It is difficult to see why his arguments do not apply to life-*enhancing* goods as well.

when Lockean-type provisos on original acquisition are added, leads us to the following position. If the accumulation of market power is morally unaccept-able, then all agents are price takers, and so none can change the price. Thus either we are in, and have always been in perfectly competitive equilibrium, with only normal profits being earned, or we must continue to live in a world of economic maladjustment, since it is morally unacceptable to acquire the power to change prices.

These concerns about the free exchange justification do not make an argu-ment, but they do suggest that free exchange, though elegant in its simplicity, must take account of deep and perhaps troublesome issues.

Fair Exchange

Another objection to the free exchange justification is that it is too simple. Free exchange, it is sometimes claimed, is not necessarily fair exchange. "Fairness involves not simply a gain to both sides from a trade, but also an equitable distribution of the gains" (Roemer 1988, p. 59). Every transaction involves a surplus—the buyer pays less than the good is worth to him, and the seller receives more than it is worth to him; otherwise there is no incentive to trade. Thus there is a surplus of "worth" created by a trade, which will be distributed between buyer and seller.[17] Experiments performed by economists and psychologists suggest that considerations of how the surplus is distributed are important in subjects' evaluation of whether or not a trade should take place. Subjects are unwilling to allow exchanges in which one party gets too much of the surplus, even if refusing the exchange makes oneself materially worse off. It is difficult, of course, to decide whether the subjects were moti-vated by moral consideration or by something else, but the results of the experiments fit well with intuitive notions of fair trade.[18]

More generally, it is often argued that for free exchange, and the distribu-tion of surplus that goes with it, to be fair the exchanging parties must some-how be "equally situated" (Hardin 1988, p. 133–34). Often, though, parties are not equally situated in the relevant sense, and this causes what appear to be inequitable distributions of the surplus. It is sometimes claimed that free exchange can, and often does, lead to situations in which one party has little choice in whether to make the exchange or not. When a worker either works or starves, he is in a weak position from which to bargain over wages if the potential employers have any monopsony power. In situations like this, it is

17. We refer here to "pure surplus," which arises simply from differential valuations of a good.
18. See Frank (1988) for a discussion of some of these experiments.

reasonable to expect that because the two parties are differently situated—one needs the exchange and the other does not—the employer would get the lion's share of any surplus.[19] More extreme examples might be of the following sort: A very sick (but not terminally ill) person can be saved by use of a drug owned by someone who is well and extremely unlikely to contract the disease. Assume that the drug was delivered fortuitously to the latter. The former is clearly willing to pay a very high price to obtain the drug, and suppose he does so. Here, the exchange is free, exhibits no coercion, and both parties benefit from it. On the face of it, though, one can see why the gains from trade appear to be unfairly distributed. On the part of the buyer, a high price was paid for something valuable—good health. But on the part of the seller, a high price was obtained from something of very little use value—a drug he was unlikely to use (and perhaps would never use, and is thus of no value, if he is guaranteed never to get the disease). Intuitions that arise in cases like these argue that free exchange is not enough to guarantee fair exchange; something more is needed. Often, the market takes care of this problem by providing substitutes for the drug so that the seller cannot demand such a high price. In cases of monopoly buying or selling, or with thin markets in general, it is more difficult to make this kind of defense work. This having been said, it has proved extremely difficult to pin down what more is needed to make free exchange fair. While many have attacked the free exchange justification on grounds of fairness, attempts to lay out what, exactly, a fair exchange is have had difficulties of their own.

Marxian attacks on the moral status of profits take a different form and point to another problem with which the free exchange justification must deal. The fundamental Marxist theorem states that exploitation exists if, and only if, profits are positive.[20] It is not the case, however, that every instance of exploitation is unjust. "The injustice of an exploitative allocation depends upon the initial distribution [of productive assets]" (Roemer 1988, p. 57). Exploitation can exist if there is inequality in the distribution of capital holdings. Whether the exploitation that follows is just or unjust depends how the initial distribution came about. If it came about through a process considered immoral, then the exploitation (and so the profit that comes with it) that follows

19. See Reiman (1981) for a development of this argument and an attack on Nozick's response to it.

20. An input is said to be exploited when the payments it receives are less than would be necessary to reproduce itself. Roemer (1988) notes that "exploitation" is an unfortunate word, as it comes loaded with ethical baggage whereas it is in fact a technical term. He also notes that not only labor but any input good can be exploited.

will be immoral. The crucial questions are two: In general, how has the unequal distribution of capital come about? Is this process immoral?

Differential Links between Profit and Holder

The importance of the initial distribution from which exchanges take place is widely acknowledged. Thus while it may be that the disposition of justly owned assets (where all parties to the transaction have entered voluntarily) generates morally acceptable profits, it does leave the problem of how just ownership comes about in the first place.[21] Kirzner points to the common intuition that "in order for an individual to have a just claim to a certain holding, he must be able, in principle, to establish some differential link to that holding that sets him significantly apart from others" (1989, p. 136). Any old link will not do though—being the only person to have stolen a particular object is not the kind of link we want. There are two strong suggestions for the kinds of links we believe generate acceptable moral claims to an object: that the owner have worked for it, or that the owner have found or discovered it. Both of these types of links have been used as moral justifications of profits.

Sweat of the Brow

P. T. Bauer, while not defending profits per se but rather a more general inequality of income distribution, states that on the whole incomes are earned. What people own or receive they have worked for. Incomes are returns to factors of production and are thus simply what a particular factor has produced. This might be called the "sweat of the brow" justification of profits; if an agent works hard to produce something, and in selling that thing makes a profit, surely he is entitled to the profit, he deserves it, and justice demands that he get it. This intuition is strongest when imagining Robinson Crusoe alone on his island, working by himself with tools that he made. Most production, however, is joint. It involves many different factors and typically many different agents. It is not possible, in this situation, to determine how much of the total production should be ascribed to each factor. The marginal calculus used by economists to determine profit-maximizing allocations states that the per unit payment to an input should be set equal to the marginal product of that input. Adding one more unit of labor, for example, should increase output (in value) equal to the wage paid to that additional unit. The additional labor cannot be said to produce that output, though, for the marginal product presup-

21. Here Nozick's strong demand that the entire history of an asset, and the inputs that went into producing it, be untainted is often weakened in favor of a more intuitive notion that demands only an examination of relatively recent history; historical wrongs cannot be righted.

poses some amount of capital (and perhaps other inputs) which is also contributing to production. While intuitions about sweat of the brow justifications are strong, they run into trouble in the face of sorting out exactly who produced what, when production is joint.

Creation or Discovery

The second type of significant link between owner and object mentioned above was one of creation or discovery. The creator of an object certainly seems to have a very strong claim to ownership. Similarly, a person who discovers something, assuming this discovery is *de novo*—there are no previous claims to it—has what appears to be a very strong moral claim to the object. That this principle applies explicitly to pure profits has been argued by Kirzner (see Kirzner, this vol.). Pure profits arise when an alert entrepreneur discovers a profit opportunity and acts on it. In making this discovery he is, in effect, creating an economically valuable commodity where none before existed.[22]

Two things are worth pointing out in response to this line of argument. First, this is not merely the sweat-of-the-brow justification in a different guise, though there may be an element of sweat of the brow in the entrepreneur's implementation of the opportunity. Second, ideas from action theory, with its emphasis on the intentions of agents, suggest new insights into the nature of this justification of profits.

Windfall profits are often thought to be morally different from other profits because of the weakness of the link between windfall profits and their owners. These profits are neither the result of working for them, nor the result of speculative investments. The link between owner and profits seems to be morally weak and not enough to provide a strong justification for ownership.[23] A link between object and owner is considered strongest when the owner is the primary source of actions undertaken in order to secure the existence of the object. The owner is the cause of the existence of the object. Another strong link exists when the rightful owner deliberately gives the object (either as a gift or in a trade) to a new owner.[24] Windfall profits, of course, have neither

22. Clearly he is not involved in the physical creation of goods out of nothing, but he is involved in transforming a noneconomic item into an economic one and, depending on the metaphor, either adding a new object to the economic world, or adding to an object a property—that of being economically valued—that it did not have before.

23. It may be, of course, that ownership comes by default—no one else has a claim to the profits—but this could not be called a strong claim to ownership.

24. There is some debate about whether this is an acceptable source of a link when the gift is an inheritance.

of these features. Oil companies were not the cause of the OPEC oil embargo (which caused a world shortage, causing prices to rise), nor were the actions of OPEC deliberately aimed at raising the profits of the oil companies. Thus one might feel that the claims of the oil companies to these profits are weak.

Profits from apparently entrepreneurial activities can be divided in two ways. Consider profits arising from the purchase of a piece of land which increases in value. Under the first division these profits can be intentional, where the expectation of the profit motivated the purchase; unintentional, where the profits, while expected, did not motivate the purchase; or accidental, where the profits were a complete surprise. Accidental profits have the features of windfalls discussed above, and perhaps should be characterized as such, even though they followed the action of the entrepreneur. The different moral implications of intentional and unintentional actions have been widely discussed, both in the ethics literature and in the literature on tort law. Briefly, while agents must take responsibility or credit for unintentional consequences of their actions, the moral link between agent and consequence is stronger when the consequence motivates the action than when it does not.[25] It would seem to follow that the link generating the moral claim of an agent to his profit is stronger when the profit motivates the action than when it does not.

The second division focuses on an agent's beliefs about how the profits will come about, and so it does not apply to accidental profits. Suppose the agent expects the value of the land to increase because a shopping mall will be built nearby. If the mall is built, the projected causal chain materializes and profits are made. But suppose that the mall is not built; a housing development on the other side of the land is built instead. The entrepreneur's projection of the causal sequence is incorrect, but profits emerge nonetheless.[26]

That this second distinction may be morally relevant can be seen by examining the nature of discovery and what is discovered. What entrepreneurs discover is not simply a profit opportunity per se but rather a fact or facts about the world—a potential sequence of events or causal chain at the end of which is a pot of gold. Discovery does give claims, it is true, but only to that which is discovered—the pot at the end of this particular chain. When the shopping mall is not built, though, that causal chain is broken, and profits associated with that chain do not materialize. To the good fortune of our agent, another

25. Clearly, an agent is not legally or morally responsible for *every* unintentional consequence of his actions. Some consequences are simply too far removed. For a discussion of this point see Hart and Honoré (1985, pp. 259–84).

26. This distinction among types of entrepreneurial intentions is due to Michael Bratman in discussion.

one does, but not one that he can claim to have discovered. The sequence of events leading to his profits, then, has two aspects. First, that of a failed investment; what the entrepreneur expected to happen fails to happen—the expected shopping mall does not materialize. But the second aspect is that of a windfall. A set of events quite different from those expected took place, and from these events profits arose. The profits in this case are like those that arose from owning oil on the day of the OPEC embargo, there was no other party whose goal it was to give profits to the maker of them, and the cause of the profits was unexpected and unplanned-for by the maker of them. A significant part of the cause of these profits was ''pure luck.''

These distinctions about the types of profits that follow what are normally called entrepreneurial actions suggest that discovery as a source of justification for profits must be used carefully.[27] The intentions of the entrepreneur may be important, but his beliefs are also very important. Profits that follow apparently entrepreneurial actions may in fact be windfalls, in which case the claims of the entrepreneur to those profits are significantly weaker.

This summary of arguments attempting to justify profits is exhaustive neither in the sense of considering all possible positions from which to argue, nor in the sense of considering all possible arguments for or against these positions. It does, nonetheless, indicate that a wide variety of ethical starting points can be used to argue for the moral acceptability of profits and profit making, and that an equally wide variety of arguments can be deployed on the other side. As was suggested above, many arguments about the moral status of profits are by-products of arguments about more general issues. The papers in this collection address the general issue of the moral status of profits explicitly, and in doing so they address many of the arguments described here.

The Papers in This Collection

The moral status of profits is a complex issue, understanding of which demands examination both of profits and of aspects of morality. All of the chapters in this volume deal explicitly with profits and morality but do so from different points of view. Because the issue is complex, different chapters focus attention on different aspects of it. Some have little to say explicitly about ethical theory but much to say about the nature of profits, and some the reverse.

The chapters by Kirzner and Hammond do not attempt any innovations in ethical theory. They are both discussions of profits and the way profits originate

---

27. One should note, of course, that the importance of these distinctions may be different depending on whether one is considering legal or policy aspects of profits, or whether one is considering fundamental moral justification.

and function. The chapters by Narveson, Mack, and Cooter and Gordley, by contrast, are explicitly about ethics. These take questions about profits as answered and argue for various ethical views, showing how profits fit into these views.

The chapters that focus on profits, by Kirzner and Hammond, employ different ethical positions. Kirzner uses the finders-keepers rule as his guiding principle, while Hammond uses a modified Pareto principle. Within the chapters that focus on ethics there is similar variety, Narveson building a deontological theory, Mack making an argument about contractarianism (by appeal to rights), and Cooter and Gordley making a utilitarian argument. The collection of papers, then, covers a wide range of starting points for this discussion.

Kirzner and Hammond both simply state an ethical position and argue about how profits fit into this position. For Kirzner, the position, or guiding ethical principle, is the finders-keepers rule. Concerned with the creation of a morally significant link between entrepreneur and profit, Kirzner suggests that it is intuitively appealing that the creator of an object take moral responsibility (either praise or blame, reward or punishment) for it, and that this is enough to create a differential link and so confer ownership. This link formed by creation or discovery corresponds to what is colloquially known as finders-keepers. Kirzner argues that profits, when properly understood, should be seen as the creation of a new object. He argues not for finders-keepers but rather that finders-keepers applies to pure profits, when profits are not simply returns to factors of production.

The ethical position adopted by Hammond is the Pareto principle, but to this general principle Hammond adds the proviso that there not be extremes of poverty and degradation. Using this as his ethical criterion, Hammond asks what economic theory tells us about the pursuit of profits (and other rewards) as a means of promoting ethically acceptable outcomes. Hammond raises objections, some of them suggested above, to the blind application of efficiency arguments in order to justify profits morally. Even using the ethical principle common to standard welfare economics, Hammond argues that only in very special cases will the pursuit of profits lead to the ethically desired outcome.

Both Kirzner and Hammond argue about the nature and function of profits, but they use different ethical yardsticks and arrive at different conclusions about the precise status of profits. Both acknowledge, though, that their conclusions are only as strong as the ethical premises on which they are based.

Narveson, Mack, and Cooter and Gordley all employ simple definitions of profits and raise different ethical criteria by which to judge them. These three chapters are not intended to offer insights into the (nonmoral) nature or function of profits; they are explicitly about ethics. In Narveson's paper, profits are defined as the net monetary gain from free, voluntary exchange, and encompass all of the types described above with the exception of profits from immoral activities. His moral criterion is desert, and Narveson asks whether profits are morally deserved. To address this question, the paper includes a detailed examination of the nature of desert. This examination concludes that the place of the bestower of the thing deserved is often neglected in discussions of desert, but that this role is an important one. Disposition of justly owned assets, or free exchange, occurs when each party to the exchange believes that trading with the other will further his own ends, and thus that the other deserves his custom. When custom is deserved, so are the profits arising from it. When trade is viewed this way, and the role of the "customer" is acknowledged, the conclusion that profits are deserved follows.

From a rights-based position, Mack argues that agents who earn economic rents are morally entitled to keep them. Mack attacks here a position defended by Gauthier, namely, that the confiscation of rents—payments derived purely from ownership—is morally justified. Gauthier arrives at this conclusion through a distinction between "rights in" and "rights to" natural endowments. If this distinction stands, then confiscation of rents (but not payments for services rendered) is morally justifiable as part of the social contract. After describing an internal inconsistency in Gauthier's account, Mack argues that this distinction between rights in and rights to, at least when applied to one's natural endowments, cannot hold. It follows, then, that rents are the rightful property of their owner.

The chapter by Cooter and Gordley, while similar to those of Narveson and Mack in arguing about ethics, differs in that it adopts a more consequentialist morality. Here Cooter and Gordley argue for the existence of "merit goods" and model their existence as a form of externality. Profits here are defined as pure rents and are significant in the model as a means of lowering the relative prices of merit goods: They are used, for example, to endow libraries and universities and similarly subsidize other merit goods. Profits attain moral acceptability, then, by the way they are used, that is, by encouraging the production and consumption of socially valuable goods.

Each of the papers attacks the issue of the morality of profits from a different starting point and a different perspective. The collection does not exhaust all of the possible points of entry to the problem, but it does represent a very broad spectrum. Because each chapter focuses its attention narrowly on a particular issue, the general applicability of each chapter's conclusions are dependent on some issues not discussed. (Each conclusion has its own "To the extent that . . ." clause.) Some of the issues not directly addressed here are empirical (Do profits support merit goods? Are profits the result of free exchange?), and some are theoretical (What counts as free exchange? Is utilitarianism, with the "nonextremes" proviso, an acceptable moral theory? Is finders-keepers more than just intuitively plausible? Are rights-based moral theories workable?). Many of these issues have been extensively discussed elsewhere, and the specific conclusions of each chapter about the morality of profits may rise or fall with the resolutions of these other questions. In the course of coming to their conclusions, though, the papers examine many important issues which must be addressed in any attempt to understand the moral status of profits.

REFERENCES

Arnold, N. Scott. 1987. "Why Profits Are Deserved." *Ethics* 97 (January 1987).

Arrow, Kenneth J. 1978. "Nozick's Entitlement Theory of Justice." *Philosophia* 7.

Bauer, P. T. 1981. *Equality, the Third World, and Economic Delusion.* London: Weidenfeld and Nicolson.

Bauer, P. T., and A. K. Sen. 1982. "Just Deserts: An Exchange." *New York Review of Books,* June 10.

Blackorby, C., and D. Donaldson. 1988. "Cash versus Kind, Self-Selection, and Efficient Outcomes." *American Economic Review* 78, no. 4.

Dworkin, R. 1978. *Taking Rights Seriously.* London: Duckworth Press.

Frank, R. 1988. *Passions within Reason.* New York: W. W. Norton and Co.

Gauthier, David. 1986. *Morals by Agreement.* Oxford: Clarendon Press.

Gibbard, Allan. 1985. "What's Morally Special about Free Exchange?" In *Ethics and Economics,* ed. E. F. Paul, F. D. Miller, and J. Paul. Oxford: Basil Blackwell.

Goodin, R. E. 1985. *Protecting the Vulnerable.* Chicago: University of Chicago Press.

Hammond, Peter J. 1987. "Markets as Constraints: Multilateral Incentive Compatibility in Continuum Economics," *Review of Economic Studies* 54, no. 3.

Hardin, Russell. 1988. *Morality within the Limits of Reason.* Chicago: Chicago University Press.

Hart, H. L. A., and A. M. Honoré. 1985. *Causation in the Law.* 2d ed. Oxford: Clarendon Press.

Hausman, D. M. 1992. "When Jack and Jill Make a Deal." *Social Philosophy and Policy* 9.

Hicks, J. R. 1959. "A Manifesto." In *Essays in World Economics.* Oxford: Clarendon Press.

―――. 1981. *Wealth and Welfare.* Oxford: Basil Blackwell.

Kirzner, I. M. 1989. *Discovery, Capitalism, and Distributive Justice.* Oxford: Basil Blackwell.

Kronman, T. 1978. "Mistake, Disclosure, Information and the Law of Torts." *Journal of Legal Studies* 7.

Locke, J. 1980 [1690]. *A Second Treatise of Government,* ed. C. B. Macpherson. Indianapolis: Hackett Publishing Co.

Matthews, R. C. O. 1981. "Morality, Competition and Efficiency." *The Manchester School* 52, no. 4.

Nell, E. 1987. "On Deserving Profits." *Ethics* 97.

Nozick, Robert. 1974. *Anarchy, State and Utopia.* Oxford: Basil Blackwell.

Rawls, John. 1971. *A Theory of Justice.* Cambridge, Mass.: Harvard University Press.

Reiman, Jeffrey. 1981. "The Fallacy of Libertarian Capitalism." *Ethics* 92 (October).

Roemer, J. 1988. *Free to Lose.* Cambridge, Mass.: Harvard University Press.

Ross, W. D. 1930. *The Right and the Good.* Oxford: Clarendon Press.

Sen, Amartya K. 1982. "Just Deserts." *New York Review of Books,* March 4.

———. 1985a. "Rights and Capabilities." In *Morality and Objectivity,* ed. T. Honderich. London: Routledge & Kegan Paul.

———. 1985b. "The Moral Standing of the Market." In *Ethics and Economics,* ed. E. F. Paul, F. D. Miller, and J. Paul. Oxford: Basil Blackwell.

———. 1987. *On Ethics and Economics.* Oxford: Basil Blackwell.

Spencer, H. 1978 [1897]. *Principles of Ethics.* Vol. 2. Indianapolis: Liberty Press.

Wall Street Journal. 1990. August 1 and August 7.

Wiggins, D. 1985. "Claims of Need." In T. Honderich, ed. *Morality and Objectivity,* ed. T. Honderich. London: Routledge & Kegan Paul.

2 The Nature of Profits: Some Economic Insights and Their Ethical Implications

Israel M. Kirzner

In everyday business terminology, the term ''profit'' has a fairly well-understood meaning (constructed, in the main, out of accounting categories). In considering the ethical acceptability of business profits, however, it is necessary for the economist first to disentangle the various analytically separate elements that together comprise such business profits. As is well understood in elementary economic theory, most of these separate elements turn out to be identical, in their economic significance, to nonprofit elements. The owner of a business may work long hours; at least part of his business profits must be seen as the equivalent of the wages he could have earned by working for another firm. The owner of a business may have his own funds invested in his firm; part of his business profits must be seen as the equivalent of the market interest income he could have obtained by investing at the market rate of return in, say, corporate bonds. It is plausible, therefore, to assume that ethical acceptability of such nonprofit elements of accounting profit raises no new questions beyond those generally relevant to nonprofit incomes in capitalist society. The sense in which business profits pose a special challenge for an ethical appraisal of capitalist distribution, therefore, arises strictly from the residual ''pure economic profit'' element contained in business profits. After filtering out, from accounting profit, all elements that can be construed as market return on capital owned, or implicit wages of management, there remains the possibility of a residual category that cannot be imputed to any factor owner; it appears to be related to the role of the entrepreneur in a way that does not permit it to be treated as his wage, or as market return on his investment. In the last analysis, the ethical evaluation of business profits thus revolves around the nature of ''pure economic profit''—both in regard to its economic function and its economic causes. As we shall see, understanding the economic nature of pure entrepreneurial profit may well open up fresh insights concerning the ethical acceptability of business profits as broadly understood in everyday discourse.

ETHICS AND ECONOMICS INTERTWINED

Much of what we shall argue here depends on recognizing the ethical implications of economic insights. We shall not, that is, attempt to offer any innovations in ethical theory. We shall not attempt to persuade the reader to modify any ethical principles to which he subscribes. Instead, we shall proceed to suggest to the reader that the *application* of these ethical principles to the evaluation of pure profit demands, as a prerequisite, an appreciation for the true *economic* nature of entrepreneurial profit, along lines that may appear novel and even strange. Once the economic insights necessary for this apprecia-tion have been accepted, we believe, the appropriate ethical evaluation— different though this may turn out to be from that reached conventionally— follows entirely without strain.

It is because of this that the "nature of profit" becomes so central to the task of its ethical evaluation. As we shall see, it is only as a result of careful attention to the economic nature of pure profit that we find ourselves forced to reject standard defenses of the ethics of pure profit. And it will turn out to be the case that from still more careful attention to the economic nature of pure profit there will emerge an understanding of it which opens up fresh dimensions of ethical relevance. It is toward this latter understanding, and a perception of these fresh dimensions of economic relevance, that this chapter sets its aim.

The beginning of wisdom in regard to pure profit is a full appreciation of how difficult it is to understand profit—or, at least, to understand profit in the way we are accustomed to understand the economics and the ethics of other kinds of incomes under capitalism.

THE ECONOMIC AND ETHICAL PROBLEMS OF PURE PROFIT

Let us begin with two commonplace observations. The first observation is that many of us regard as justly earned those receipts which can be attributed to the efforts of the recipient. To the extent that a person's sweat is solely responsible for a particular output, we tend to regard it as unjust for that particular output to be appropriated by anyone else. The second commonplace observation is that many of us regard the fruit of a tree justly to belong to the legitimate owner of that tree. If a justly owned asset spontaneously yields a return, without the effort of any human being, we tend to regard it as entirely acceptable for that return to accrue to the owner of that asset. We do not need, for present purposes, to delve into the philosophical underpinnings supporting these two widespread convictions.[1] They are together sufficient to highlight the

---

1. We take these widespread ethical intuitions for granted, not because we believe they are self-evidently true and correct but because our goal is to understand pure profits in terms of widely held ethical convictions. (This will hold, in particular, also for our use of the finders-keepers ethic later on this chapter.) It follows, of course, that our arguments will properly be held at least partly irrelevant by those who, in fact, refuse to accept those widely held ethical institutions.

problem—at once ethical and economic—raised by pure profit. The *economic* problem raised by pure profit is that it seems to be *uncaused*. We can neither trace it to anyone's effort, nor to the spontaneous fruitfulness of any productive source. This is so, as we shall emphasize, simply as a matter of sheer definition. To the extent that a receipt *can* be attributed to the effort of the recipient, it qualifies immediately as a wage (implicit or explicit). To the extent that the receipt can be seen as attributable to the pure spontaneous fruitfulness of an owned asset, it qualifies immediately as a property-income component of accounting profit. It is only after all such elements have been filtered out, as we have seen, that we arrive at pure profit. This pure profit then appears to present an economic puzzle: if it was not created by any human effort, nor emerged as the fruit of any kind of "tree," how could it possibly have come about?

But at the same time this very difficulty presents a strictly ethical aspect. Whoever grasps this pure profit can lay claim to it on the basis of neither of the two intuitive convictions referred to earlier. He has not expended effort in its creation or acquisition, nor is he the owner of any asset from which it spontaneously emerged. The economic dilemma thus turns out to be matched by a mirror-image ethical difficulty.[2] If this pure profit, economically uncaused as it appears at first glance, must be attributed to pure chance, or to the exploitation of buyer ignorance, this very circumstance appears to render its grasping by an individual seriously vulnerable to ethical challenge. Exploitation of consumer ignorance, of course, raised issues of fraud. And even the beneficiary of pure good fortune does not at all enjoy that intuitive ethical approval of his fortunate situation which, for many of us, attaches to the recipient of that produced by the sweat of his brow, or to the owner of the fruit-bearing tree. We can no longer appeal to a widely shared notion of simple justice to support his grasping of profit. Let us return to ponder on the apparently "uncaused" character of pure economic profit.

If we begin with an institutional framework which recognizes private self-ownership rights and the possibility of acquiring ownership rights in productive

---

2. Throughout this chapter we will be referring to the ethical "difficulty" or "problem" associated with pure profit. Of course, no difficulty or problem will exist for one who, indeed, believes that the phenomenon of pure profit is ethically undefendable. Although we will be using the terms "difficulty" and "problem," it is not our intention, in so doing, implicitly to beg the ethical question involved. From the perspective reached by the end of this chapter, suggesting a possible line of ethical justification for pure profit, it seems useful to introduce discussion by focusing on what will eventually be seen, we shall argue, to have been only apparent difficulties and problems.

resources, we have no difficulty in accounting for the emergence of factor incomes. The worker is able to command a wage for his labor because that labor produces an item for which a consumer (and hence an entrepreneur intending to sell to the consumer) is prepared to pay. Because labor services are scarce, market competition ensures a positive wage to productive labor. The owner of a fruit tree is able to command a price for the fruit of his tree because, given his ownership of the scarce fruit, consumers are, in competition with one another, prepared to pay positive prices to acquire that fruit. Given widespread preference for earlier rather than later receipts, the market for loanable funds yields interest income to lenders, because the borrowers find it worthwhile to offer interest, and scarcity of loanable funds makes it necessary for them to do so. But there seems, on the face of it, to be no earthly reason why, when a consumer buys an item, he should pay a price for it which is *more* than sufficiently high to cover *all* costs of resource services (including the borrowing of necessary capital funds) needed to deliver that item to his doorstep at the time he wishes to buy it. The portion of this purchase price which accrues as pure profit is paid, it appears, for nothing at all. It does not pay for the performance of any productive service rendered. It does not pay for the use of capital funds. It cannot be rationalized as being paid in return for the provision by the seller of necessary information—because, to the extent that this *is* the reason why this payment is being made, it follows that it is payment for a service rendered and thus not pure profit after all. It seems that the pure profit portion of the purchase price can emerge only as the result of a fluke, an aberration, and/or of virtual fraud on the part of the seller (who somehow, as the result of consumer ignorance, extracts a price higher than that strictly necessary to provide the consumer that which he is buying). And it is here that the ethical side of the problem of profit comes clearly into focus. It follows from the very circumstance that there appears no economic justification (in the sense of ''valid explanation'') for the payment of pure profit, that the grasping of such profits must necessarily fail to meet both of the two commonly held criteria for deservedness mentioned earlier. A payment is economically justified if the relevant conditions of supply and demand mark out a positive market clearing price. The circumstance that such justification is absent in the case of pure profit leaves pure profit in an ethical limbo. One is simply unable to point to any quid pro quo (such as effort, or the fruit of an owned tree) corresponding to the grasped profit. The ethical problem of profit emerges directly from the economic nature of pure profit.

Pure Profit and the Entrepreneurial Role

The problematic nature of pure profit is mirrored, of course, in the problematic nature of the entrepreneurial function itself. From the perspective of conventional economic theory this function is a notoriously elusive one. The entrepreneur assembles all the productive services needed to produce a product. He assumes the cost represented by the market values of all these services and receives the market value of the produced output. He retains whatever surplus remains, as pure entrepreneurial profit (or, if the residual is negative, he suffers entrepreneurial loss). But in stipulating that he assumes the costs embodied in the market value of *all* productive services needed for the product, we of course mean to include also all those services provided by the entrepreneur himself which could, in principle, have been hired in the marketplace. His labor services and the services of the assets he owns could have been provided from the outside. In identifying the peculiarly entrepreneurial character of his role, we must certainly not obscure this role by failing to distinguish it analytically from the provision of these nonentrepreneurial services with which the entrepreneurial role is often in real life packaged together. The computation of residual pure profit, as we saw previously, requires that we net out, from the gross revenue obtained from the sale of output, not only out-of-pocket expenditures made by the entrepreneur to command the productive services he buys in the market, but also the market values of the nonentrepreneurial services the entrepreneur himself provides. The pure profit residual accrues to the pure entrepreneurial role played by the entrepreneur. But of what does this role consist? What does the entrepreneur, qua entrepreneur, contribute to the emergence of the product? After all, the productive services he assembles (including his own nonentrepreneurially contributed services) are, by stipulation, together *fully* sufficient for the production of the product and its delivery to the purchaser. The list of assembled services *must* be a complete one. Inputs produce output; the entrepreneur assembles *all* the inputs needed for the output. With *all* the needed inputs in hand, what else could possibly be needed? It appears, at first glance, as if the purely entrepreneurial function disintegrates into nothingness as soon as we attempt to grasp hold of it.

Pure profit accrues to the entrepreneur. But we cannot seem to perceive what it is that the entrepreneur *does*. And, as seen previously, we seem to be unable to understand why the prices paid by purchasers are high enough to leave a residual pure profit. We don't know what the function of the entrepreneur is, and we don't understand how and why he is ever able to retain his residual pure profit. The ethical problem we found to surround pure profit thus parallels our mystification concerning the function and role of the entrepreneur. Much of what follows here is concerned with the explication of the entrepreneurial function.

Some Leading Theories of Entrepreneurial Profit

It will be useful, both for its own sake and as preliminary to our own theory of profit, to provide a brief review of the principal economic theories of entrepreneurial profit developed during the heyday of entrepreneurial theorizing (1890–1920).[3] The several major approaches we shall identify attest to the intense interest displayed by the early neoclassical economists in the pure profit concept and in the entrepreneurial role. This contrasts sharply with the virtual silence on these matters which characterized the subsequent half-century of economic thought. We shall identify what we believe to be weaknesses in these approaches but also point out the valuable insights contained in them. Wherever possible, we shall take note of the possible implications which these theories hold for the ethical evaluation of pure profit.

J. B. Clark

Clark's observations on profit occur peripherally to his exhaustive analysis of distribution under conditions of static equilibrium.[4] Under static conditions there is no profit. All incomes are marginal productivity incomes. "Profit has no place in such static conditions. The two incomes that are permanent and independent of dynamic changes are the products, respectively, of labor and of capital. Each of them is directly determined by the final productivity law . . ."[5] Profit emerges only as a result of dynamic change. Suppose a new invention improves the methods of production. This may result in permanently higher wages. "Wages now tend to equal what labor can now produce, and this is more than it could formerly produce."[6] However, as a result of "economic friction," wages may be temporarily lower than their new, higher, static level, leaving a profit margin between output value and production costs, which the

3. This section draws substantially upon the material in my *Discovery, Capitalism and Distributive Justice* (Oxford: Basil Blackwell, 1989), chap. 3. The history of theories of profit and entrepreneurship is a rich one. See in particular R. F. Hebert and A. N. Link, *The Entrepreneur: Mainstream Views and Radical Critiques,* 2d ed. (New York: Praeger, 1988). My brief review makes no attempt at completeness in coverage; instead, it identifies several key approaches, an understanding of which (and of the shortcomings of which) can, I believe, conduce to an appreciation of the Misesian theory discussed here.

4. J. B. Clark, *The Distribution of Wealth* (New York: Macmillan, 1989).

5. Ibid., p. 201.

6. Ibid., p. 405.

entrepreneur is able to grasp. "The interval between actual wages and the static standard is the result of friction; for, if competition works without let or hindrance, pure business profit would be annihilated as fast as it could be created—entrepreneurs, as such, could never get and keep any income . . . Dynamic theory has to account for the whole of that friction on which *entrepreneurs'* shares depend; while static law determines what wages will be, when the friction shall have been completely overcome, and what they would be at this instant, if friction were immediately to vanish."[7] Clark is apparently satisfied with the justice of such entrepreneurially grasped profit—despite the circumstance that it does not fit into his own marginal productivity ethic (which declares wages, for example, to be justly earned only because they correspond to what labor has contributed to the total output). Clark notes that were it not for the friction which permits a temporary profit to entrepreneurs, the latter "would have no incentive in self-interest to make any improvements, and it is clear that additions which are difficult and costly would be in danger of not being made. Profit is the lure that insures improvement . . . To secure progress, this lure must be sufficient to make men overcome obstructions and take risks."[8] Yet it is not clear how this renders the grasping of these profits ethically acceptable for Clark. Clark does not appear to recognize any productive service to have been rendered by the entrepreneur, even when he has introduced improvements in productive methods. After all, all that is produced through the new methods is produced by the input services being used. So we do not quite understand how Clark's productivity criteria for distributive justice have been met by the entrepreneur, permitting him to enjoy (the admittedly temporary) profits made possible by economic friction.

On the other hand, Clark *has* provided a solution to the problem of what causes profit to exist at all. Profits are not uncaused; they are caused by economic frictions which prevent the immediate disappearance (through competitive activity) of the profits initially generated by dynamic change. Clark has, importantly, identified pure profit as a disequilibrium phenomenon, and has at least given a name to the source responsible for the temporary persistence of disequilibrium: "economic frictions."

F. B. Hawley

Hawley was an important (but now almost forgotten) U.S. profit theorist at the turn of the century. He is prominently cited by Frank Knight in his survey of profit theories, and Hawley's theory, while sharply criticized by

7. Ibid., pp. 410–11.
8. Ibid., p. 411.

Knight, is recognized by him to contain a valuable element of what Knight believes to be a correct theory.[9] Hawley's work had a profound influence on subsequent U.S. textbook treatments of profit, an influence continuing well after World War II.[10]

Hawley identifies the "distinguishing function of the *entrepreneur*" as the "assumption of risk," and saw pure profit as "the economic reward for services rendered by the assumption of industrial risk."[11] Were no one to be prepared to assume this industrial risk, it would not be possible for production to occur. Profit provides a reward for this entrepreneurially provided service, and thus also an inducement persuading the entrepreneur to provide this service. It is important, Hawley contends, not to confuse this reward and inducement with the amount an unwilling risk bearer pays in order to insure himself against the risk of loss. This latter payment, "a sum sufficient to cover the actuarial or average losses incidental to the various risks of all kinds necessarily assumed by the entrepreneur and his insurers," is already included among the costs of production.[12] Hawley maintains that production will not occur unless the entrepreneur can be induced to assume risk, through the prospect of a surplus over and above *all* costs, including the cost of insurance. This is so, Hawley argues, because there is an "irksomeness of uncertainty" attached to each *particular* business project, even where the businessman has confidence in the validity of his actuarial judgment over the long run (during which time losses and gains will tend to offset each other).[13] It is because of this that Hawley asserts that "industrial risks will not be assumed without the expectation of a compensation in excess of the actuarial value of the risk."[14]

It will be observed that Hawley's theory of profit does, within its own framework, adequately address the economic (and, by implication, also the ethical) problem surrounding profit and the entrepreneurial role. The entrepreneur does provide a service, a service that is both essential for the emergence of output and not able to be purchased on the market. Profit is not uncaused, it is caused by the need, if product is to be forthcoming, for the (inescapable)

9. Frank H. Knight, *Risk, Uncertainty and Profit* (Boston: Houghton Mifflin, 1921), pp. 41–48.

10. On this see Martin Bronfenbrenner, "A Reformulation of Naive Profit Theory," *Southern Economic Journal* (April 1960): 300–309.

11. F. B. Hawley, "Enterprise and Profit," *Quarterly Journal of Economics* 15 (November 1900): 75.

12. F. B. Hawley, "Reply to Final Objection to the Risk Theory of Profit," *Quarterly Journal of Economics* 15 (August 1901): 610.

13. Ibid., p. 604.

14. F. B. Hawley, "The Risk Theory of Profit," *Quarterly Journal of Economics* 7 (July 1893): 460.

risk of business to be assumed. The consumers are forced to pay prices high enough to permit profits, or else they would not find the products they wish to buy. Hawley does not appear to have much concerned himself with the ethics of profit. He wished to teach economists how correctly to characterize the phenomenon of profit. Yet we can see for ourselves how an ethical defense might be constructed on the basis of Hawley's theory. The entrepreneur provides a special service, one irksome for him to provide; he may be deemed entitled to the reward the market provides as an inducement to him for so providing this needed service.

Yet the framework that Hawley has offered seems unredeemably flawed. Knight put his finger on its central weakness. Hawley assumes "that the 'actuarial value' of the risks taken is known to the entrepreneur."[15] Knight was himself to emphasize, however, that there is a fundamental difference between risk and uncertainty. For Knight "uncertainty" is a term reserved for that which is, as a consequence of the utter unpredictability of future events, inherently indeterminate and immeasurable. So long as Hawley provides no room, in his analytical scheme, for such open-ended, uninsurable uncertainty, he has not rendered plausible the nature of the peculiarly entrepreneurial function. As Knight pointed out, "[A] little consideration will show that there can be no considerable 'irksomeness' attached to exposure to an insurable risk, for if there is it will be insured; hence there can be no peculiarity income arising out of this alleged indisposition."[16]

Frank H. Knight

Knight constructed his own uncertainty theory of profit out of elements he found in Clark and Hawley. Clark was right in associating profit with dynamic change; Hawley was right in associating the entrepreneurial function with the residual bearing of uncertainty. But it was left for Knight to forge out of these ideas what he believed to be the correct theory of profit and of the entrepreneurial role. Clarkian dynamic change is, by itself, not enough to generate profit, because it is possible for change to be anticipated.[17] If an increase in the productivity of labor can be generally anticipated, competition among prospective employers will immediately force wages up to the new, higher level. It is only to the extent that change is responsible for ignorance of the future that it can be associated with the phenomenon of profit. And this insight leads Knight to locate the source of profit not in dynamic change itself but in the open-ended

15. Knight (1921), p. 43.
16. Ibid., p. 46.
17. Ibid., pp. 35–37.

uncertainty of the future for which such change is responsible. For Knight it is this inescapable difference between what has been anticipated and what actually occurs, which is responsible for entrepreneurial profit (and loss). So that profits are not forthcoming because an inducement must be offered to overcome some irksomeness of uncertainty bearing; profits and losses are forthcoming because the uncertainty of life continually generates unexpected gains or unexpected losses. The entrepreneur has (certainly as a result of the inducement offered by the prospect of possible profit) placed himself in the position of residual claimant. Knight goes into considerable detail concerning the qualities required for the entrepreneurial function, involving, as it thus does, both *responsibility* for and *control* of an enterprise in an uncertain world.[18] But for an understanding of Knight's view of the nature of entrepreneurial profit it is sufficient to focus on the extent to which entrepreneurial *judgment* (which for Knight appears to refer to the judgment required for the successful carrying out of routine managerial tasks in an uncertain world) and *pure luck* are inevitably intertwined in the generation of residual profit.[19] Because the entrepreneur exposes himself to residual uncertainty the element of luck plays a decisive part in determining whether the residual left, after paying all contractual income, will be positive or negative.

So that, for Knight, pure profit is not exactly uncaused. It is an implication of the need to operate in a world of uncertainty. In such a world somebody, or everybody, must be left exposed to the vagaries of pure luck. Entrepreneurs choose to occupy such exposed positions; their luck may be good or bad—profits may be positive or negative. Consumers do not deliberately pay a price higher than necessary to cover all costs of production; if they pay such higher prices this is because the course of events happens to have been such as to force the current output price up higher than had been anticipated when the contractual income payments for factor services were agreed upon. Profit emerges because a world of uncertainty is necessarily one in which "a condition of perfect equilibrium is no longer possible."[20] A world of continuous disequilibrium is one in which residual incomes are continually being subjected to unanticipated shocks and readjustments. It is not correct to characterize profits as "having to be paid" in order to induce entrepreneurs to enter (although the *possibility* of such profits may indeed provide such inducement); in fact, Knight believed rather strongly that, on balance, losses outweigh profits. Profits (or losses) emerge simply because, in an uncertain world, mat-

18. Ibid., p. 271.
19. Ibid., pp. 277–83.
20. Ibid., p. 272.

ters never do turn out to be exactly what the best judgment anticipated as being likely to happen.

What Knight has given us, then, is a theory of profit which sees it as caused by uncertainty-bred conditions of market disequilibrium. It should be noted that while this certainly does explain how the phenomenon of profit arises, it does so in a way which does *not* see profit as the market value offered in exchange for the fulfillment by the entrepreneur of any valuable social function. To be sure, profit and loss are inseparably associated with the entrepreneurial role, and, to be sure, Knight sees a *most* important place for this role in the capitalist process of production.[21] But the nature of these associations is such that even where profits, rather than losses, have been achieved, these can hardly be seen as payment for the entrepreneurial services rendered. We would rather have to say, according to Knight, that the provision of entrepreneurial services is inseparable from consequent exposure to the possibility of loss and the possibility of profit. Since, on balance, there never may be net profits won by the entrepreneurs in the economy, these net profits cannot, even if they occur, be seen as market generated payments made for, and necessary to induce the provision of, the services of entrepreneurs.

In other words, Knight has, in his own way, solved the purely economic problem of pure profit without being concerned with, and without offering any clues to the solution of, the ethical problems we identified earlier. Where an entrepreneur has won profits there still seems no way of subsuming these profits under the category of justly received incomes (according to the everyday consensus mentioned earlier as providing rough criteria for ethical acceptability). Although by focusing upon uninsurable uncertainty (rather than upon insurable risk) Knight has no doubt restored legitimacy to Hawley's "irksomeness of uncertainty," nonetheless Knight's perspective does not, as we have seen, permit profit to be seen as paid for (and thus ethically justified by) the provision of this service of irksome-bearing. While we now understand what Knight wishes us to see the entrepreneur as doing, we are, therefore, still unable to see how this renders the winning of profit legitimate. In fact, it would seem eminently plausible for a critic to argue that the entrepreneur has no inherent right to the lucky profits that came his way. (Knight himself may well have felt that the entrepreneur's vulnerability to the losses generated by bad luck, somehow makes it not unfair for him to be permitted to keep the

21. In fact, Knight (1921) argued that it is the entrepreneur (who, while himself owning no inputs, assembles them to generate output) who must be considered the real "producer" of capitalist output (p. 271).

proceeds of good luck.[22] But this surely depends on the validity of Knight's conviction that, in general, losses more than cancel out profits.)

J. A. Schumpeter

We list Schumpeter's well-known theory of profit not because his theory offered a fundamental insight not already covered in our brief review of the literature but because of the centrality and prominence of his theory, and because of certain important fresh nuances to be noticed in that theory. For Schumpeter profits are created by entrepreneurial innovations. He sees the entrepreneurial function as consisting in the "carrying out of new combinations," which change the methods of production and/or the products produced.[23] The energy and leadership qualities of the entrepreneur provide him with the initiative and the will needed to break away from the routine activities of everyday business. It is not so much a matter of originality and ingenuity of invention as of power and determination "in getting things done,"[24] of introducing into practice the inventions that others can see as well as he can.[25] These entrepreneurial innovations together make up the "perennial gale of creative destruction" which, for Schumpeter, is an unmistakable characteristic of capitalism.[26]

The profits won by the Schumpeterian entrepreneur are not windfall profits; they have been deliberately created. By innovating a new technique or a new product the entrepreneur creates a profit-surplus of revenues over costs, for as long as it takes the nonentrepreneurial "imitators" to compete away that difference. For Schumpeter risk and uncertainty have nothing to do with profit (although he would not deny that entrepreneurial activity is inseparable from exposure to uncertainty). Schumpeter believed that the risk associated with an entrepreneurial venture is borne by the capitalist, not the entrepreneur. The profits of innovation are not a reward paid by the market but a gain created by jolting the economy out of its routine pattern.

22. See Knight's statement: "Both in abstract ethics and from the standpoint of social interest in adequate motivation, a proposal to reduce high profits raises the question of using the proceeds to reduce losses" ("Profit," in *Encyclopedia of the Social Sciences* 12, reprinted in *Readings in the Theory of Income Distribution,* ed. W. Fellner and B. F. Haley (Philadelphia: Blakiston, 1949), p. 546.

23. See Joseph Schumpeter, *The Theory of Economic Development* (Cambridge, Mass.: Harvard University Press, 1934), pp. 74ff.

24. J. A. Schumpeter, *Capitalism, Socialism and Democracy,* 3d ed. (New York: Harper and Row, 1950), p. 132.

25. Schumpeter, *Theory of Economic Development* (1934), pp. 88–89.

26. Schumpeter, *Capitalism, Socialism and Democracy* (1950), p. 87.

The similarity between Schumpeter's understanding of the nature of pure profit and that perceived by J. B. Clark is obvious. For Clark, too, as seen earlier in this section, profits emerge as the result of the dynamic change associated with industrial progress. Schumpeter was to recognize this similarity. In surveying neoclassical contributions to the theory of enterprise (in his monumental *History of Economic Analysis*), Schumpeter described Clark's contribution as being "the most significant of all: he was the first to strike a novel note by connecting entrepreneurial profits, considered as a surplus over interest (and rent), with the successful introduction into the economic process of technological, commercial, or organizational improvements."[27]

What distinguishes the Schumpeterian view of pure profit from that of Clark seems to be entirely a matter of nuance. Clark does not seem to emphasize as Schumpeter does the *deliberate* character of profit creation; he does emphasize, more than Schumpeter appears to do, the *temporary* nature of profit, noting (as we have seen) that it is only "economic friction" which somehow prevents its instantaneous disappearance. The lure of profit stimulates the entrepreneur to introduce technological innovations, with the impression somehow being conveyed that the market is already clearly *offering* these fleeting profit opportunities in exchange for innovation (rather than their being deliberately engineered by the Schumpeterian entrepreneur's leadership and determination). As we saw earlier, Clark's theory solves the problem of what causes profits: profits are caused by economic frictions which prevent the immediate disappearance (through competitive activity) of the profits initially generated by dynamic change. For Schumpeter, it would seem more accurate to describe his theory as solving the causal problem in profits slightly differently: profits are caused by entrepreneurial innovations; they tend to be ground down to zero by the competition of imitators. As we have seen, Clark's theory of profit was not more than a footnote, as it were, to his comprehensive marginal productivity theory of income distribution under static equilibrium conditions. Schumpeter's theory of entrepreneurial innovation, on the other hand, was the central element in his understanding of the capitalist process.

SOME LESSONS LEARNED FROM THE LEADING THEORIES

Consideration of the theories briefly sketched in the preceding section can significantly advance understanding of the phenomenon of pure profit. These

---

27. J. A. Schumpeter, *History of Economic Analysis* (Oxford: Oxford University Press, 1954), p. 894. See also Schumpeter, *Theory of Economic Development* (1934), pp. 128–29, where Clark's theory is described as the closest to Schumpeter's own.

theories point unerringly to the *disequilibrium* character of profit. It turns out that the problem which we encountered, at the outset of this chapter in explaining the economic causes of profit, was a problem only because we were, at least implicitly, seeking for causes that could operate steadily under settled circumstances. We were looking for a service provided steadily by the entrepreneur that could be understood as commanding a settled market price. Inevitably, we found ourselves forced to acknowledge that, to the extent such a steady service and such a settled market price could be identified, we were no longer dealing with the purely entrepreneurial role and with pure profit. The work of Schumpeter and Knight (in whose ideas, as we have seen, we can find echoes of insights present in the work of Clark and Hawley) incisively identifies profit as a gain that has no place at all in the settled scheme of the equilibrium state. Profits appeared to be without cause, because in the settled scheme of things that was the background of our quest, there can in fact be no profit. Real world profits do exist; they have their cause in the circumstances responsible for and which accompany the real world state of disequilibrium. For Schumpeter profits are created through the leadership with which the entrepreneur propels the economy away from its earlier somnolent, state of equilibrium. For Knight profits are caused by the inevitable failure of market participants, in the disequilibrium world of uncertainty, to correctly anticipate subsequent conditions.

Yet these solutions to the *economic* problem of pure profits have not provided any help in decisively establishing ethical justification for profit. The ethical challenge, we saw, arose out of the circumstance that profit is neither a property income (comparable to the fruit that grows on a tree that is legitimately owned), nor an income paid as compensation for a productive service rendered. It was this that seemed to place pure profit under an ethical cloud. Consideration of the Schumpeterian and Knightian disequilibrium theories of profit appears, at first glance, to suggest that, indeed, even after as economists we understand how profits arise, one might yet conclude that they lack ethical justification. For both Schumpeter and Knight it is still the case that profits cannot be defended as the fruits of any owned tree, nor as the market value of any provided service. It is true that a consistent defender of private property rights could claim that, since no violation of property rights occurs either in the Schumpeterian or the Knightian scheme of things, the resulting ownership patterns cannot be pronounced unjust. (This is, indeed, the central thesis of Nozick's entitlement theory of justice.)[28] But in regard to pure profit it seems

28. Robert Nozick, *Anarchy, State and Utopia* (New York: Basic Books, 1974), chap. 7.

safe to say that many people are, at the intuitive level, simply not satisfied by the entitlement theory. (Perhaps their intuitive misgivings about profits are such as to lead them to question the very property system, consistent application of which appears to legitimize these apparently undeserved gains.)

In the Knightian theory of profit, with its emphasis on the consequence of sheer luck, the undeserved nature of profit appears particularly bothersome. It seems, to critics of capitalist distribution, entirely arbitrary to declare one individual to be the just owner of that which came his way only as a result of a chance occurrence in no way attributable to his efforts.[29] (As noted earlier, it is likely that Knight found himself able to defend profits on the grounds that those who stand to win profits are exposed to losses which, on balance, more than offset the profits.)

Schumpeterian profits are certainly not primarily a matter of luck; they are deliberately created by determined entrepreneurs. As such they might seem to be ethically defendable as the outcome achieved by deliberate effort. Yet such a defense presents something of a puzzle. Once the "imitators" will have absorbed and duplicated the innovations pioneered by the entrepreneur, equilibrium will once again have been attained; no portion of output revenue will then revert to the entrepreneur. It must appear puzzling that the contribution made by the entrepreneur is somehow held to cease as imitators copy his trade secrets. If it is eventually obvious that the nonentrepreneurial factor services are by themselves entirely sufficient to generate the new product or the new production technique (so that the full value of the output becomes justly imputed to them alone), this might be held to be equally valid and relevant immediately after introduction of the entrepreneurial innovation. If, on the other hand, it is held that, absent the pioneering effort of the entrepreneur, the new technique might never have come to pass at all, and that this entitles him to a share of the output revenue, then it is not clear why this does not entitle him to a similar share for as long as the revenue stream endures. In a nutshell, the Schumpeterian concept of profit does not facilitate its being easily fitted into a productivity-return ethical category. Let us turn to yet another theory of profit, similar in spirit, to a degree, to both the Schumpeterian and Knightian theories, but yet providing a unique twist that can perhaps help us in solving not only the economic problem of profit but also the ethical problem as well.

29. Critics of capitalism have, indeed, even challenged the notion of self-ownership on precisely these grounds; see for example J. Roemer, *Free to Lose: An Introduction to Marxist Economic Philosophy* (Cambridge, Mass.: Harvard University Press, 1988), p. 154.

THE ARBITRAGE THEORY OF PURE PROFIT

This theory of profit is that of the Austrian economist Ludwig von Mises. It seems appropriate to call it the *arbitrage* theory of profit[30] because it focuses on the sense in which profit is simply the price discrepancy between two markets, today's market (in which, say, productive resource services are bought and sold) and tomorrow's market (in which the output of these productive services will be sold). Arbitrage opportunities arise when today's market prices are (after taking interest expense into account) out of line with the true, higher values that will be revealed in tomorrow's market. As Mises said, "What makes profit emerge is the fact that the entrepreneur who judges the future prices of the products more correctly than other people do buys some or all of the factors of production at prices which, seen from the point of view of the future state of the market, are too low. Thus the total costs of production—including interest on the capital invested—lag behind the prices which the entrepreneur receives for the product. This difference is entrepreneurial profit."[31]

The Misesian theory shares with Schumpeter's theory and with Knight's theory the insight that profit is a disequilibrium phenomenon. (Arbitrage profits are possible only because arbitrage activity has not yet squeezed them out of existence.) But the emphasis in the Misesian discussion is on the ability of the superior entrepreneur to identify, more correctly than others are able to do, where today's market undervalues future output. "An entrepreneur can make a profit only if he anticipates future conditions more correctly than other entrepreneurs. Then he buys the complementary factors of production at prices the sum of which, including allowance for the time difference, is smaller than the price at which he sells the product."[32]

Schumpeter's emphasis was on the leadership and determination expressed by the entrepreneur in creating new procedures of production. Mises's emphasis is on the superior perception on the part of the entrepreneur as to where resources services are currently undervalued.

Knight's emphasis was on the extent to which luck can benefit the agent who exposes himself to residual uncertainty. Mises's emphasis is on the vision exercised by the superior entrepreneur. Mises does not, of course, underesti-

---

30. On this see further Israel M. Kirzner, *Competition and Entrepreneurship* (Chicago: University of Chicago Press, 1973), pp. 85–86; Hebert and Link (1988), p. 152.

31. Ludwig von Mises, *Planning for Freedom and Other Essays and Addresses,* 2d ed. (South Holland, Ill.: Libertarian Press, 1962), p. 190.

32. Ludwig von Mises, *Human Action* (New Haven: Yale University Press, 1949), p. 291.

mate the role of uncertainty in creating opportunities for profit.[33] "The ultimate source from which entrepreneurial profit and loss are derived is the uncertainty of the future constellation of demand and supply. If all entrepreneurs were to anticipate correctly the future state of the market, there would be neither profits nor losses."[34] But for Knight profit appears to arise, *after* the entrepreneur has taken up his exposed position, by a fortunate change which everyone (including, very possibly, this entrepreneur) has failed to foresee. For Mises, on the other hand, the profit-making entrepreneur is he who (while everyone else has failed to see the course of future events) sees the opportunity created by the errors of the other market participants. For Knight luck is a decisive factor generating profit; for Mises superior vision is the decisive factor in the grasping of profits.

We emphasize these nuances of difference between Mises, on the one hand, and Schumpeter and Knight, on the other, because, as we shall try to show, it is these differences which hold important implications for the ethical evaluation of pure profit.

Pure Profit and the Ethics of Discovery: An Overview

Once we identify profit as the result of the circumstance that the entrepreneur "anticipates future conditions more correctly than other entrepreneurs,"[35] we have within our grasp the solution to the ethical problem of profit identified earlier in this chapter. The entrepreneur "sees" the future more accurately than others do. Because others see the future inaccurately, there is generated a gap between the present market value of resources and the (discounted) market value of output (as it will, in fact, turn out to be in the future). The entrepreneur, in seeing the future more accurately, in effect sees this gap. (Indeed, it is the very prospect and incentive of gaining from such perceived gaps which concentrate and focus the entrepreneurial vision to more accurately glimpse the future.) What the entrepreneur sees is a prospective increment of value which others, although in no way handicapped as compared with our

33. Murray N. Rothbard ("Professor Hebert on Entrepreneurship," *Journal of Libertarian Studies* 3, no. 2 (Fall 1985): pp. 281–86) has argued that this recognition and emphasis by Mises on the role of uncertainty in the generation of pure profit is inconsistent with the interpretation which the present writer has given Mises's theory. For Rothbard, an "alertness" theory of profit must do away with uncertainty. Although I have not been able to follow Rothbard's reasoning on this matter, the reader may wish to explore this issue further. See also Hebert and Link (1988), pp. 132f.

34. Mises, *Human Action* (1942), p. 291.

35. Ibid.

entrepreneur, have somehow failed to see. (In fact, the increment of value is nothing but the market expression of this failure on their part correctly to see the future.) We argue that profits grasped by the entrepreneur are in the nature of an unowned, unperceived object first discovered by an alert pioneer, who, in the view of many, becomes the legitimate private owner of that which he has discovered, on the basis of the "finders-keepers" ethic.

Up until now our discussion concerning ethics referred to only two criteria on the basis of which general opinion seems prepared to endorse ethical accept-ability of gain. These were (a) compensation for productive service rendered, and (b) gain directly derived ("fruit from an owned tree") from private prop-erty legitimately possessed. We now wish to recognize a third criterion, a criterion that (although apparently widely accepted in everyday discourse) ap-pears alien to the world scheme of economics but is, we believe, crucially important to the evaluation of outcomes in an uncertain world. It is on the basis of this "finders-keepers" criterion that we shall argue the ethical defensi-bility of pure entrepreneurial profit. In the following pages we shall develop somewhat more fully (a) the nature of discovery, and (b) the discovered charac-ter of pure entrepreneurial profit.

THE MEANING OF DISCOVERY[36]

In the world of standard economics there is a widely employed scheme of classification the assumed exhaustiveness of which we wish to challenge very vigorously. In this scheme it is assumed that economic gains can be understood either as the deliberately achieved goals of human effort, or as windfalls attrib-utable to sheer luck. (In addition, of course, this scheme recognizes the possi-bility of sequences of events in which luck and effort intertwine.) No other category of cause besides planned result of deliberate activity, and fortunate outcome of sheer good fortune, is recognized. If an outcome was not deliber-ately aimed at, it must be seen as purely lucky. We wish to insist that a third possible source for economic gain, a source entailing ethical implications of an entirely different character, must be recognized. This source is deliberate human discovery, not to be attributed to unaided luck but (at least in part) to the alert attitude on the part of the discoverer. It is the alertness of human beings that enables them to notice and profit by what they find.

Standard economics understands the meaning of search activity. One de-cides to search for an object, or for an item of information, in exactly the same way as one decides to engage in every other kind of deliberate productive

36. This section draws substantially upon chap. 2 of my *Discovery, Capitalism and Distribu-tive Justice* (1989).

activity. Such a decision is seen as rigidly determined by the value of the prospective find to the searcher, in conjunction with the relevant costs of search. The determination is, in the economics of search, seen as being made in the context of assumed probabilities governing the techniques of deliberate search.

Deliberate search, however, is not at all the same as spontaneous, alert discovery (although, certainly, the two may occur together). Someone looking up a telephone number in a telephone directory is engaged in deliberate search. Someone who, walking along a city boulevard, notices a public telephone and realizes that this will permit him to make an important telephone call, has made a discovery. (Someone who notices the availability of a telephone directory and is thereby spurred to undertake a search for an important telephone number presents an example of how discovery and deliberate search may be inter-twined.)

The special ethical relevance of spontaneous discovery arises precisely from the circumstance that it can be classified neither as a deliberate activity nor as an occurrence strictly attributable to blind chance. If I deliberately produce output using only legitimately acquired productive resource services, common-place ethical intuition is inclined to recognize my just title to what I and my resources have produced. If I am lucky in the sense that a fortune has fallen from heaven directly in my lap, commonplace ethical intuition is not at all clear on the legitimacy of my claim to sole ownership of this fortune; after all I did not lift a finger in achieving this windfall. Critics are often inclined to argue that such windfalls somehow belong to "all mankind." It is not a simple matter to rebut such a position on the basis of commonplace intuition. What I claim here is that he who alertly grasps an opportunity for gain—an opportu-nity in principle available to others but which has remained ungrasped because as yet not noticed—occupies a distinct ethical box, neither that labeled "pro-ducer of output with legitimately owned resources," nor that labeled "lucky beneficiary of windfall gain." The ethical box occupied by the alert discoverer of an available opportunity might well be labeled "finders-keepers."

The finder (i.e., the discoverer) of this opportunity might lay claim to what he has discovered, not because he deliberately produced it but because he alertly noticed it. He might reject the criticisms of those who denounce private appropriation of lucky windfalls on the grounds that these criticisms are not relevant to his situation. Criticism of ownership based on pure luck cannot apply to the gains won by alert discovery. The lucky winner in a *purely* chance situation has done *nothing* to generate this outcome, which is unrelated to his efforts, his actions, his thoughts, and his purposes. The opportunity noticed by the discoverer is the direct creation of that discoverer's alertness, vision, and self-confidence. He was not deterred by the opinions of others; he saw what he saw and grasped it. He did not produce it deliberately; his unique vision brought it into economic existence. In a very real sense, he created what he discovered.

The creative aspect of alert discovery deserves to be emphasized. It seems plausible to attribute the finders-keepers ethic to the insight that the discovered object owes its very existence, as it were, to the discoverer. Had he not discovered it, that object would, for all *human* intents and purposes, be nonexistent; it would not figure in anyone's plans, purposes, or evaluations. An object produced out of the producer's owned resources is considered the just property of the producer because it *is* those resources, simply in different form; the pie *is* the sum of the ingredients out of which it has been baked. But a discovered object has been created, as it were, ex nihilo; its discoverer is considered its owner, not because he owned the inputs from which it has been produced but precisely because it has *not* been produced out of inputs. The discovered object has been brought into existence from nonexistence, simply through its having been discovered. Its discoverer is, in an ethically relevant sense, its creator.

The person into whose lap falls a valuable object has *not* created that object (assuming that others notice its fall just as soon as that person himself does). He is simply the location where sheer, blind luck has placed that object. The person who, owning resources, has deliberately employed them to produce output has not created that object out of nothing; he has deliberately fashioned it out of owned inputs. The discoverer of an object, available to but unnoticed by everyone else, has, in the relevant sense, created that object out of nothing, simply by virtue of the alertness of his personality. That alertness links the discovered object indissolubly with his personality; commonplace ethics finds this link sufficiently convincing to place the discovery in an ethical box entirely distinct from that labeled "windfall gain."

The Discovery Character of Pure Profit

The arbitrage theory of profit, which we identified earlier with Ludwig von Mises, permits us to see entrepreneurial profit as a wholly discovered gain. Both the economic problem of profit and the ethical problem of profit dissolve once one recognizes the discovered character of pure profit. Profits, we found, cannot conceivably arise in equilibrium conditions; this is because equilibrium is, by construction, a state in which nothing (that is relevant to the analysis) remains to be discovered. Profit arises strictly in disequilibrium precisely because disequilibrium conditions are the directly implied consequences of as yet ungrasped opportunities "waiting," as it were, to be discovered. The appearance of an arbitrage opportunity between two markets is simply the manifestation of the failure of those selling in the low-priced market to be aware of buyers in the other market who are prepared to pay more; of the failure of those buying in the high-priced market to be aware of sellers in the other market who are prepared to sell for less. These failures in mutual awareness constitute an as yet undiscovered opportunity for pure profit. The entrepreneur who notices the price gap is making the relevant discovery. In grasping the profit constituted by this price gap he is, by his superior alertness, bringing into existence and into reality something of which no one was aware. It seems intuitively appealing to see the entrepreneur as the just owner of what he has discovered, not because he has provided a productive service, not because he claims the benefit conferred by pure luck, but because he is the finder, the creator of what he has discovered, and is thus entitled to be its keeper.

Our assertion that discovery-generated profit is not to be understood as the market value of a productive service provided by the entrepreneur perhaps may be challenged as an unnecessary complication. It perhaps may be argued that, even if one grants the crucial role of discovery in generating profit, this need not prevent us from seeing profit as a factor income. So that all that is required in order to understand pure profit within the traditional, Clarkian scheme is to recognize its emergence as due to deployment of a newly identified factor, the entrepreneurial propensity to discover. There is no need, it may be held, to justify pure profit in terms of a finders-keepers (i.e., a creators-keepers) ethic. Pure profit may be justified, surely, as being simply the additional value we can attribute to a factor service furnished by a particular class of factor owners, that is, to the service of discovery provided by entrepreneurs. We believe this argument to be faulty; it is *not* possible, we maintain, to treat entrepreneurial discovery as a productive factor.[37]

The key point is that, by its very nature (following from the sharp distinction drawn above between pure discovery and deliberate search), the pure propensity to make discoveries—or alertness—*is not capable of being deliberately deployed.* If one focuses on any such deployable propensity, in fact one must not be thinking of pure discovery at all but of a kind of deliberate search. In the market context pure entrepreneurship is not for hire—because if "entrepreneurial" services are, in fact, the object of sellers' offer to sell

37. For further discussion of this point see Israel M. Kirzner, *Perception, Opportunity, and Profit* (Chicago: University of Chicago Press, 1985), pp. 187–88; and my *Discovery and the Capitalist Process* (Chicago: University of Chicago Press, 1985), pp. 27–28.

and buyers' offer to buy, then clearly the true entrepreneurs *are those doing the buying*—the services they are buying are not the relevant entrepreneurial services at all. It is these buyers' alert discovery (of the worthwhileness of deploying the services they are buying) which constitutes the element of pure discovery in the situation. To put the matter somewhat differently, an entrepreneur never perceives his alertness, his discovery potential, *as a valuable, available factor able to command incremental value.* Either he already perceives the available incremental value or he does not. (If he perceives the existence of this incremental value but must now search to ascertain the precise route to its realization, what we have is the *already* perceived opportunity of *producing* valuable knowledge through search, not a potential pure discovery at all.) If he does not yet perceive the availability of any incremental value, there is nothing, in the range of deliberate actions available to him, which promises any such gain at all. An engineer asked to identify the productive agents "needed for" the production of a product may certainly list, as one of these agents, an intangible such as "knowledge." But he will not list "initiative," or "awareness of the opportunity to produce the product," because the very notion of what is needed in order to produce a product presupposes the *prospect* (based, obviously, on an *already* existing initiative, on an *already* possessed awareness of the productive possibilities) of producing (if the listed necessary productive ingredients are forthcoming).

It is for these reasons that the pure profit perceived and grasped by the successful entrepreneur cannot be justified as simply the market value of a special kind of productive service he was able to provide. The notion of a market value (which presupposes sellers knowing they can provide the service they propose to sell and buyers knowing the service is available for purchase) is simply not applicable to pure discovery (to which we have seen the pure profit must be traced).

FURTHER REFLECTIONS ON THE DISCOVERED NATURE OF PURE PROFIT

This insight into the discovered nature of pure profit is closer to the Schumpeterian than to the Knightian view of profit, but it permits us to see something not so easily seen in the Schumpeterian view. The difference between the Misesian view and that of Knight is a decisive one. Although for both profit is a disequilibrium phenomenon associated strictly with the open-ended uncertainty of an unexpectedly changing world, it emerges quite differently for each of them. For Knight it emerges because the world has changed in a way that was expected by nobody, including the profit-winning entrepreneur; his profit *is* in the nature of a windfall. For Mises, on the other hand, profit is won through the superior vision of the entrepreneur, through his power to *transcend* the uncertainty which has misled other market participants to undervalue present resources.[38] The relation between Misesian profit and Schumpeterian profit is a more subtle one. For Schumpeter profit is deliberately created as the pioneering, innovating entrepreneur disturbs the somnolent calm of the existing routine. This disequilibrating activity consists in acts of creativity, or at any rate, in introducing into practice the creative novelties thought up by others. (Schumpeter labeled the entrepreneurial process the "perennial gale of creative destruction.")[39] So that one might be tempted to apply a creation ethic to Schumpeterian profits, too. We must not, however, forget that Schumpeter insisted that it is no part of the function of entrepreneurial leadership "to 'find' or to 'create' new possibilities. They are always present, abundantly accumulated by all sorts of people. Often they are also generally known and being discussed by scientific and literary writers. In other cases there is nothing to discover about them because they are quite obvious."[40] Clearly, it would be difficult to apply a finders-keepers ethic to this kind of picture of the entrepreneurial function. On the other hand, the arbitrage view of profit is not inconsistent with the notion of innovative production possibilities. Earlier discussion of this view of profit by the present writer have sometimes been misunderstood in this regard. The emphasis placed on the superior vision of the entrepreneur has been interpreted as denying him genuine creativity, since that which can be seen presumably exists, in *some* sense, before it has been noticed. For similar reasons, critics often wish to emphasize the inherent unknowability of the future; the future, they insist, is *not* to be considered as a rolled-up tapestry to be gradually unrolled as time passes but as something that is being continually created out of nothing in the course of the events and decisions which make up the flowing sequence of human history. They are thus unhappy with the arbitrage view on the grounds that it appears to deny this inherent unknowability and inescapable uncertainty of the future. How can we ascribe

38. I have sometimes been (justifiably) criticized for making it seem as if the Misesian entrepreneur can win profits but never suffer losses. The superior vision of the entrepreneur sees profit opportunities; this explains profits but does not account for losses. The truth is, of course, that losses arise in exactly the same context as do profits, namely, when entrepreneurs, acting in an uncertain world, act to grasp what they think they see. Those who correctly see what others have not seen make profits. Those who "see" what, in fact, is not there to be seen (so that they buy resources at prices not justified by subsequent output values) suffer entrepreneurial losses. It is because we recognize that entrepreneurs are *interested* in making profits rather than losses that we are unable to treat losses and profits, as Knight does, as being wholly symmetrical.

39. Schumpeter, *Capitalism, Socialism and Democracy* (1950), p. 87.
40. Schumpeter, *The Theory of Economic Development* (1934), p. 88.

to the entrepreneur the capacity of seeing into the future when the future is not yet "there" to be seen? If we insist on viewing the entrepreneur as arbitrageur, are we not thereby suppressing the entrepreneur's role as innovator and creator of new products, new techniques, and new ideas?

Our view is that while entrepreneurship may very well (and in the real world certainly very frequently does) manifest itself in acts of innovative and technical creativity, the economic significance of such acts is yet to be seen in the strictly arbitrage aspect of such activity. The innovator is entrepreneurial in that he believes he has discovered a new way of deploying inputs—a way that will reveal the present market as undervaluing these inputs. The creativity we have emphasized in regard to entrepreneurial profit grasping consists not in the concrete innovative creations through which profit opportunities are identified and gasped but in the circumstance through which these innovative creations compel us to recognize how the market has (in regard to these innovative possibilities) undervalued the relevant inputs. It is the discovery of a price gap which others have failed to see which makes up, for the pure theory of entrepreneurial profit, the relevant creative aspect. So long as one is confined (as one is within the Schumpeterian framework) to recognizing entrepreneurial creativity only insofar as it is manifested in changed techniques of production, one's attention is deflected from the pure discovery element contained in every successful entrepreneurial venture.

It is true that the future is not a rolled-up piece of tapestry. Rather it is a tapestry that is being continually woven by the actions of individuals who are able to choose freely. Yet it should be clear that the successful entrepreneur, who located a new store in an area he believes will shortly become rather heavily populated, is in fact "seeing" the future. Although that future must be created by the further choices of many freely choosing persons, the entrepreneur has "seen" it—more correctly than others have. His purchase of the land on which to build his store has taken advantage of the market's failure to value that land at its full value—in terms of the services it can and will provide to this larger future population.

In talking of "more correct" or "less correct" entrepreneurial vision, in referring to noticing opportunities others have failed to notice, we are not, of course, attributing any kind of *moral culpability* to those who have failed to see the future correctly. If we use the term "error" to describe the failure of others to see what the successful entrepreneur sees, this term is used strictly as a metaphor. No one can be "blamed" for not fore-seeing the future course of events correctly. But, on the other hand, we must not deny "credit" to the entrepreneur who *does* correctly see the future. He is not simply the lucky beneficiary of a chance turn of events. He really did guess the future correctly, not perhaps with certainty but with sufficient conviction to inspire him to undertake his venture. When that venture turns out to have been a profitable one, we are entitled to describe the successful entrepreneur as having made a discovery; he should, for many of us, be entitled to keep that which he found.

Toward a Broader Theory of Distributive Justice[41]

Although this chapter has focused narrowly on the ethical acceptability of pure profit, its central insights point to a broader issue, that of distributive justice in general. We conclude this chapter by briefly drawing attention to this broader context. The truth is that the traditional approach to distributive justice has suffered, we maintain, by failing to incorporate considerations relating to the ethical status of discovered gains. Once we recognize the nature of discovery, we appreciate that the total "pie" which is being "distributed" is, in fact, a pie the very size of which is being discovered, in fact created, during and through the very process of distribution. By this we do not mean simply that (as is, of course, well recognized in the literature of distributive justice) the size of the total social output, being a function of the incentive system, is itself determined, to some extent, by the distributive pattern adopted. Instead, we are referring to the circumstance that a significant proportion of production activity is inseparably intertwined with the pure discovery engaged in by market participants in their entrepreneurial roles. Real world production is, almost inevitably, partly a matter of entrepreneurial vision in identifying where resources can be obtained, what products are worthwhile producing, what techniques will be most successful and most economical, and so forth. The size of total output and, in particular, the size of the total complex of available resources is something that cannot, even in principle, be thought of in isolation from the system of rewards assigned to entrepreneurial discovery.

There never is a "given pie," or even a given complex of resources (from which to "bake the pie") available to society. So that the notion of "distribution" (and hence "distributive justice"), a notion presuming something "there" to be distributed, is a highly problematic one.[42] The notion of a given pie or given available resources rules out any possible query as to whether, perhaps, any of the output attributable to the resources ought to accrue to he

41. For an elaboration of the broader agenda appealed for in the text see, in general, my book *Discovery, Capitalism and Distributive Justice* (1989); see especially chap. 7 for certain qualifications to the ideas set forth perhaps too unequivocally in this chapter.

42. For an earlier criticism of the notion of distribution, based on considerations not emphasized here, see Mises, *Human Action* (1949), p. 255.

who *created* the resources ex nihilo, as it were. After all, the resources are seen as somehow "given," before the issue of distributive justice makes its entry.

It is our position, indeed, that in confining attention to the issue of how given output, or given resources, are to be justly distributed, theorists of economic justice have illegitimately blocked from consideration a most important series of possibilities. These possibilities arise out of the circumstance that, in our real world of open-ended uncertainty, an enormous contribution to the total size of output is made by those whose alertness has brought to society's attention the availability of resources, the availability of techniques, and the desirability to consumers of specific kinds of output. Appropriate rewards (and incentives) for this kind of contribution requires that we step outside the framework of a given available set of goodies that must be shared out. We require a perspective which recognizes that, quite apart from the attribution of these goodies to relevant inputs, there is also the primordial issue of how it came to be discovered at all, that these inputs and worthwhile output possibilities were, in fact, available. The theory of pure profit outlined in this chapter finds its place in such a broader-gauged approach to economic justice.

3 Deserving Profits

Jan Narveson

THE CHALLENGE

"It is a peculiar smugness—and lack of theory—on the part of many of the well-off in advanced societies that leads them to suppose that they somehow deserve the luxury in which they live." So says Russell Hardin (1988, p. 132), echoing a widely shared attitude. It is a matter of some interest, I would think, whether he is right about this, and we may take his remark as a suitable backdrop for the forthcoming deliberations on the desert or nondesert of profits in particular. Making a profit, as great a profit as possible, is at least one of the major objectives in business activity and is often written up as the defining objective, and to acquiesce in the disconcertingly popular view that profits are not deserved would be to undermine business quite fundamentally. And with it, as I would insist, our prosperity.

The thesis that profits are not deserved has been argued for, explicitly or implicitly, at different levels, of which I shall distinguish two. (1) The more specific charge holds that desert is an important concept in social philosophy, perhaps that justice consists in giving people all and only what they deserve ("their due"); but that profits in particular, say because they are not worked for, are not properly deserved. Thus the "capitalist" economic system is unjust. (2) But there is also a more general charge, stemming from Rawls, to the effect that desert can play no basic role in social philosophy on the ground that the fundamental bases of desert would have to be "morally arbitrary." The upshot for the case of profits in particular is held to be that they too are undeserved.

And if they are not deserved, what would follow? Presumably that it would then be O.K. to take them away from those who happen to have them, to "redistribute" them, deprive those who get them of the businesses which produce them, and the like. The resources in question would be regarded as available for public use, and the complaints of the dispossessed could be ignored. Plainly, it is important to decide whether that is so.

In the present essay I will respond to this charge and uphold the thesis that profits can be deserved and often are so, though, of course, not always. And I shall try to correct, by setting in the appropriate perspective, the errors leading to the opposite view. The inquiry will require us to think rather closely about (1) the concept of desert, especially in relation to the neighboring but not identical notion of *entitlement;* (2) an influential argument of Rawls that has been widely taken to undermine the notion of desert, or at least its applicability to most important issues about justice; and (3) certain famous attacks on capitalists' roles in the productive system, to the effect that only those who do the "work" should be getting the rewards.

My strategy will then be twofold. One, to query how much it *matters* whether profits are "deserved"—to raise a question about just what is supposed to *follow* even if we were to grant that they are not so. On the other, I shall argue that in any case they (often) are, and are so in ways that are perfectly straightforward and not particularly problematic. Here I will complain that philosophical treatments of desert tend to leave out or soft-pedal the crucial role of the provider of the things deserved, the person from whom they are supposed to be deserved. Leaving out that person's interest in the matter turns out to be the root of the problem. When that is corrected, the case for the "capitalist" is, I think, complete.

A CENTRAL DISTINCTION: DESERT AND ENTITLEMENT

No discussion of the present matter would pass muster without attention to a distinction made famous by Joel Feinberg (1970), and receiving well-deserved attention in George Sher's important recent book-length study, *Deserving* (1987): the distinction between *deserving* something, on the one hand, and *being entitled* to it, on the other. We begin our investigation with it. Entitlement may be characterized roughly as follows:

> For individual A to be *entitled* to something, *x,* is for it to be the case that some structure of legitimate rules calls for A's getting or having *x,* so that appropriate persons acting within that structure *owe x* to A, or (if A already has *x*) must acknowledge A's right to *x.*

There is no logical entailment that A has *done* something and that *x* is conferred on A in recognition of A's contributions, though A might have, and might have had to, do something so as to be eligible for the titled item.

One could eliminate the word "legitimate" here, so that people could say, "I agree he's entitled to it: but entitlement has nothing to do with whether he should get it!" But it is more intuitive to use the term in such a way that one who speaks of entitlement presumptively thinks that the rules awarding the item in question are somehow justified, and would thus need to take back any claims to entitlement were the relevant structures shown to be invalid or shot through with injustice. What matters here is simply that nothing, so far, is implied about the *desert* of *x* by A. "That desert and rights are distinct," observes George Sher, "is suggested by the fact that persons often deserve such things as success, competitive victory, and wages, to which they have no rights, and equally often acquire rights to property and opportunities that they do not deserve" (Sher 1987, p. 194).

Sher goes on, following Feinberg, to suggest that the concepts of desert and entitlement belong to "different parts of our ethical vocabulary": namely, to the parts concerning *value* and *obligation*, respectively. Most desert claims, he notes, "are grounded not in anyone's obligations, but rather in the value of persons' coming to have what they deserve" (Sher 1987, p. 195). The most prominent and, for our purposes, nearly paradigmatic example of entitlement is where an agreement between A and B calls for *B* to receive *x* from person *A* where *A* previously had legitimate control over the disposition of *x*, as when B buys something from A. Larger structures of agreement cover many further cases: various people have made arrangements, the terms of which are such that *A*, who is a party to that agreement, is required to transfer *x* to *B*, who is happy to accept it. Whether there are entitlements from nonvoluntary structures is another question. But where profit is in question, the agreement of the persons concerned is a sine qua non.

Deserving x, by contrast, is a considerably more difficult notion to pin down. When we argue for someone's desert of something, we point to such factors as the person's efforts to get it, or to other personal qualities which, we think, constitute relevant considerations that favor giving it to him. Indeed, desert needn't be attributed to persons at all: a starry night could deserve our taking time out from other activities to gaze at it. It is not so surprising that a philosopher such as Sher can devote several hundred closely argued pages to exploring this subtle and interesting concept. Nevertheless—building in part on Sher's labors—I shall hazard an initial characterization (to be modified below), which will perhaps serve as an approximate definition:

> To say that *A deserves x* is to say that some fact about *A* is such as to constitute a reason for *A*'s getting or having *x*.

Well, which facts about A? Either some action(s), or some relevant feature or quality; especially, in the case where *A* is a person, some other nonadventitious personal quality. Among prominent examples: having worked for *x*, exerted oneself toward the acquisition or bestowal of *x* in some relevant way, or displaying some appropriate quality of character bearing on *x*. It is natural to say, when desert is queried, "What has he done to deserve it?"; but also "Well, what's so great about him that he should get such treatment?" The treatment need not be good: for "great," substitute "awful" for the converse case. The general point is that those questions require answers when a case for desert is made. Desert needs a "case": that is, we must be able to point to features, qualities, or actions of A that constitute good reason for the bestowal of x on A by those who control the supply of x. These constitute the "merits" on the basis of which x is to be given. The more merit(s) of the relevant kind, the stronger the case for giving x to A.

Feinberg offers the classic example illustrating the distinction of entitlement and desert: a (formally organized) race. Suppose that Jones crosses the finish line first. He is thus, by the rules of the competition, *entitled* to the prize. Jones may also have exerted himself mightily, trained countless hours, and in general gone all out to win. That would count toward making it true that he deserved to win. But the one who actually does win does not merely "deserve" the prize: the organizers actually *owe* it to him: it would be flying in the face of the constituting rules of the activity in question if he did not get it.

Suppose, by contrast, that Jones wins by a fluke. It was, instead, Smith who went all out, trained assiduously, etc.; but alas, appendicitis strikes Smith at the halfway mark, or he stumbles on a stray stone. Fate or accident intervenes to prevent him from realizing his goal of winning. Sad. He *deserved* to win; but alas, he did not. So he does not get the prize. He is, unfortunately, not *entitled* to the prize. Everyone will sympathize at this unhappy outcome. But few will object that the prize should instead go to Smith, and Jones would certainly have a legitimate complaint if the organizers, going back on their own rules, were suddenly to give the prize to Smith on the ground that Smith deserved it. For he did not *qualify* for it.

The race example involves one of the most characteristic bases of desert: effort. Sher observes, "Of all the bases of desert, perhaps the most familiar and compelling is diligent, sustained effort. Whatever else we think, most of us agree that persons deserve things for sheer hard work" (Sher 1987, p. 53). But is it the *only* basis of desert? Can one, for instance, deserve something by virtue of what one *is* rather than what one *does?* The example of the starry sky, I believe, shows that we can. What, after all, are the stars supposed to have *done?* Come out and twinkle for us?

But we may dwell on an equally compelling example involving persons: the beauty contest.[1] Of two competitors, Ms. H and Ms. K, suppose that Ms. H is by nature irresistible, while Ms. K, not so well favored, works away at everything—her figure, her smile, the works. The judges nevertheless award the prize to Ms. H, despite her almost total lack of effort toward that end. Do

---

1. Which also figures in Feinberg (1970) but with my own twists.

we say that *H* deserves the prize or not? If the judges declare *H* the winner, then, of course, she is *entitled* to it. But that's not all. Being, let us suppose, clearly the more attractive of the two, she also *deserves* it. The judges might, indeed, feel that Ms. *K* deserves a prize—an award for effort, say. But it is, after all, a beauty contest, they reflect, and not, say, a self-improvement competition; and if so, then the prize should go to Ms. *H,* who might reasonably feel hard done by were the clearly less attractive Ms. *K* to get it. The one who is in truth more beautiful is the one who ought to be pronounced to be so and to get the prize in *this* competition. Surely that's clear, even though effort and assiduity have little to do with it.

The specifics of the example should be set aside here. In a different contest, points may be reserved for talent, intelligence, moral character, or what have you. And whether there should be contests for beauty at all is, of course, a debated issue. But we aren't debating it here. Indeed, part of the point of using this example, which will undoubtedly be thought in bad taste by some, is to illustrate another important feature of the notion of desert: it doesn't just apply in contexts of which we approve. We might be totally uninterested, or quite negatively interested, in bestowing any sort of favor or approval upon those who excel at certain things: the Mafia chieftain who gives an extra pat on the back to a favored assassin for a "job well done," or Mr. Universe 1991. But that those who do figure in these cases recognizably employ the concept of desert rather than something else is perfectly clear.

That it is perfectly clear brings up an extremely important question about this matter: it seems that to say someone deserves something is not only not to say that he or she *will* get it, but also it is not even to say that he (morally) *should;* or, at any rate, not just like that. "Meritorious" gangsters should *not* get rewards. But must we stick with this? Can we say in our hearts that *A* in truth deserves *x,* yet seriously deny that *A* should get *x?* Perhaps not. We can understand others' employment of desert criteria without internalizing them ourselves. What the Mafia lieutenant "deserves" is perhaps the hit-man-of-the-month award, but what he *really* deserves, we might say, is not a pat on the back but a lengthy stay in prison. Within the Mafia enterprise, one can hardly dispute the schedule of merits employed; but morally, we want to reject the whole enterprise.

Those who are inclined to downrate beauty contests may feel that sex appeal, say, is not the sort of thing that should be publicly displayed, or that there is something morally criticizable about elevating some individuals above others in that respect. But they may also feel, more germanely to the present discussion, that the way one is physically structured is essentially a matter of one's genetic endowment, something that one has no control over. And they may advance the view that to make the contest depend on what is beyond the control of the contestants is somehow *unfair*.

To put such charges in perspective from the start, no case better illustrates the nature of entitlement than a pure lottery. Each buys a chance to win, and the holder of the number matching the one drawn by the appropriate randomizing mechanism reaps the prize. Every participant agrees wholly to the rules, and we can easily imagine them all contributing to the pot from an identical set of resources. Yet the prize is clearly not awarded for effort or merit but simply for happening to be the holder of the correct number. Everyone has made whatever effort was involved in chipping in and acquiring a ticket, so *that* isn't what the prize "rewards." Yet the participants have no possible complaint about fairness. Nobody deserves the prize; the winner is merely entitled to it.

This leads us in the direction of the kind of issues brought up in a now-famous argument of John Rawls (1971): Can we justly base desert on qualities wholly beyond the control of the agent, qualities that are, as he puts it, "morally arbitrary"? We will devote specific attention to Rawls's argument later. But before doing so, we need to return to the distinction of desert and entitlement, and to ask, What really *justifies* these distinctions? Thus far I have only produced examples that, I suppose, most readers will find persuasive. But some may not, for they may think that the examples are tied to an ideology they reject. And that, I have recognized, is a relevant complaint, if it can be made out. As arguments, the preferred examples have the familiar shortcomings that "intuitive" arguments always have: they persuade only those who are, or are nearly, already persuaded. Can we do better?

At this point, then, we have two jobs to do. The first is to defend the "entitlement" idea, specifically in regard to the domain in which lie profits. What I have said above may in general be described as having been said from *within* an approach to our subject that includes recognition of entitlement as a proper basis for the goods in question. But what if someone wishes to reject the entire view? Have we anything to say to him? I think the answer is in the affirmative, and moreover that quite a lot of what there is to be said has been said. But I hope that the further bit I add will help further to nail it down (knowing perfectly well, to be sure, that it won't do so for all). I pursue that in the next section.

The other job is to try to get a good handle on the notion of desert—to develop a view of desert which will explain where it belongs in the theory of morals. This we will pursue in the section on Desert in Relation to Entitlement. Having done those two things, we will be in a position to address ourselves to the question whether profits are deserved, or better, when in general they are deserved and then whether it is reasonable to pronounce that they generally are or are not. And, perhaps more important, we will be in a position to say how much and why that matters.

JUSTIFYING ENTITLEMENT

Should we ever give things to people on the ground that they are entitled to them, as distinct from the ground that they deserve them? The answer will require an excursion into moral theory. My excuse for doing so here is that it seems to be essential; but my hope is that it can be done briefly enough to provide a reasonable glimpse at the answer, and yet keep the end of this essay from disappearing over the horizon. The answers to both the question about entitlement and the question about desert on bases other than effort are, I believe, of a piece. We take up the first and more fundamental of them in this section.

The general answer I propose to give holds that a rational morality must be based on our interests; where "our" means, in particular, the interests of *agents*—thinking decision makers. Those are the central, generating interests for morals; it is we, to use a now familiar computer metaphor, who have the central processors in this operation. We gather data from the outside, to be sure: how this is going to affect us is important, and something over which we have limited control. What we are going to *do* about it, on the other hand, is what we have full control over. The control, of course, is in turn exercised, if we are rational, on behalf of our interests or values (for this purpose the two need not be distinguished).

Among these interests will be some that it is reasonable to describe as "commitments" and others that it is not, such as breathing—crucial, but not something we deliberate about; still others are of varying degrees of importance, from trivial to overwhelming. Adjusting the mix of interest pursuits is, generally speaking, what decision making mainly consists of. That we have a certain interest is often obvious to us, but even when it is, how we are to pursue it when we must make trade-offs between that and various other interests will often be a perplexing matter. And it is by no means claimed that we will always or even usually settle such things by calculation or anything much resembling it. Reflection is often low-level: we get a few more facts, we find ourselves deciding to do this rather than that, and it is only retrospectively that we conclude that our "maximum utility," say, lay in that direction.

What about the interests of other people? For us agents, that is, in principle and in general, a live issue—meaning by this that it is not to be solved by a priori argument. The interests of others *in general* do not come stamped with normative force. We can realize that another person's interest will be much affected by a certain action, and we can react so as to promote it; but we might also decide to impede it, or we might remain indifferent: its effects on our practical life may be essentially nil. Are any general policies—policies for *all,* regardless of their particular concerns—to be recommended in this area, and if so, on what basis?

The word "general" occurs several times in the preceding short paragraph and is to be taken seriously. "Others in general" are, simply, others regardless of their specific relation to us. We may love some few of them, perhaps dislike some others; but toward most we have neither attitude. They are miscellaneous people, people we don't know as particular people, but still people with many of whom we nevertheless interact. Not with all at once, of course or, indeed, in most cases, ever on a one-to-one basis. There is, however, no telling whom we might cross paths with next among all these people, and there is the extremely important additional point that we benefit from the prior interactions of all sorts of people that go to enable the particular ones we do deal with to benefit us. What aspects of people in general, then, might concern one?

The answer to that question is, in form, obvious: we are concerned about their potential effect on our interests, our "projects," on what we value. To affect those interests is to affect them for better or worse. And to gauge this, we need to invoke a notion of our "status quo." A change for the better is an improvement on where we are; a change for the worse is a decline from there. When we act, we do so, we hope, for the better and in any case not for the worse. We each find ourselves with an assortment of resources, a major subset of which is our repertoire of personal assets and powers, and with a sizable and fairly amorphous set of interests, desires, goals. When we act, we utilize those powers, which can reasonably be regarded as really "us" if anything is—our bodies and minds; and we utilize such other resources as may be available. What makes a resource "available" is that it responds to our commands, roughly speaking. The set of resources we command is what enables us to act. Accordingly, we are concerned that their availability be unproblematic.

Now consider the notion of desert. As noted, it is a *value* notion. Whether someone deserves something is a matter of how well that person meets certain relevant conditions; very often it is how well he meets them in relation to various other individuals. Whether we will measure up, in any particular case, is in general and in principle uncertain, to greater or lesser degree. If our ability to act in any particular way were always conditioned on our maximally meeting some normatively significant conditions, life for most of us would, in a word, be impossible. We would have no assurance of where we stand; we could scarcely get up in the morning with any confidence that we could do anything at all, for sure. We would continually be subservient to variable value judgments, and those not our own.

When we are *entitled* to something, on the other hand, these questions of value are shoved to the rear. With an entitlement, we know where we stand, because where we stand doesn't depend on whether, on this particular day, we have earned an "*A*" instead of a "*B*+" or even a "*C*−." An entitlement is comparable to a *decision:* when we have made up our minds, we are ready to act. The work of deliberation, whether it was done the best it could be done or not, is now done. The item in question is, simply, one's own, and what happens to it next depends only on one's own decision. From the point of view of the rational agent, entitlement secures one, to a reasonable extent, against the unpredictable decisions of others, and thus against utility losses due to lack of coordination with those others. The others, especially the ones we don't know and have no particular personal interest in, are kept, so to say, at a safe operating distance by one's entitlements, and, of course, they are similarly protected from you. Whether to become involved with them at some other level is then *up to us*—both we *and* they must agree to specific modes of interaction involving each other. No moral theory lacking these concepts can manage that feat, and this is, I think, a decisive objection to these other theories.

It has become customary among moral theorists to distinguish between "teleological" and "deontological" theories, and to identify the former with systems in which values are regarded as *impersonal,* the paradigm example being utilitarianism. They then identify deontological theories as, for instance, "right-based" or "duty-based." A right-based theory has it that morality suspends from fundamental rights, whereas a teleological system holds that morals issue from value principles.

This seems effectively to saddle the deontological theorists with, in effect, either an intuitionist or a natural-law basis. In fact, the two come to the same thing: a normative "natural law" is one which is supposed to be true just in the nature of things: fundamentally, one just "sees" that the principle in question is true—it's "self-evident." But that's exactly what an intuition is: a moral principle or judgment that presents itself without further reason. I have long complained about proposing to *found* moral theory on intuition and will merely reiterate the main objection here (see Narveson 1988, chap. 10). We need, most especially, to distinguish two employments of the term "based." In one of these, a moral system is "based" on its most fundamental ("first") *moral* principles. In this respect, whether a moral theory is teleological or deontological is a matter of what those normative principles look like on which, according to the theorist, all the others depend by deductive links. If an act of type *F* is right only because, given certain facts, such acts turn out also to be of type *G*, then the principles claiming the rightness of *G* are more fundamental, in this sense, than those about *F*. If what makes an act right is held always to be that it meets certain value criteria, for example, maximization, then we have a "teleological" or "value-based" system in this sense; if not, then it is "deontological" (or mixed).

But that is not the only relevant place to apply the term "based." For if we now turn our attention to the question, What makes those fundamental moral principles *themselves* true?, then we have a very different question: What is morality based on? To claim that the most fundamental principles of the system are "based on rights," for example, would be to hold that rights are somehow just "there," metaphysical "facts" not capable of further explication. Indeed, it would be to say that the most fundamental principles of morality are not "based" at all: they are based on *nothing* beyond themselves. It is to proclaim self-evidence for them. It is, in short, to affirm an intuitionist "basis" for morals.

To hold, as I do, that morality is based on something rather than nothing, and specifically that it suspends from our *interests,* is to deny that there are any such self-evident moral truths, such ethical-metaphysical "facts" apprehended by the appropriate intuitions. But it is also *not* to commit oneself to utilitarianism, which is widely treated as if it were the sole alternative to an intuitionistic deontology. Just the contrary is true, however: for utilitarianism *is itself a "right-based" system* in this second sense of the term. Thus, when Henry Sidgwick, widely regarded as the most acute of the classical utilitarians, asks why we should regard the like utility of others as morally equal to our own, he cites a *deontic* constraint: it simply *is* thus equal, he in effect says. That is as much as to say that morality requires us to regard it so. But *why* does it thus require us? To this he has no further answer (Sidgwick 1961, p. 382). A more recent theorist, R. M. Hare, misleadingly talks as though we can prove this by the "logic of the moral concepts"—as though it were a purely *conceptual* truth that morality obliges us to accept Sidgwick's axiom. He's wrong about this. A morality need not be utilitarian. Its principles can permit people to *ignore* the greater utility of others.[2]

Whether and in what ways their utility should be taken into account is an

2. I have criticized Hare's argument in Narveson (1981 and 1991a).

open question in particular cases. What answers that question, then? Briefly, it's *the way they are likely to affect us,* given considerations of interaction. Others impinge on us, bump into us. Some of them get, as the song says, "under our skin": we have emotional reactions to them, and our utility is directly affected by our perception of their utility—we share their happiness and misery. But most do not. With most of them, our interactions must be, in a sense, more superficial than that. Our main concern about all these others is that they not affect us adversely, that our interactions with them be on the whole for our good or at least not for our ill. And they, similarly, want this of us.

Some seem to suppose that it is rational for us to demand that those others not only refrain from making things worse for us but also that they make some contribution, perhaps a substantial one, to our well-being. For instance, some even appear to think that what they owe us, or we them, is an equalization, along some dimension or other, of our respective levels of well-being. But it is evident that this is not a reasonable demand. If you are the party with the initially better situation, why should you accept such a requirement? Why *must* you do anything for me? If you have your choice to start with, and are given your choice between simply leaving me to my devices and working hard for me with no return on the investment, why wouldn't you leave and be done with me? What we do need with others, though, are general principles of *cooperation:* constraints from impinging on others to their disadvantage, thus enabling us all to improve our lot from these interactions. These principles must be adopted in *mutual* interest, not out of a hunch about "general utility."

This specifically means that considering our general situations, it is not only in my interest that my entitlements be recognized and respected but also that it is in *my* interest to recognize and respect *yours.* I benefit from your agreement to refrain from deciding whether to deprive me of my life exclusively on the basis of whether that happens to serve your interests at the time; but a necessary condition of your reasonably agreeing to this is that I likewise recognize your right to exist, agreeing not to contemplate the same practical issue regarding your life in that same myopic way.[3]

When we propose to insist to others, as a prerequisite for interaction, that

---

3. Much of my inspiration for accepting this "social contract" view stems from the work of David Gauthier (1986). I do not concur with all of his views. A valuable compilation of recent reflections on his work is to be found in Vallentyne (1991). One particularly important point of dissent relevant to our present subject concerns Gauthier's views about "economic rent." While I have expressed criticisms of it (Narveson 1988, pp. 203–6), a far more trenchant critique is in Mack (1991).

they not feel free to injure us in respect of our bodies and any other resources we may have, this cannot rationally be based on notions of desert or value. I do not know how you value me, and I do not, in a sense, care. I do not need to claim to "deserve" to be who I happen to be; indeed, the whole idea of deserving such a thing makes no sense. Were *all* rights to be based on desert, then nobody would have any fundamental rights at all. Small wonder that we shall repudiate the general thesis that all rights must be based on desert.

Yet this is not because rights are metaphysically basic features of the world. It is because it would be irrational to leave one's prospects entirely to the vagaries of desert-based notions, or for that matter to considerations of "general utility." Entitlements do not depend on such things. They are, instead, *recognitions, agreements* about who gets what: they draw lines and allot the desired things bounded by them to particular persons, not on the basis that those are the "best" persons to occupy those areas but on the basis that they in fact, as it happens, *do* occupy them, have the strongest interest in continuing to do so, and will thus rationally utilize their powers to prevent the rest from dislodging them. The fact that one is the particular person one is must, of necessity, lie utterly beyond any possible considerations of personal desert. If our persons are to have the protection of morals, that cannot depend on desert.

That the "Social Contract," the general "agreement" to be made with all, has the general form of conserving and protecting what one has rather than supposed rights to the care and promotion of one's interests by others is likewise not due to metaphysics. It is, instead, because this is the best deal we can practically expect from everyone, given one's own and most people's typical lack of emotional concern for furthering others' projects. Drawing a moral line around one's own concerns, insisting on the noninterference of others, enables one to operate without the constant predatory and defensive activities that would be necessary in the absence of morals. But it also enables one to operate without the continual oppressive burden of having to respond to the interests of others regardless of those other people's relation to one's own interests (Gauthier 1986; see also Buchanan 1975).

Note that it would also be irrational to depend on metaphysical claims about "natural" rights, or intuitions of same, for these purposes. Whose untestable and incontestable intuitions would I go by, after all? Mine? But why should *you* go by those? Or I by yours? If intuitions have any force at all, it has to be because they constitute a somewhat inchoate exercise of practical reason at work, a more or less dim hunch that this is the way to go, considering our respective interests and situations. They may be regarded as more or less educated guesses that this or that represents a *reasonable joint principle for interaction.* As such, they are subject to further explication and justification, but do not depend on an immediate ability to provide it. Also, they cannot, as such, possibly be regarded as foundational.

DESERT IN RELATION TO ENTITLEMENT

The question will naturally arise, What is the relation between desert and entitlement—or is there one? The answer, I suggest, is that we need such concepts as desert in order to arrive at decisions about what to do with whatever we *are* entitled to do anything with: minimally, with our own bodies and minds. Entitlements constitute the framework within which such notions of desert can operate. That framework is common to us all; what happens within it depends on the decisions of individuals who are free to do as they please within the broad limits it imposes. Your and my *entitlements* do not answer the question whether I should cut you in or out of my will: you quite simply are not entitled to any of my estate, as things stand. But if I happen to decide to do so and alter the terms of my will accordingly, or if I just decide to give you something, then, my having signed on the dotted line, it's yours. Whether the executors should hand over the money, or whether the bank should cash my check to you, are not matters for them to determine on the basis of your merits, your deserts: those are settled by considerations of entitlement (they need only know that you are indeed the individual to whom the check is made out, or is named in the will as beneficiary). But my original decision to include you among my beneficiaries is clearly not settled, nor can it be settled, by entitlements alone. Entitlements frame the limits on our actions. I cannot decide to cut you in on my neighbor's will, for instance. But having command of some resources, my question what to do with them can only be rationally addressed in value terms, such as whether you *deserve* a share. Once I have invested in a certain company, I am entitled to dividends, as decided by its board of directors. But should I invest in it in the first place rather than in some other? To decide that, plainly, I must turn to considerations of whether this is the best company for my purposes. And I may quite properly include the matter of whether it deserves my support among those considerations.

Philosophers have talked as though they must choose between "teleological" notions like desert and "deontological" ones like entitlement. But it simply isn't so. We really need both. Proceeding exclusively with entitlements would be irrational if it were intelligible; but preceding exclusively with notions such as desert, as I have argued, is impossible and, therefore, also irrational. In the later sections of this chapter, I shall try to sort out the bearing of these notions on the question of profit. Whether we ever are *entitled* to profits, however, is surely part of what was intended by the broad question this chapter addressed. We should hardly have settled the broad question to anyone's satisfaction if our result were that many deserved them, but none were ever entitled to them!

Our result so far is that entitlement and desert are logically independent of each other in the specific sense that for any given item, *x*, and person, *A*, *A* may be entitled to *x* but not deserve it, deserve it but not be entitled to it, or both, or neither. But, to anticipate, it is often true, as in the case of the prize in a race, that the rules entitle persons to be accounted winners on the basis of a competition designed in such a way that we would normally expect the person who wins also to be the most deserving. Whether the free enterprise system, with its opportunities for profit, is one of those is an important question which will be addressed later.

"NATURAL" DESERT?

Now let us turn to the second question: Can we ever deserve things by virtue of natural qualities as distinct from achievements and efforts on the part of the deserving person? May we reasonably regard Harry as "deserving" his prize, or his reward, or his paycheck for that matter, on the basis of his native gifts? To do so goes somewhat against the natural grain, as it were, of the concept of desert. George Sher, as we have noted, says, "Of all the bases of desert, perhaps the most familiar and compelling is diligent, sustained effort. Whatever else we think, most of us agree that persons deserve things for sheer hard work" (Sher 1987, p. 53). And he goes on to note a "natural suggestion": that "the diligent deserve what they were striving to get by their efforts" (Sher 1987, p. 54).

But why should we attach so much weight to diligence, industry, persistence, and the like—to committed and directed activity? Sher offers the plausible observation: "Unlike other resources, our time and energy are not just means of augmenting the effects of our actions. They are, instead, the raw materials of those actions themselves . . . the very stuff of which we fashion our lives. . . . By single-mindedly pursuing the goal, he is weaving it into the fabric of his life" (Sher 1987, p. 61). And this, in the end, is "the correct explanation of why the diligent ought to succeed. . . . because their sustained efforts are substantial investments of themselves—the ultimate sources of value—in the outcomes they seek" (Sher 1987, p. 62). When such things are said, though, how are we to read the "ought" in this claim that the diligent "*ought*" to succeed? *Not*, Sher agrees, in such a way as to "imply either that the hard worker has any special right against anyone else or that anyone else has any special obligation toward him . . . In itself, diligent effort creates no entitlements'' (Sher 1987, p. 54). And he quite properly points out that diligence *of itself* is not normally enough to constitute a case for deserving reward or even, in a sense, success. The cases of "the untalented poet, the mediocre tennis player, and the political hack,'' he suggests, show that "the two sources of value conflict. If we focus on their diligent efforts, we are led to believe that these agents ought to succeed, while if we focus on the easy predictability of their failure, we are led to believe that they ought to fail'' (Sher 1987, p. 67). That easy predictability is due, however, to lack of talent.

Return for a moment to our beauty contest of the second section above. Perhaps Ms. *K* deserves to win in that she worked the hardest, put most effort into it, and wanted most badly to win; but Ms. *H* deserves to win because she simply, despite lack of significant effort to get that way, looked better. Similar cases readily crowd to mind: the prodigious violinist who plays better at age seven than the normal symphonic violinist who has worked hard over a long life, the naturally talented writer to whom the felicitous phrase leaps effortlessly to mind when the less gifted must sweat over every phrase, and so on. In all of these cases, the assigned criterion of merit is such that some will almost certainly have a *natural* advantage over others, one that no amount of hard work on the part of those others will ever overcome (and no amount of hard work on the part of anyone can ever account for).

These cases are real, so far as ordinary experience and evidence can decide the matter. Natural beauty of person, talent, intelligence, strength of body, even sweetness of character are all *real* phenomena, facts of life. Some people are born in such a way that given any chance they will display these qualities in a degree far above average; others such that no amount of training or supplied aides will get them even to square one. And the same goes for undesirable qualities. Those who claim that this is not so invariably argue that it *cannot* be so—that the whole idea of natural differences of valuable qualities among people is a nonstarter. Though the evidence for such differences' often being natural seems overwhelming, we need not decide this for present purposes. What does matter is that it might well be so, that it is very, very widely thought to be so, and thus that our view of what to say if it is so matters, practically speaking. A moral view based on the contrary supposition would be, practically speaking, a nonstarter.

It matters both whether there are appropriate responses to what we take to be natural inequalities and whether the sort of responses we currently think to be appropriate to them really are so. They might be inappropriate without this inappropriateness being a function of misperception of the facts: perhaps there is some *conceptual* inappropriateness, so that we respond wrongly even if we are right in thinking the phenomena in question to be natural. Such is the view of those who hold that to employ such criteria of desert is *always unfair*. Are they right? Can someone be said to "deserve" anything by virtue of possession of a natural trait?

We should first point out that it is never the mere *possession* of such a quality or talent that, just like that, does the "deserving." The possessors of the talents or other attributes that make things that are difficult for everyone else easy for them still have to have done *something,* though it might be trifling compared to those who hoped to succeed by diligence. At the very least one must come forward, sign the entry blank, and the like. Besides, there are no qualities whose display by humans is totally passive. The deserving have always done *something* relevant. And recognitions of possession of such qualities does, in a minor way, serve to motivate people, at least not to destroy or hide them; and preferably, as in the beauty contest, to put one's qualities on public display, benefiting many more than would otherwise be the case.

In these rather marginal ways, then, we can say that all desert is conditional upon effort of *some* kind. But it is indeed marginal: what really turns the trick, given the perhaps tiny input of effort, may be the natural talents or qualities display of which earns the prize. Is this morally acceptable? Does the naturally beautiful or naturally talented competitor then "deserve" the prize? Certainly. Both Mozart and Ms. *H* deserve their first-rate reputations. The criterion is beauty, or whatever, and however she or he came by it, there they are, displaying that quality or talent in sufficient abundance to beat out all comers.

What do those who object have in mind against this familiar observation? Some, as we noted above, may be questioning the purpose of the whole exercise: Who cares about "beauty" anyway? they may ask. It's just "in the eye of the beholder," after all, and carries little weight against more important qualities like character or intelligence. Why, they may ask, are we wasting our time in this trivial pursuit? The replies to such objections are, I think, conclusive. The answer to the first question, "Who cares, anyway?" is: those who cared enough to go to the trouble of organizing the contest, attending it, putting up the prize money, and so on. As to the second, those concerned may simply say that it's not trivial to *them,* or that even if it is, it's amusing, interesting, or whatever. And that will be answer enough.

In point of fact, most people, of whichever sex and of whatever age above childhood, are likely to have an interest in beauty of person, and there is likely to be a fair amount of agreement among them as to who has more of it than whom. There is, in short, a general human interest on which such contests may have a rational bearing. Beauty of person is in its modest way a very widely recognized value, and it is hardly surprising that it is recognized in public contests. But in any case, it is not necessary for the concept of desert to be wielded that the deserving qualities be of such general interest. For all we need is that it matters to *those concerned.* From their point of view, there is no good reason to exclude, and every reason to include, the naturally advantaged. The possession of certain qualities is what they are interested in, and their interests are what make the whole thing go round.

The point, then, is this: desert must not be thought of as a fundamentally two-place predicate, "*A* deserves *x.*" That is suggested by our opening characterization ("To say that *A deserves x* is to say that something about *A* is such as to constitute a reason for *A*'s getting or having *x*"). It's right, so far as it goes, but it doesn't go far enough. We need to give explicit recognition to the fact that desert is fundamentally a *three*-placed affair, at a minimum. The "something about *A*" that constitutes the reason in question does so *for* those whose possible bestowal of what is deserved is in question. The proper formula, then, is "*A* deserves *x* from *B*," where *B* is the bestower of the benefit in question. And our opening formula needs to be fleshed out thus:

> To say that *A* deserves *x* is to say that there is some person(s), *B*, such that something *about A* is such as to constitute *a reason* for *A*'s getting or having *x from B*—in other words, it constitutes a *reason for B* to bestow *x* on *A*.

And that person, *B*, bestows this benefit on the basis of *B*'s own *interests. B* singles out the "more deserving" on the basis of criteria of importance *to B.* For talk of desert to make sense, then, we need a point of view and an agent who can act to forward the interests recognized in that point of view, an agent who discerns aspects of the environment—for example, of various other humans in her environment—whose qualities and doings can or do make a contribution to things that matter to her.

This is not to say that the concept of desert applies every time any rational person decides, for whatever reason or for none, to bestow some benefit on some person. To say that someone deserves something is to say that that someone meets the criteria laid down by the rewarder. What the sponsors, the providers, of the reward say is, "We are looking for persons with such-and-such qualities; so we will count this list of talents, accomplishments, or features as the basis upon which we will bestow the reward." Absent an understanding of that kind, nobody would be able to recognize the case as one of meriting or deserving in any sense. The reward would be a sheer windfall, indicating no merit of any sort, just good luck. (One could stretch things and regard "luckiness" as itself a rewardable attribute—consider how the audience applauds the door-prize winner, though that individual did nothing except happen to get the right ticket.)

Of the qualities in persons that interest people, some consist outright of capacities to exert effort, and of the rest, some are more improvable by effort than others. Our interest in recognizing them, by expressions of approval, formal public recognizances of merit, or more substantial benefits, consists considerably in encouraging people to make efforts in the appropriate directions. That's a major part of it, certainly. But not all. Just as we may admire the sunset, going so far as to exclaim enthusiastically to no one in particular at its beauties, so we may admire human qualities even if they are not ones that can respond to deliberate cultivation.

And that, in a nutshell, is why desert is not confined to achievement requiring substantial and directed effort. From the point of view of those who do invest effort in this or that object, such as the worker in some employment, it may seem that all that matters, the only relevant desert base, is effort. But that is *never* true; the rewardee is never the only one who matters. On the contrary: it is the *rewarder* whose interests crucially determine the nature of the competition or other social undertaking that creates the context in which the notion of desert is applied. Sometimes this is the same person: one can have a sense of achievement, give oneself a pat on the back (or a kick in the backside). But those *receiving* rewards are not the only ones who matter in the context of reward and desert.[4]

RAWLS ON DESERT

Rawls's famed argument against desert starts from the indisputable premise that nobody can conceivably be said to "deserve" their genetic endowment,

---

4. A cautionary note may be in order here on the subject of "meritocracy." Nothing that has been said has any tendency whatever to support the idea that we, either collectively or individually, have a duty to bestow political power, or any power, on individuals of natural ability, energy, beauty, or the like. One reason for this is that nobody deserves anything for merely being whatever she or he happens to be: we must, as we have seen, do *something*. And in the case of political or any sort of power, as in any other, what is done must serve the interests of those bestowing it. All must earn their way, though it be far easier for some than others. Thus the rich, for example, do not deserve anything just for being rich. Having money, they are in a position to make offers for things they want that somebody out there is unlikely to refuse; and they are in a position to fund this or that venture. But they must actually *do* so before so much as a dime is forthcoming to them. Meritocracies, like aristocracies, would require the rest of us to bestow benefits—praise, social position, money, whatever—on some persons *for free,* that is, irrespective

parentage, or existing social and natural environment, since prior to being "given" those things, there was no individual to give them to, since "they" are what make that person the individual he or she is; and, of course, afterward it's too late to do anything about them. Then the argument proceeds to point out that whatever we may do to deserve anything, the possibility of doing it is contingent upon our having a natural endowment of a relevant type. So much is uncontroversial. But it then goes on to argue that if one's desert *basis*, D, for benefit x is one whose very existence, or one's very capacity to display it, is in turn contingent on some further undeserved attribute F, then one doesn't deserve D; and since one doesn't deserve D, then one doesn't deserve x either. "The assertion that a man deserves the superior character that enables him to make the effort to cultivate his abilities is equally problematic; for his character depends in large part upon fortunate family and social circumstances for which he can claim no credit. The notion of desert seems not to apply to these cases." And if not, then "the more advantaged representative man cannot say that he deserves and therefore has a right to a scheme of cooperation in which he is permitted to acquire benefits in ways that do not contribute to the welfare of others. There is no basis for his making this claim" (Rawls 1971, p. 104).

Many criticisms have been launched against this remarkable argument. Sher, for instance, suggests that the claim that if F is necessary for D, then we can deny desert of x, is too strong, for two reasons. One is that if we interpret Rawls's argument as essentially one of *fairness*, then, he thinks, it can at most apply to desert bases in respect of which we *differ*, and applies only to the marginal benefits of our differential endowments (Sher 1987, p. 26) rather than to all benefits of all endowments whatever. The other is the claim that D's being conditioned by F is not enough; F should be not only a necessary but a sufficient condition for D before D gets ruled out of court. Thus of two persons with equal intelligence, say, one might apply it while the other idles. So the undeserved condition doesn't actually cause the desert of the deserver; additional effort makes the difference, and this is a real merit of the deserving person (Sher 1987, p. 30).

But these counters, I think, do not get to the heart of the matter. For one thing, the second really gets us into the Free Will problem in a major way, and that is one we should stay out of: the idea that people come in for desert by volitions of their own that are totally uncaused by any factors they can't

of what they do for us. That is an absurdity which the point of view developed here should help to expose rather than be thought to invite as a supposed implication.

control is surely too obscure, too "far out" to be relied on in serious ethical applications. It belongs very strictly to metaphysics rather than to ethics.

But more important, Sher's first objection involves a basic misunderstanding with which we must now come to grips. The problem is this: if Rawls's argument were right at all, then it would undermine *all* arguments for desert, not just those involving marginal differences. It is true that Rawls is especially concerned with fairness, and this will make him sensitive to proposals that would distinguish one person from another. But that's only what Rawls is interested in. His actual argument, however—whatever he may have intended—is *not* sensitive to such distinctions. If we do not deserve anything for which we do not, in turn, deserve the basis on which we allegedly deserve it, then it follows remorselessly that we do not deserve *anything,* regardless of how many other people are similarly or differently situated. That I deserve *x no more or less than you* doesn't yet show that any of us deserves it at all; and Rawls's argument cuts to the bone: if it is right, then none of us deserves anything at all! If justice is regarded as a matter of giving people what they deserve, and his argument is sound, then the correct inference is that so far as justice is concerned, *no one should get anything from anyone.*

An interesting further question to pose for the enthusiast who rushes to embrace this position about justice then arises: Ought we, in addition to giving people nothing new, also take away that which the undeserving—that's all of us, remember—already have? If so, then to be consistent we should commit universal suicide (or perhaps murder, should some be reluctant). We do not, after all, deserve life.

If the proponent shies away from that conclusion, holding only that we should not give people *further* things just because they "deserve" them, though they may—lucky blokes!—keep the unmerited things they already have, then we might further ask how we are to make a principled use of that idea. If we may properly give some nice things to ourselves despite our total lack of desert, why couldn't we also give them to others whom it happens to serve our purposes to give them to, despite their similar undesert? In fact, why couldn't we just do whatever we liked with them? There is, I think, no reasonable reply to that query.

But if so, then nothing really stops us from being allowed to give anything we want to anyone we want, and to retain what we have (namely, our very selves) together with whatever we can get by utilizing those selves. We are home free, so to speak. And what will we do with our freedom? One thing will be to recognize an entitlement to be what and who we are as the basis for all further givings and exchanges. And another is to reestablish notions of desert *without* the Rawlsian rider, feeling free to reward those who do things useful or interesting to ourselves, regardless of the metaphysical underpinnings of those actions or displays. In particular, we will feel perfectly free to reward those who, being gifted by nature, did not have to work nearly so hard as others to do the useful services for which we reward them—including, as may be, mere display of desirable features possessed in unusual degree by the rewardee.

If we are to use notions of desert at all, then, Rawls's argument must be rejected entirely. We must admit that persons may indeed deserve things without having also "deserved" all, or for that matter *any,* of the various personal qualities by virtue of which they come to have done or exemplified whatever we think makes them deserve the item we propose to award them on that basis. The proper way to look at desert is from the point of view of the holder of the assets or benefits to be distributed. Why should we reward individuals who do *x,* or who have property *G?* The answer, fundamentally, is that it *serves our purposes to do so.* Desert is not a one-way street. That is the view which stems from forgetting that it is a three-place and not a two-place predicate. That third place is vital, for it is what makes sense of the whole thing. It is we as agents who bestow praise and blame, rewards and punishments, and if we are rational, then we will do so on the basis of the contributions such activities make to what *we value.* "Desert bases" do not operate all by themselves: people do not deserve things of nobody, or of abstract entities or "brooding omnipresences in the sky." If they deserve things, they deserve them from *us*—the people who have them to give and the motivation to give them.

BEING ENTITLED TO PROFITS

So far, I have attempted to explain why we have major use for (1) the general notion of entitlement as distinct from desert, and (2) for the coherence and rationality of awarding things on the basis of the possession of properties or the exercise of capacities which may not themselves have been, in their turn, deserved by the rewardee. What does all this have to do with our present subject, the desert of profits?

I take this present subject to concern not only desert in the narrower sense investigated above but also more generally with the moral grounds, whatever they may be, for recognizing the legitimacy of profits. Those denying the desert of profits do so in a spirit of denying their legitimacy, denying that we should let people "get away" with them. "Property is Theft," says Proudhon;

and so are profits, says Marx. The implication is that they are morally bankrupt or at least suspect, and that we either shouldn't permit them at all or should at least feel free to tax, regulate, or possibly confiscate them. The question is whether they are right about that and not just whether they or others are right about the narrower thesis that profits are not, technically, "deserved."

The outlines of my answer to this important question are as follows. First, if people are ever *entitled* to profits, then it may not matter whether they also deserve them; and they sometimes are. If the entitlement system by which they are so is defensible, then profit will be defensible as a corollary. And second, when they do deserve them, if they ever do, then it need not be by virtue of exerting great effort or of applying skills or qualities acquired only as the result of earlier effort or even of any intentional, directed activity at all. We may have perfectly good reason to bestow "rewards" of the specific type that profits exemplify, upon the particular agents who serve us in the ways in which their profitable activities do. In this section, I consider entitlement.

Let's first remind ourselves of the general idea of ownership. It is, to begin with, clearly in the Entitlement rather than the Desert category. To Own something is to be *entitled* to do as we wish with it, of course within whatever restrictions are imposed by others' rights. Some have pointed out that we can disassemble the set of possible things that might be done with anything into various different subsets: for example, specific use, disposal, transfer, rental, and whatnot.[5] This truth has led them into a falsehood: that the notion of ownership is *wholly synthetic*—actually, so to speak, *composed* of a set of wholly distinct rights, the uniting of which is (*a*) logically unnecessary, and (*b*) wholly conventional, in particular, due solely to the operations of legal systems. That inference is wrong. The fact that A can be broken down into B, C, and D, does not prove that A is essentially nothing but the adventitious sum of B, C, and D, and especially does not prove that A has to be put together by convention. Nature does it all the time, despite natural objects' being decomposable into simpler elements; and while it is not exactly "nature" that puts together the various separable powers of ownership, neither is it simply convention.

In the case of property ownership, the unifying feature of these diverse possible acts is very easy to identify. No matter what we do with items, what unites them all is simply that we (can) *do* them. The fact that I have x within my power when I do one thing with it also enables me to do other things with it, if it occurs to me to do those things. And if a moral case can be made for

5. See Waldron (1988, p. 49) for the classic list, which in turn is due to Honoré (1961). Waldron does not make the mistake I mention, but see Gibbard (1976).

allowing people, in general, to do things that they want to do, then we have a moral case, prima facie, for property. For me to have the right to *x*, where *x* is an object of some sort, is simply for me, in general, to have the say-so on what happens to *x*. Where *x* is mine, whatever use can be made of *x*, the person wanting to do it has to "clear" it with me. If I want to go fishing with it, my own "permission" is automatic; but if someone else wants to, it is not, and the permission must be obtained or reasonably inferred. Such is the nature of the entitlements of ownership.

Why should we accept a general right of liberty, anyway? And even if we did, does it indeed lead to a right of private property? These are much disputed matters, and I have elsewhere entered my argument at length (Narveson 1988, p. 1). But the case can be quickly sketched here. The answer to the first question is simply that liberty is being permitted to do what we like or want. But "what we like or want" is *us*. To ask the question why one has an interest in being allowed to do what one wants is to ask a self-answering question: that one has an interest in doing something is precisely that one wants to *do* it, and not to be allowed to do it is to be disenabled from doing it. Accepting a *general right* of liberty will, of course, not allow one to do certain things that one might have wanted: namely, to interfere with others' liberty. To say that there is a *general* right of liberty is to say that everybody has it, not just certain people or oneself. Acceptance of this general right is rational, then, only if one stands to gain more than one loses by embracing it. And why think that? A large question, to which, again, I think there is a good answer. For to say that we may interfere whenever it pleases us is to license and, given people with conflicting *interests,* is in effect to invite war, conflict, aggression, and defense. But these are inefficient activities. We will do better if we mutually refrain, instead of permitting each other to get on with all those activities that can be pursued by peaceable methods, namely, by agreement with those affected.

But we can make sense of this, indeed, make it possible, only with property rights. You and I cannot bargain about anything if we have nothing that is ours to bargain with. If I have nothing to offer, I can make no offers, and so the question whether the offer is good enough for you to accept cannot arise. A general right of liberty, however, does give each and every one the right to himself or herself, at a minimum: to use our own persons as we think best, free from arbitrary depredations.

Does it also lead to property rights in external things, things other than selves? Here what people have insufficiently appreciated is that a "right to an external thing" is not a different, separate kind of right from "action" rights, rights to do. On the contrary, it is simply a further right to one's own actions, namely, to do all those things that you can only do with the objects in question. We have property when we are allowed to do things *with* particular external things. To say that those things are ours is to say that those are doings we are to be allowed to engage in. The doings are what count, at bottom.

But if we are disposed to allow others to do what they want, to pursue their lives as they see fit, then this means that we are disposed not to interfere with their activities, unless and until those activities in their turn interfere with others. To make sense of this, however, is to recognize the classic principle of First Occupancy—First Come, First Served, as it were. Those who begin performing activities that involve the use of things that are not previously used are not, thereby, interfering with anyone else. (To suggest that they may be "interfering" with *future* people is to redefine the ordinary notion of "interference," rather than to convict the advocate of liberty on a charge of inconsistency.) They are, of course, preventing others thereafter from utilizing that very thing. But we cannot all utilize that very thing, so that's not an objection unless one objects to anybody doing anything with anything—which, of course, would be to object to anyone's doing anything at all. Others, who come later, will just have to confine their actions to the use of *other* things, either things they can arrange for the use of with their current owners, or other unowned things. A property rights scheme based on first acquisition, that is, on first use, is the only scheme that can coherently claim to incorporate a general right to liberty (Narveson, 1989).

Once we have something that we may do as we please with, it may please us to trade it with someone else who would be more pleased with what we have, while we are more pleased with what he has. The right to do that is a simple entailment from full ownership, as defined above. If I may do *what I please* with *x,* and you may do *what you please* with *y,* then obviously we may exchange it, again with the usual restriction that in the process we may not violate the rights of others not party to the transaction. Our entitlement rights to what is ours include, then, the right to lend or otherwise conditionally transfer what we own to others on whatever conditions we mutually accept, by trading them to others in return for what we find more suitable. So long as certain fundamental restrictions are observed—namely, that no fraud or force is employed in the exchange process, both parties acting (sufficiently) voluntarily, and provided that no significant negative side effects (or "externalities") on third parties are involved, such as to amount to an imposed and unaccepted using or destroying of what those other parties legitimately have—then the parties come as a result to be *entitled* to their respective new bundles of goods or services.

What about profit, then? Profit, I take it, is the difference between what it cost me to acquire item *x* and what I get—call it *y*—from selling *x* to someone else. In the special but familiar case where the costs are monetary and where *y* is money, then the monetary value of *y*, minus the cost of *x*, is the profit to the original owner of *x*. Of course, the customer supposes that his newly acquired *x* is better than *y*, the money he paid for it, from his point of view. He too profits, though not, of course, monetarily—unless, as is often the case, he purchased *x* for investment purposes which turn out to be successful. If we grant the case for a general right of liberty and that this makes for a general right of property, then the in-principle legitimacy of profit, in this generalized sense, automatically falls out. It is quite unnecessary for profits to be deserved in any further sense than that the person making them supplied, fair and square, a service or item for which the purchaser was willing to pay, and did pay, the price that afforded that profit.

But I have thus far used the term "profit" in a broad sense, and it will be objected by some that it is too broad. What, they will want to know, about profit in the *special* sense in which profit is not just "return" but that very special return which is neither interest nor wages nor rents (at going rates)? Here I wish to endorse the general view of Professor Kirzner, advanced elsewhere in this volume. The entrepreneur should be regarded as "finding" something, "discovering" it. What he finds, and takes advantage of, is an opportunity to provide people with services that no one else has as yet thought to provide (or if they have "thought" to, have not actually done anything about it). So viewed, our account makes clear why these too are things to which people can be entitled. Those to whom the entrepreneur sells his newly created items judge them to be worth the agreed price, a price which, let us suppose, yields the entrepreneur a greater return than would such familiar investments as lending out his capital at specified rates, or performing familiar services for others at "going" rates of pay. And after all, why not? The customer is under no obligation to buy. If he buys, nevertheless, it is because at the time he judges the newly available item to be worth what is asked for it in comparison with any other purchase or other use of his money that, so far as he knows, he could have made instead. He thus agrees to the exchange. No more is needed. The entrepreneur has made a profit to which he is entitled, for the same reason as he is entitled to a newly discovered mineral or piece of land he arrived at and put to use prior to anyone else's putting it to that or any competing use.[6]

We are, then, often entitled to profits. Profits can be legitimate. But entitlement, as we have seen, does not entail desert. Do we ever *deserve* profits, then? The stage is now set for a clear answer—in the affirmative.

Deserving Profits

In some cases of legitimately owned goods, we might do nothing with them, but in most we will do something, either using them as they are or using them to better our situations. So far as miscellaneous other people are concerned, we ordinarily do not see any direct point in simply giving them useful things of our own. That comes under the heading of gift or charity, not business or investment. On the other hand, in the absence of charity we may nevertheless do well to share the use of our worldly goods with others, on favorable terms. The things available for profitable use are diverse. "What profiteth a man if he gain the whole world but lose his own soul?" asks the New Testament. The implication is that he would profit more were he to take the option that leaves him with his soul, minus the whole world, rather than vice versa. Here the profit is spiritual. And the passage makes no bones about it: in spiritual matters, we are to maximize our returns on investment, whatever the implications for more mundane concerns. Again, one can have a profitable afternoon discussing the theory of universals with a colleague: the profit is intellectual. Another can have a profitable session with a famous ski instructor. The profit is athletic. All of these are reasonable uses of the term "profit": all imply that a certain disposition of one's resources, including one's time and energy, has had the result that you are now, as a result of your investment, better off in some valuable respect than in the situation ex ante, and all suggest that this is a good thing to do.

If we turn now to the possible desert of profits of the normal, monetary variety, we will note, first, that some who do very, very well might quite possibly have been, in the main, very, very lucky. But then, if we can point to those, we can point also to others who have done well because they have

---

6. Of course, many would dispute that we are ever entitled to acquire things in that way; and many more would want to impose such conditions as the "Lockean proviso," which allegedly limits what one can do along that line. In fact, I find discussions of the proviso confused (and attempt to sort things out, to the advantage of the "finders-keepers" view, in Narveson (1991b); but in any case, there is no question of an entrepreneur not leaving "enough and as good for others," for of new ways to do things there is literally no end. (See also Child 1990.)

been very, very acute, shrewd, persistent, imaginative, enterprising, even rather courageous, and so on. The ones who succeed for these reasons are the ones of whom we are inclined to say that they "deserved" their success. Are we ever right to so conclude? Russell Hardin, as we saw at the outset, apparently thinks not, and his skepticism is widely echoed.

Now, one might suggest that the facts adduced above *show,* all by themselves, that we are correct about this. After all, we might say, what I have noted are paradigm cases of the use of the word "deserves." If I am right in what people would likely say in such cases, so this argument would go, then there is no more to be said. But as is clear from the foregoing, I reject this easy way with the subject. I do want to allow for the possibility that somehow we are all making some kind of mistake. I don't think that what we have is essentially, let alone exclusively, a matter to be settled just by noting what we say, and I do think that it is appropriate to ask Why. But still, I do think that we have good answers, that the answers have been given, in general outline, and that they do support such ordinary cases as the one I have described.

Of course, they will support them only if the activities which make profit possible meet the conditions of legitimacy imposed earlier. Profits may not be made at others' expense. Or rather, they may not be made by fleecing, defrauding, and so on. The earlier conditions are often enough met, we think. But what about the "and so on"?

There are, I think, two major candidates for plausible objection. The first is that profits are always made in some way *at the expense* of others, and thus never meet the legitimacy conditions: profits are a form of theft. The second is that there is only one legitimate kind of desert basis for material goods, namely, Labor; and profiteers, necessarily, do not exemplify it. Profits, as such, *cannot* be deserved. Both are familiar charges from assorted quarters on the Left. Both, I think, can readily be shown to be either baseless or to require extraordinary assumptions or attitudes unmotivated from the point of view of ordinary people.

What about the first charge? Presumably it is not being maintained that profits are typically earned through violence or fraud. That is too obviously subject to refutation at the hands of the observable evidence to take seriously at this level. Of course, some profits are so made and are thus illegitimate; that they are so is central to the entitlement view. But in the same sense that some are illegitimate, lots of others are not. Cheating and chiseling do happen, but they are atypical. What the proponent of this kind of objections needs is some kind of inevitable, inherent side effect of profit making that undermines the legitimacy of all such activity. On the face of it, all parties to profit making act voluntarily enough—customers aren't forced to buy, entrepreneurs to invest, or employees to work. (Some may object that even this isn't so. But it is difficult to see how any sense in which it is not so can be relevant. In the sweat of thy brow, says a familiar and much-admired source, shalt thou eat bread. But though everyone must, in some way, sweat, they don't have to sweat for any particular employer in a free-market system—none of them has the power to force him to stay, with whips or jails awaiting those who try to leave; and in a nonmarket system, after all, everyone sweats for the same employer—the state. On the whole, we must look elsewhere for a reasonable objection of this type.)

Most who think to do so quickly turn in the direction of "fairness" and "equality" (recent Marxists tend to, seeing the difficulty of making much independent use out of notions of "exploitation"). Exchange systems, of course, permit that goods are "distributed" in ways that many will regard as "unequal." Somehow, they think, exchanges between A and B are such that A winds up with "more" than B—even though what A has more of isn't the same as what B has "more of," so that a question arises how this estimate of inequality is to be got off the ground in the first place, and even though both parties are satisfied that they have made the best exchange possible in the circumstances. Still, the theorists we have in mind don't like this. They nevertheless suppose it to be "unfair."

But wrongly. For one major thing, the proponents take insufficient account of the fact that exchanges that were precisely equal would be pointless. Why don't we trade five-dollar bills? What could be more equal? But precisely because what we end up with is absolutely "equal" to what we started out with, the proposed exchange would be completely pointless. For exchange to make any sense, each party must see himself or herself as *gaining* by transferring what he had before to the other party. And on the other hand, our interests typically take no regard whatever of the relative holdings of the parties to the exchange, either ex ante or ex post. When the newsboy sells the millionaire a newspaper for 50¢, both the newsboy and the millionaire reasonably think themselves to have made a good deal. The justice of assorted holdings simply is no particular function of their relative "sizes" as such. If all relevant parties are agreed, and none act with eyes closed or with wool drawn over them by the other, then charges of unfairness, we may reasonably argue, are irrelevant. It is not amiss to point out that they are also of dubious meaning. Each of us is different. We do not measure what we have in terms that are directly transferable to others. Even equal amounts of money mean very different things to different people. The aspiring egalitarian will find it impossible to mint a suitable common coinage for his theory.

Those who think otherwise may have one of two sorts of reasons for thinking as they do. One is that there is some sort of natural right to an "equal share" of valuable things. But resorting to natural rights is not helpful if we seek a common basis of rules for interaction among diverse people, many of whom will not recognize the Natural Right in question. Can it be *defended*, as distinct from merely *asserted?* I think not. How else, if not by the rejected appeal to intuition? Of course, one defense would be that we all deserve equally, that our desert base, our relevant merits, are in all cases identical because, say, there is only one such base, and it is the same in all of us. We have considered one special form of this argument previously, which holds that they are identical because they are nil. We will shortly consider a variant, in the view that there is just one relevant desert basis, labor, which implies that we should all get, if not straightforwardly an equal share, at least a share "equal to our labors." The only third option is the one that would indeed be germane if its premises were true: namely, that we each really are equal to each other in all sorts of specific and familiar variables, of talents, capacity for industry, alertness, and the rest of what we might call the productive virtues. But this is the way that is empirically refuted on all hands. Reality stubbornly refuses to cooperate with anyone seriously wishing to maintain the Equality of All Humans in all contexts of distribution on the basis of desert. It just isn't so.

No matter who has what and no matter how they came by it, one can relate to the de facto possessors of resources one would like to have in only two ways: by using force, or by voluntary methods. And among the latter, again, there are two: persuade them that there is some good reason for yielding up, say, the excess of their resources over one's own to oneself, simply because they are such "excesses"; or else make them an offer, one that makes it worthwhile for them to trade. The trouble with the first of the Voluntary methods is that there are no good *arguments* for equality, though the field resounds with assertions. Those who are to be persuaded of its merits will not be rationally persuaded. No steelworker is about to split his hard-earned income with lower-paid fieldhands, say, for the sake of "equality": he doesn't *care* about equality, and he does care about the condition of his house, the fact that his wife is pregnant and new bills are about to come upon him, and so on.

It has not been sufficiently usual in moral philosophy to pay extensive attention to the interests of ordinary people. But they, I submit, are what *count* for our purposes. If there are no good reasons that would be acknowledged by them for insisting that you and I and they must all have the "same," then we have no moral basis for requiring equalization. The equalitarian can provide no reasonable premises from which ordinary people could find their way to insisting on Equality as the watchword of justice. It is human nature to envy those with a good deal more, no doubt; but it is also human nature to be extremely averse to parting with what one has merely in order to equalize one's situation with the less fortunate. There is no similar problem, though, about exchange and property, which respect the rights of individuals and whose capacity to cater to our interests is clear.

As to force, we should first point out that anyone who agrees that *x* may not morally be *required* has already agreed, in effect, that force may not be employed to bring *x* about. Besides, most will be disposed to agree that the use of force to pursue our various private purposes is immoral. But a deeper inquiry might be sought. Why morally proscribe the use of force for whatever there is no moral warrant for requiring people to do? In effect, I have addressed this in making the case for a general principle of liberty, which of course implies precisely such a proscription. But I want to add that the case for liberty consists in showing that using force has problems, of which the most fundamental is that *it doesn't pay*. The victims of force will, for one thing, resist, and if they are the rich, the possessors of greater resources, then there is the little problem that they are more likely to win anyway. But otherwise, and in general, the problem, as Gauthier (1986, chap. 6) and others (notably Buchanan 1975, chaps. 1 and 2 especially) point out, is that force is *suboptimal*: the two parties waste resources fighting, which cuts into the supply of produced goods and services that might otherwise be distributed to mutual advantage. There is the most excellent reason for ruling it out.

Of course, isolated uses of force succeed in the short run from time to time. But they succeed only because they are violations of a general prohibition that is widely observed (and because the victims or their agents have not been able to catch and punish them). There is no excuse at all for thinking that we shouldn't even have the prohibitions in the first place. In their absence, who can doubt that communities would experience their share of the horrors of Hobbes's famed "war of all against all"? But once the prohibitions are in place, then violators of those prohibitions are cheaters, despoiling others of what is reasonably regarded as theirs.

And that leaves us with voluntary exchange, which is justified by considerations of *advantage*. No fancier reason is needed. For it to make sense for me to want to trade with you, all we need is that I suppose I would be better off as a result, if you will agree; and the same for you vis-à-vis me. So both you and I reasonably think that we would, respectively, be better off with what we would have afterward than with what we have now. What better reason could there be? Considerations of the ratio ex post of your to my goods, is on the face of it irrelevant (but see Frank 1985). Obviously I will think that I have more than you after the exchange in at least one respect since, after all, by hypothesis I value what I have more than what you have, which is what I had before, and my lesser valuation of which is precisely what occasioned the exchange from my end. And the same with you. But we are both right, for the relevant values to bring to bear here are, surely, yours and mine. If we both think we have come out ahead, how could any other consideration be relevant?

This is, to be sure, excepting the fairly important case in which our activities generate significant negative externalities. Naturally they are objectionable. Indeed, our account is precisely what shows them to be so. The lungs, for example, of those on whom pollution unpermittedly falls, are the private property of those whose lungs they are, and so pollution is a prima facie violation of the very same rights we are upholding here. It has to be pointed out, however, that there is no necessary connection, nor much of any empirical one either, between externalities and equality. Nor is it at all evident that in order to deal with such special problems we need to abandon the market system. What we do need to do is find suitable ways for reasonably estimating and then satisfying the damage claims of those who are damaged by such negative externalities, and of measuring potential ills in such a way as to make possible rational decisions about how much in the way of pollution and the like we should permit. While this is not easy, there is no reason to think that the result must impugn the system of free exchange with its potential for profit. Indeed, the prospect of making profits by producing the desired clean-up equipment, etc., needed to eliminate the damages is likely to be the chief stimulant to their elimination.

Once we regard people's resources as properly *theirs,* then the case for claiming that they are ''harmed,'' damaged or injured by free exchange, as such, falls to the ground. By definition, free exchange does not deprive people of what is theirs. The worst that can be said of it is that (1) it might not give you as much as you would have liked; and (2) if you had nothing to start with, then no benefits from exchange are possible for you. In those cases a system insisting that all transfers of goods be by agreement leaves you only with the option of asking for charity. Which is incontestably bad for you—but, we should note, not necessarily a state that any others have *put* you in, and second, not as bad as some states they could put you in even so, given sufficient ill will. Not giving *B as much as B would like* hardly counts as a "harm" or "deprivation," so long as we don't beg questions. Neither does giving him nothing when he has nothing. In order to so count it, we must presuppose that *B* had a *right* to move, for example, to "enough," or to an "equal amount." But that is the view which, as I have argued, lacks general rational support. The "support" we see for it always consists in sheer assertion, in the end.[7] If we look under the rhetorical surface, nothing meets the eye but fallacy or irrelevance.

LABOR, DESERT, AND VALUE

Well, what about the other thesis, then? Do we not think it just that people get what they deserve, and unjust that they get anything else—namely, either more or less (or something qualitatively different) than their deserts? That the expression "just deserts" is essentially pleonastic? As we have seen, the short answer to this is No: "we" do not, indeed, think this. The race goes to whoever crosses the finish line first, whether or not that person is a distinctive case of The Swift, who may have had a bad day. Nor do the organizers of the race necessarily care whether the winner worked harder than the others to become so.

But it is much more important to point out that in any case we are not always—for most of us, not even usually—engaged in a "race." We are, instead, just *getting on,* and what we have in the way of resources are considerably assets which we have done no "racing" for but simply happened to find ourselves with. Whoever wishes may think this *"unfair"*; but in it there is certainly nothing *unjust.* If we turn to the subject of holdings gained from operations on a free market, then, we can take a similar line. We can insist that what people are entitled to is one thing, what they deserve another, and that sometimes, or perhaps often, the twain do not particularly meet, or have at best a nodding acquaintance. When they don't, the relevant "prizes" nevertheless rightly go to those entitled to them—even though we may often add, as a further thought, that it would be nice if those who get them would do something for the deserving but unrewarded persons who lost out. But then, it would also be nice, if niceness is in question, to do something for the *un*deserving and unrewarded who likewise "lose out."

But this is perhaps not an adequately satisfying answer. For one thing, we

7. For a notable case in point, see Nielsen (1984). Norman (1987) provides another instructive example.

will surely feel that if desert and entitlement run *too* independently of each other, then perhaps something is wrong. And for another, entitlement can't be self-justifying. There have to be good reasons why we should have such a system. Of course, I have attempted to provide some of those good reasons in the preceding sections. One might even translate those reasons into the vocabulary of desert by suggesting that we *deserve* to have an entitlement system! Nevertheless, the first point is important.

Let us turn, then, to the special case of workers versus profit makers, by considering the classic thesis known as the Labor Theory of Value, a theory that has been much discussed even in recent years as well as in the last century.[8] That all such theories fail if intended as explanatory theses about exchange values in market societies is, I take it, something that can be taken as simply established by now. But it may be useful to put the basic criticisms in a nutshell, helped by our discussion of the notion of desert: the trouble with the Labor Theory is, in brief, that it focuses exclusively on what we may call the "input" side, the production side of the value transaction. Indeed, it seems to be doing its best to forget that it is a *trans*action we are talking about here at all. And for that reason, it actually fails to give anything like a proper account of the deserts of labor itself.

The idea that labor of itself "creates value," when one takes into account the two-sidedness of exchange, is a sheer fallacy. True, labor is indeed normally *intended* to create value, or rather, to create valuable *things*.[9] But alas, it can fail. We can spend years in fruitless effort; and as Sher observes, no prizes are given to "someone who excels at balancing a telephone on his nose" (1987, p. 119). It doesn't matter how much effort and ingenuity is put forth, nor how clearly it displays "autonomy," for when the product goes to market, people will decide on the basis of their own interests, paying no independent attention to the "quantity of labor" that may have been embodied in the items they choose to purchase.

It is futile to point out, as Jeffrey Reiman does in a recent contribution, that a person's labor is "his very life." "In capitalism," says Reiman, "Marx held that workers work without pay because they give their bosses more labor-time than the amount of labor-time they get back in the form of their wage. . . . The worker gives a surplus of labor over the amount he receives in return, and this surplus labor is held to be unpaid" (1987, p. 6). As Reiman goes on to recognize, it only follows that the surplus given is "unpaid" if labor is

8. For a few (of many) examples from the mainline journals: Cohen (1979), Reiman (1987), Hunt (1986).
9. As G. A. Cohen, himself a Marxist, established so decisively in Cohen 1979.

"the proper measure of what my boss and I have exchanged" (1987, p. 6). To this end, Reiman seeks "a neutral way of characterizing what it is that people give one another," where "[b]y neutral, I mean a way of characterizing that does not presuppose the validity of any of the systems of ownership that are under inspection." He comes up with the suggestion that "all that remains that workers give in production is their time and energy, in a word, their labor" (1987, p. 9). And, he suggests, "this labor-time is really given in the sense that it is "used up" . . . workers have only finite time and energy, and thus less left over when they have given some up." This contrasts, he thinks, with their talents, which "[f]irst of all . . . are the result of their natural gifts plus the time and energy they devoted to developing those gifts. . . . But the 'natural gifts' themselves are . . . given to the worker and thus merely passed on by him. What's more, talents are not used up in exercising them. . . . Outside of ownership, labor and talent, all that is left in any part of the social product are the natural materials that went into it" (1987, pp. 9–10).

Let us grant most of this. But what does it prove? Even if we suppose that labor is somehow what we ultimately exchange—and only a very stretched use of the term would support that—and even if we supposed that we could measure this life labor in some meaningful way, what Reiman forgets is that he's asking us to buy it; and from our point of view the sheer fact that the worker's labor is his, is the very stuff of his life, may be of no particular interest to us, the buyers—the other party involved. We have our own lives to live. And we are interested in a range of things having no necessary relation to degrees of effort, ingenuity, persistence, or whatever, either in the abstract or on the part of whoever might produce anything. What interests us is *results,* not effort. And not just any results, but only those pertaining to our own lives—our own goals, purposes, ends. What we want is a better mousetrap. We have no independent interest in the amount of work someone may have expended in trying to come up with one or in making the inferior ones that won't do.

And if we now ask, Who *contributes* to the end of bringing into existence these various goods? then the capitalist can hardly be left out of account. In providing capital, he enables various people to produce what would not other-wise be produced at all. Thinkers who sympathize with Marx on this matter are quick to point out that this function of providing the capital could conceiv-ably have been provided instead by some other means than the voluntary enlistment of individuals who own the funds or other forms of capital required (e.g., Cohen 1979; Schweickart 1980). And no doubt it could. For instance, it could instead be provided by slave labor or in plants managed by party functionaries—that is, by taxing all, whatever their interest in the matter, to supply capital out of the (supposedly) public treasury instead of from the private treasuries of persons interested in making money, and having it managed by civil servants rather than persons who have a direct personal stake in how it does. But whoever supplies it and however it is supplied, what is supplied is, in the circumstances, necessary for enabling people to engage in the direct acts of production that yield the desired products. Supplying that capital is thus a function that merits the consumer's favor—that is, his voluntary purchase of the goods it enables to be produced at the price which earns that favor.

Once we look at it from the point of view of the consumer, then, it is perfectly apparent why it is rational to "reward" the supplier of capital: for what he supplies is, unquestionably, of value to us. It's what we want. For twice the price, say, we can get a similar product from workers in a commune, collectively but laboriously constructing their own machinery and "organizing the means of production" with no outside capital. Very well: perhaps I can be persuaded of the superior virtue of doing things that way. But what if I'm not? Why *must* I, a mere consumer, be interested in such things? What if virtue isn't what I'm in the market for? (My New Testament apophthegm implies that I'm a fool not to be, and it may be right; but it may also be wrong in implying that material wealth is incompatible with spiritual wealth. In any case, I may well say, it's not the business of the people who make my shoes, or whatever, to go on about my spiritual welfare.)

Marx, of course, confined his version of the theory to the production of useful goods and, moreover, to their production by currently competitive technologies. Those two restrictions, indeed, are all that could have kept the theory in the field for so long. Without them, as Marx was aware, the theory would be a nonstarter. Obviously, the incompetent who produce one item per hour should not get paid the same as the supercompetent who turn out a dozen in the same time. But those restrictions also enable him to obscure the real issues. For Marx is thus able to keep the consumer on the shelf, as it were, looking only at producers, that is, workers and capitalists. And then, of course, the Marxist has an easy time of showing that the capitalist doesn't "do" anything (Cohen 1979), in the sense in which workers do things. Only workers produce, say the Marxists; capitalists don't really produce—they just collect the spoils.

Yet Marx, one should note, seemed to think that workers who do more should get more. But *who* "does more," in the sense relevant to this theory? The problem is that there is a sharp divide between two ways of answering:

(*a*) On the one hand, we have pure "input side" measures—the ways that are clearly more appropriate for a labor theory of value in the narrower sense. More labor is more hours spent, more calories expended, more sweat dripped.

(*b*) On the other hand, we can focus on *output* and say that by definition he who produces more has "worked" more, has "done" more—regardless of how much sweat emerges, how many hours he works, how many calories he burns up.

Once we have made this distinction, however, we can see that Marx's two restrictions preclude criterion (*a*) from being meaningfully deployed. We are only *allowed* to look at those workers who not only (*a*) produce something useful, as determined by the fact that somebody, given his choice, will buy it, but (*b*) who produce it comparatively efficiently. This comparative efficiency, of course, comes about as a result of the fact that those who buy the product do so more or less rationally—preferring it, for example, to similar items that cost more. Which means, as Robert Nozick pointed out (1974, pp. 256–62), that our criterion for assessing efficiency smuggles what was supposed to be the rival theory in by the labor theory's back door: method *X* is more efficient than method *Y* if *X*-produced goods survive on the market and *Y*-produced ones don't; product *P* has utility only if someone will actually buy *P* when it is offered for sale.

No matter how you consider it, then, the conclusion remains that (*a*) and (*b*) will give you differing results. Consider a factory, now technologically quite feasible, which employs *no* (human) production workers on its assembly line—all that work is done by alert, competent, tireless, reliable, nonunionized robots. The production-line engineers who look after the robots emit little sweat (though, contemplating my modest experience with digital-controlled equipment, probably plenty of tears!); but if we identify *them* as the only available candidates for Marx's "workers," then we shall have to say that they do vastly more work than their production-line human counterparts in less advanced factories, for one hour of their time doubtless accounts for many times the output of one hour of Detroit assembly-line worker time. But then, if we go in this direction for long, we may well have to point our finger at the supplier of capital for this operation as also having contributed mightily to production, and in that sense done "work," so counting as "labor." If the Marxist's reply is (as it no doubt is) that the "work" done by the capitalist could have been done by "society," then he becomes susceptible, courtesy of our workerless factory, to the response that the work done by Marx's proletarian can instead be done by robots. And so what? No one is eternally indispensable; everything *can* be done in some other way, and sooner or later probably will be. The only question is, Which way is the best, under the circumstances, that is, given the available alternatives? It is the judgment by the relevant parties, *namely, the consumers,* that matters.

It is, in fact, quite possible to compare the performance of private-sector and public-sector investment. And when we do, both experience and theoretical reflection strongly argue that from the social point of view the capitalist way is better. Private capital is more productive, because more efficiently deployed and allocated, than "public" capital—in addition to having the not insignificant advantage of being compatible with respect for the freedom of the participants. But the point of all this is not that in order to justify utilizing the concept of desert at all we are forced to make this case. All we have to do is to point out that the people who most relevantly apply the concept, namely, consumers, could *reasonably make* such judgments. It is their point of view that is the *source* of criteria of desert in these contexts. And it is a point of view which clearly makes good sense for regarding the profits from well-made investments as (often) deserved by those who make them. That the capitalist deserves his profits stems from the fact that his investment activity causes desirable services to be performed for people who want them—services that would not otherwise have been performed, either at all or as well.

The general effect of this argument is to show that profitable investment is a genuine case of merit. The person who invests does something with his resources that he or she need not have done, and what he does is useful to those whose enterprises are supported by the investment in question. Were it not so, of course, they would not pay him for it. Other writers have shown that and how entrepreneurs perform useful functions, notably the function of organizing production, and especially of organizing it more efficiently than it would otherwise have been, thus enabling more to be produced with the same inputs and thus more profit to be made (e.g., Arnold 1987). All this is right. But we should not suppose that we could come up with a metric of merit over entrepreneurship in the abstract. Other things being equal, we might agree, he who is more entrepreneurial—more innovative, more exploitative of market opportunities, and so on—will deserve more. But a less entrepreneurial person who makes a greater though more conservative investment may nevertheless properly make more, just as the beauty queen who had more to invest, though she had to do much less by way of getting the investment made, may nevertheless deserve the greater prize.

To repeat: we only go up blind alleys if we myopically fix our gaze only on desert factors in abstraction from what causes them to *be* desert factors, namely, the interests of the agents—in this case, ultimately, the consumers—who hold the purse strings, loosening of which is the source of the relevant rewards in this area. What is done that deserves reward is the marshaling of resources in the direction that elicits the purchasing response from consumers. No further justification on grounds of high moral character, or whatever, are required here.

At the risk of overworking an example, let's return just one last time to our beauty contest. There have been controversies about these events in recent years, the question being whether their purposes are such as to deserve public attention. These questions are, of course, relevant. Yet we can apply desert concepts in the absence of a verdict on the ultimate significance of the activities that form their background, though if the verdict is negative they do not stick very well. When people insist that the pursuit of profit is not a meritorious activity, they deserve answers. The point of this essay is that we must look in the right place for those answers: namely, into the purposes of those who supply the rewards and recognizances in question. To hold that profits do not matter is, I suggest, really to hold that the goods and services whose production and distribution makes profits possible do not matter. To those who say that profit making is not meritorious because it's "too easy," the reply is likewise easy: "O.K., then why don't you go out and make some yourself?" While it is, no doubt, easier if one begins with an inherited fortune or the like, that is by no means necessary: people have made fortunes from trivial initial capitals. Beauty crowns, as a matter of fact, are rarely[10] won by the "natural" beauties who invest no further effort in the competition, and the number of shirts lost in the pursuit of profits is enough to deter many from seriously engaging in such activities. The idea that profits are made by people who "do nothing" is not only false in conception, as we have seen, but also false to real fact. The truth is that many of us do not embark on investment programs and the like because it is too time-consuming and too demanding. There's a folk saying on this subject which we would do well to bear in mind: "If you're so smart, why aren't you rich?" The fact is that "being smart" isn't enough. To those who supply the further qualities required, we consumers—and that's all of us, remember—have reason to be grateful. Luckily, those who get the profits in question don't need our gratitude as well; but if the institutions making profits possible are under ideological threat, then a sober recognition of their foundations is not without point.

SUMMARY

We began by formulating the familiar distinction between entitlement and desert. Entitlement is the "deontic" member of this pair: its domain is the

---

10. "Never" is closer to the truth, I understand, in regard to the major ones.

right, the required, when we *owe* someone something, and so on. Desert, by comparison, is a value concept. Its implications for action are less clear and more disputable. Those very facts about it are among the main reasons we want to have entitlement notions as well. Were they to drift too far apart, however, entitlement would certainly be threatened. Rules of entitlement need justification, and desert notions will figure somewhere in that justification.

The questions about desert concern when such considerations are in order, who applies them, and why? The answer is that when someone deserves something, she or he deserves it *of* someone, there being no sense to simply "deserving" something all by itself: desert takes a minimum of two roles (though in the odd case the same person may occupy both). And those who bestow the prizes, who hold the goods in which the rewards consist, are the fundamental wielders of these notions. They apply them on the basis of the interests and values they bring to the context. This explains why desert is not exclusively reserved for such things as effort, diligence, and the application of ingenuity. It is also available for the exercise of native wit, talent, and skill, or the display of natural charm, which are not producible by effort alone. Nevertheless, those who have the relevant interests in these displays or exercises may quite reasonably see fit to reward them; though, of course, they also have reason to reward effort when it can be successful.

Thus we can rule out one-sided theories such as the Labor Theory of Value, theories which would look exclusively at the deserving individual without reference to why he deserves what he does or from whom. To understand profit and its role, we need to look at it from the point of view of the purchaser, the consumer, and not that of the producer in independence of the rest. The relevant interests of those who supply the prizes and rewards will, in turn, be such as to give rise to criteria of relevant performance, achievement, and exemplification of appropriate qualities. We must be able to grade items on the basis of the degree to which they satisfy the relevant criteria. In the case of profit, the relevant criterion is that the profiter has put his money in the right venture at the right time, thus bringing the customer the wanted products before anyone else did, or at a lower price, and so on. Our purchase of those products is likewise the supplying of the appropriate reward.

When all this is appreciated, then, the case is made: profit making, like any number of other activities, is reasonably eligible for the application of desert concepts. Those who make profits by the normal, legitimate means are not only entitled to them but can deserve them, and often do. Happily for us.

REFERENCES

Arnold, Scott. 1987. "Why Profits Are Deserved." *Ethics* 97 (January 1987): 387–402, with discussion by Edward Nell and a response by Arnold.

Buchanan, James. 1975. *The Limits of Liberty*. Chicago: University of Chicago Press.

Child, James W. 1990. "The Moral Foundations of Intangible Property." *The Monist* 73, no. 4 (October 1990): 578–600.

Cohen, G. A. 1979. "The Labor Theory of Value and the Concept of Exploitation." *Philosophy and Public Affairs* 8, no. 4 (Summer 1979).

Feinberg, Joel. 1970. "Justice and Personal Desert." In *Doing and Deserving*. Princeton: Princeton University Press.

Frank, Robert H. *Choosing the Right Pond*. New York: Oxford University Press, 1985.

Gauthier, David. 1986. *Morals by Agreement*. Oxford: Clarendon Press.

Gibbard, Allan. 1976. "Natural Property Rights." *Nous* 10 (1976).

Hardin, Russell. 1988. *Morality within the Limits of Reason*. Chicago: University of Chicago Press.

Honoré, A. M. 1961. "Ownership." In A.G. Guest, ed., *Oxford Essays in Jurisprudence,* Oxford: Oxford University Press.

Hunt, Ian. 1986. "A Critique of Roemer, Hodgson and Cohen on Marxian Exploitation." *Social Theory & Practice* 12, no. 2 (Summer): 121–71.

Mack, Erick. 1991. "Gauthier on Rights and Economic Rent." *Social Philosophy and Policy* 9, no. 1 (Fall 1991).

Narveson, Jan. 1981. "The How and Why of Universalizability." In Nelson Potter and Mark Timmons, eds., *New Essays on Ethical Universalizability,* Dordrecht: Reidel.

———. 1989. *The Libertarian Idea*. Philadelphia: Temple University Press.

———. 1991a. Review of R. M. Hare's *Essays on Political Morality*. *Nous* (forthcoming).

———. 1991b. "Property Rights: Original Acquisition and Lockean Provisos." Unpublished ms. Available from author.

Nielsen, Kai. 1984. *Liberty and Equality*. Totawa, N.J.: Rowman & Allenheld.

Norman, Richard. 1987. *Free and Equal*. Oxford: Oxford University Press.

Nozick, Robert. 1974. *Anarchy, State and Utopia*. New York: Basic Books.

Rawls, 1971. John Rawls. *A Theory of Justice*. Cambridge, Mass.: Harvard University Press.

Reiman, Jeffrey. 1987. "Exploitation, Force, and the Moral Assessment of Capitalism." *Philosophy and Public Affairs* 16, no. 1 (Winter 1987): 3–41.

Schweickart, David. 1980. *Capitalism or Worker Control?* New York: Praeger.

Sher, George. 1987. *Desert*. Princeton: Princeton University Press.

Sidgwick, Henry. 1961. *The Methods of Ethics*. 7th ed. London: Macmillan.

Vallentyne, P., ed. 1991. *Contractarianism and Rational Choice*. New York: Cambridge University Press.

Waldron, Jeremy. 1988. *The Right to Private Property*. Oxford: Oxford University Press.

4 The Moral Status of Profits and Other Rewards: A Perspective from Modern Welfare Economics

Peter J. Hammond

> 50. But . . . cases often arise in which expediency may seem to clash with moral rectitude; and so we should examine carefully and see whether their conflict is inevitable or whether they may be reconciled. The following are problems of this sort: suppose, for example, a time of dearth and famine at Rhodes, with provisions at fabulous prices; and suppose that an honest man has imported a large cargo of grain from Alexandria and that to his certain knowledge also several other importers have set sail from Alexandria, and that on the voyage he has sighted their vessels laden with grain and bound for Rhodes; is he to report the fact to the Rhodians or is he to keep his own counsel and sell his own stock at the highest market price? . . .
>
> 54. Suppose again that an honest man is offering a house for sale on account of certain undesirable features of which he himself is aware but which nobody else knows; suppose it is unsanitary, but has the reputation of being healthful; suppose it is not generally known that vermin are to be found in all the bedrooms; suppose, finally, that it is built of unsound timber and likely to collapse, but that no one knows about it except the owner; if the vendor does not tell the purchaser these facts but sells him the house for far more than he could reasonably have expected to get for it, I ask whether his transaction is unjust or dishonourable.
>
> 57. I think, then, that it was the duty of that grain-dealer not to keep back the facts from the Rhodians, and of this vendor of the house to deal in the same way with his purchaser. The fact is that merely holding one's peace about a thing does not constitute concealment, but concealment consists in trying for your own profit to keep others from finding out something that you know, when it is for their interest to know it.
>
> Extracts from pp. 318–27 of M. Tulli Ciceronis (Cicero), *De Officiis* (Book III); translated by Walter Miller for the Loeb Classical Library (Cambridge, Mass.: Harvard University Press, 1913).

INTRODUCTION AND OUTLINE

The conference organizers had originally suggested that I should discuss the moral status of profits which arise because of asymmetric information. Actually, Cicero had already discussed this issue more than two thousand years ago (at some time during the period 46–43 B.C.) in his essay on "The Conflict between the Right and the Expedient." He makes it clear that there had been an earlier debate between Diogenes of Babylonia and his pupil Antipater. I shall return to this old topic, but only in connection with some very general issues concerning the role of profits and other rewards in an economic system—especially a system that can succeed even when there is asymmetric information in the economy. This is the subject of the "modern welfare economics" which appears in the title I have chosen. Before getting to that, however, I shall say something about how I shall interpret both "morality" and "profits."

1.1. Morality in Economics

Ethics seems to be a peculiarly difficult branch of philosophy. On the whole it is easy to understand why most economists would prefer to stay well clear of it. Yet ethics is important to welfare economics because obviously there is no way of avoiding it if we are to give our evaluations of economic systems and policies, or our recommendations for improvements, any ethical force or content. Without ethics, welfare economics is reduced to, at most, propositions about how to give people more of what they seem to want, without any presumption that this would actually be ethically desirable. For example, this leaves the economist unable to say that it would be wrong to provide what drug addicts or alcoholics appear to want.

Economic welfarism is a particular and very special ethical value judgment. It judges economic systems solely on the basis of what goods and services individuals are able to enjoy, and of what labor services and resources they are required to supply. Indeed, it assumes that (*a*) in the end it is only the allocations of goods, services, and tasks to individual consumers and workers which is ethically relevant; (*b*) individuals behave in a way which maximizes their own welfare—in the sense that they choose what it is right for them to have, provided that nobody else is deprived as a result. Part (*b*) involves what is often called "consumer sovereignty"—it is assumed that consumers behave in a way that reveals their preferences, and also that they prefer what it is better for them to have. Denying this is a form of paternalism, of course.

This particular value judgment of economic welfarism has become standard in welfare economics and in most discussions of economic policy. What is being left out are many ethical considerations which may be important even in economics, such as the understandable desire of most people to be free of tax gatherers, customs officers, (potentially) corrupt bureaucrats, and tax systems far too complicated for even most intelligent and well-trained people to be able to understand fully. This desire to have freedom for its own sake will be discussed later in section 10. Meanwhile, I am willing to accept at least provisionally the ethics of economic welfarism on the grounds that, in connection with economic policy reform and the design of economic systems, there are so many other pressing issues worth discussing which may be more important. Also, economists obviously have a much greater claim to expertise about the effects of policy changes upon economic welfare than about their effects upon any more general ethical values.

A particular form of economic welfarism I shall not be using, however, is total wealth maximization. This is a commonly used criterion for making the interpersonal comparisons that are usually required in order to be able to compare different economic policies. The criterion involves simply adding up different individuals' indices of real wealth, or some alternative monetary measures of well-being. Then that policy is recommended which would make total wealth as large as possible. In this way different individuals' gains and losses are simply reduced to monetary values, and then they get added up in order to determine the total net gain, which must be equal to the (net) increase in total wealth. No attempt at all is made to see how gains and losses are distributed between rich and poor, or between individuals who are less or more deserving. This procedure, therefore, amounts to "one dollar, one vote" instead of "one person, one vote." It is a very particular way of making interpersonal comparisons on the basis of wealth alone. It equates the extra money a rich man wants to spend on a superior bottle of wine to the same sum of money a poor mother needs in order to buy medicine which will save the life of her child. For this reason, most people would clearly find it ethically unacceptable. You may notice that I have carefully avoided calling it an "ethical" criterion. Yet too many economists in the past have become accustomed to making interpersonal comparisons in this way. Indeed, it is precisely this kind of value judgment which lies behind the usual comparisons of economic performance simply on the basis of GNP or national income statistics.

Actually, a rather weak form of economic welfarism will suffice for most of the arguments contained in this paper. All that they require is the usual Pareto criterion based on consumers' own preferences (i.e., consumer sovereignty) but supplemented by some concern for distributive justice. In particular, the ethical claims that I shall make will apply whenever there is a social welfare ordering which both respects individuals' preferences and seeks to avoid extremes of poverty and degradation, even among a minority of the population. No specific social welfare ordering, however, is assumed.

1.2. Profits and Other Rewards

Before proceeding further, I should now say something about what "profit" will mean throughout this chapter. It will not necessarily be one of those measures of profit accountants are expected to report and governments tax, adulterated as they are by somewhat arbitrary provisions for depreciation and for valuing a firm's capital equipment. Indeed, as Griffiths (1986) for one has pointed out, accountancy standards are extremely lax over how to treat many important components of firms' profits, and about what to include in measures of profit and earnings. Nor will "profit" be the usual economists' ideal of "supernormal" or "abnormal" profit, which is what is left over after excluding those "normal" profits accountants would include, even though they actually represent payments for some of the firm's inputs such as its financial resources and (the efforts and skills of) its management.

All such attempts to define profit as some kind of residual, or to give it some justification, are rather *too* subtle for the points I want to make, however. In fact, on grounds of relative easy observability, profit in each single time period will be regarded here as simply net cash flow—or the difference between income received and expenditure incurred within that time period. Of the normal profits discussed above, this only deducts actual payments for services rendered. This cash-flow measure of profit also deducts the payment of taxes but includes dividends. Then, however, intertemporal models still present serious problems in defining profits, because cash flows in different periods and in different events have to be weighed against each other in order to determine the total contribution of a firm to its shareholders and to the economy as a whole. This will be discussed in section 7 below.

In fact, as discussed previously, in economics it is natural to make judgments on the basis of allocations of goods and services. Profits, therefore, matter to the extent that they affect such allocations. Profits' effects can be direct, such as when a producer who sells at a higher price earns a higher profit which is then really a transfer of resources from buyer to seller. Profits can also have indirect effects, as they do when opportunities to create profit get exploited by profit-seeking individuals and firms who take labor and other resources others are willing to supply, and then convert them into goods others wish to buy. Even the indirect effects, however, arise because profit seekers anticipate the transfers which constitute the direct effects of profits.

It follows that profits matter because they are transfers. So it is really the dividends that are actually paid to the owners of the company which should be counted as profits, and not any retained earnings which are used to finance investments intended to generate profits—or dividends—in the future. Moreover, the distinction between normal and supernormal profits is not after all so important. Either is a form of payment or transfer. It is true that one is a payment in exchange for a specific service, whereas the other is a residual after all inputs have been paid for. Yet it will turn out that the arguments to be advanced below do not need this distinction to be maintained at all. They suggest instead that payments generally are right if and only if they improve the allocation of resources. Such improvements may occur because there is more distributive justice. Or, as is more in accord with traditional neoclassical economic theory, the payments or transfers associated with profits may have favorable incentive effects. They can make the allocation of resources more efficient by encouraging resource owners and producers to increase their supplies and by encouraging consumers and firms to limit their demands.

What this suggests is that profits do not need to be regarded as morally different from many other kinds of payment. The right way to judge profits is essentially the same as the right way to judge royalties, professional earnings and salary payments, rents, interest payments, even wages. Either they do or do not improve the allocation of resources, both directly and also indirectly through incentive effects. That is why I have chosen to add, "and Other Rewards," to the title. And why "profits" will mean "profits and other rewards" for most of the rest of this chapter.

There are important implications which follow from this simple observation. It matters how profits are earned because the activities that earned them may or may not have been morally desirable. The profits earned from producing penicillin have a different moral status from those earned by producing cocaine. It matters who earns the profits, since profits earned by the deserving poor are not the same as those received by the wealthy owner of a large company who has inherited it all and never contributed anything to its management. It even matters how profits are spent—profits which some of the rich use to found institutions like the Liberty Fund or Stanford University seem much more acceptable than those spent on excessive amounts of alcohol, even by somebody who is otherwise poor and deserving.

1.3. Issues

After these preliminary remarks, I would like to distinguish between two important and separate ethical questions: (*a*) Should firms be encouraged to make as much profit as possible? (*b*) Should firms and their owners be allowed to keep those profits which do result from their production and trading activities? There are, however, a number of important subsidiary questions which would also have to be settled in the course of a complete discussion. Of these, two which relate to (*b*) are: (*c*) Who should be responsible for making the firm's production and financial decisions? And (*d*) should the people who control the firm, or somebody else, be the ones to receive its profits? When the firm is small and is run by a worker/owner who is responsible for all its capital and labor, the answer is quite different from when the firm has become a large enough organization to have agency problems in its own administration. Then profit-sharing schemes can have important incentive properties in encouraging managers, workers, even customers, to ensure that the firm is being well run. Those who supply the firm with capital would seem to have no special claim to the firm's profits, over and above the usual return to suppliers of financial resources such as loans. When the firm risks failure, and the financiers' stakes are, therefore, also at risk, this should certainly be taken into account. But so should the limited liability of shareholders—and even the limited exposure of those who are partners in a firm with unlimited liability, since bankruptcy laws also afford them some protection.

Another subsidiary question is considerably more subtle. Of course, for profits to be maximized in any reasonable sense, a necessary condition is that the firm must be making efficient use of its inputs in producing its outputs. And it is easy to show that, if all firms are maximizing profits taking as given the same set of "producer prices," all of which are positive, then there is aggregate production efficiency. That is, the production sector as a whole is using its inputs and organizing its outputs in a way which implies that it would be impossible to increase the total output of any good or service without decreasing some other output or else increasing total inputs, and it would also be impossible to reduce the total input of any good without substituting more of some other input or else producing a smaller total amount of some output. It turns out that the following question needs to be considered: (*e*) Is it desirable that the production sector as whole, or at least the typical firm, should organize its production efficiently? For even this question may have a much more subtle answer than has yet been widely recognized within the economics profession.

Having posed these five questions, they will be discussed eventually in their logical order, which is first (*a*), then (*e*), and finally (*b*), (*c*), (*d*) as a group. That is, I shall begin with the desirability of profit maximization, or at least the weaker property of production efficiency. The distributional issue of who should receive the profits earned by a firm is left until last, following the usual (and usually mistaken) separation of efficiency and distributional issues in public economics.

Before these main questions can be considered properly, however, it is necessary first to introduce the reader to some of the subtleties involved in what I have chosen to call "modern welfare economics." This label is used to describe recent work on the theoretical principles of economic policy, taking into account the reality that policy makers will naturally be ill-informed about

the relevant tastes, endowments, and opportunity sets of economic agents—
information that is really essential in bringing about any allocation of resources
which is optimal in the traditional sense. Particularly because this work is
being addressed to readers whose first specialization may not be economics, a
nontechnical summary of recent ideas seems in order. Let me comfort those
who wonder if their economic background may be inadequate by pointing out
that such a background may not always be helpful, since it has been my
experience that most members of the economics profession have yet to adjust
their thinking to the new insights which it seems to me that this work can
provide. Let me also freely admit that to a large extent I shall merely summa-
rize ideas already expounded more extensively elsewhere (see Hammond 1979,
1985, 1987, 1989, 1990a, 1990b, 1990c, 1993a).

1.4. Outline

For this reason, sections 2 and 3 below begin by reviewing the two neoclassical "fundamental efficiency theorems of welfare economics." These are
what lie behind the usual justification for the role of profits in the economic
system that most textbooks and most courses in microeconomics provide, even
at the graduate level, not excluding some that I have taught myself.

Section 4 considers how limited information gives rise to additional "incentive constraints" restricting the set of possible economic systems which can
be used to allocate resources. As many economists have remarked following
the work of Samuelson (1954, 1955), such constraints arise in connection with
public goods because of the "free-rider" problem. But they also seriously
limit the policy instruments that can be used to move the economy around
what is usually thought to be its Pareto frontier—instruments that are certainly
needed in order to remedy excess poverty or other instances of distributive
injustice. Indeed, incentive constraints even change the proper notion of Pareto
efficiency and so shrink the Pareto frontier, except at those few points (actually
only one, if competitive equilibrium happens to be unique) where no attempt
is made to redistribute resources. Once this becomes recognized, it seems at
first that almost all links between perfect competitive markets and Pareto efficient allocations become severed.

Section 5 argues that markets generally exert a negative influence on the
economic system. This is because they put further constraints upon those
schemes of quantitative controls, rationing, price control, taxation, etc., likely
to be typical of an incentive constrained Pareto efficient economic system.
Really one needs to expand the set of incentive constraints and so shrink the

relevant Pareto frontier even further. This is in order to allow for the difficulty or expense in preventing individuals using tax evasion, black markets, etc., in order to subvert controls on their trading behavior.

These theoretical preliminaries would seem to suggest that the usual neo-classical case for having firms maximize their profits and then pass them onto their capitalist owners rests on extremely shaky foundations. The incentive constraints due to private information force us into a kind of second-best world—or even third-best, bearing in mind the constraints markets themselves can create. Because of negative results such as those due to Little (1957), which were later formalized by Lipsey and Lancaster (1956), it might be thought, therefore, that nothing at all would remain of the standard argument for profit maximization, or even for production efficiency. Nevertheless, Diamond and Mirrlees (1971) were able to produce a very powerful argument for the desirability of production efficiency and also for profit maximization at suitable producer prices. A generalized version of this argument is considered in section 6. A condition for it to work in any great generality is that all of a firm's (supernormal) profits must be taxed away—or, perhaps somewhat less restrictively, that any extra profits which result from increased efficiency must be confiscated, so that dividend payments after tax remain unchanged. This leads to the paradox that (increases in) supernormal profits can only be justified as a desirable target for a firm if those who create them are not allowed to keep any of them.

Up to now, the discussion has been concerned solely with a static economy. This severe restriction has been all too common even in modern welfare economics for the simple reason that sequence economies seem only too likely to add to the vast complications without yielding many new insights beyond those of some rather special models. Yet some general ideas may finally be beginning to emerge, of which a few are briefly considered in section 7. Unfortunately the attempt to extend the discussion to intertemporal economies raises one last particularly vexing question: (f) what exactly is the definition of the profits we may be wanting firms to maximize?

Another important restriction is the almost exclusive use of equilibrium models. This is another rather questionable feature of modern welfare economics. It can only be justified by the continuing lack of suitable disequilibrium models general enough to allow the effects of policy changes to be analyzed comprehensively. Section 8 attempts to consider the extent to which the role of profits may be stronger in economies which do not adjust quickly and automatically to equilibrium. Section 9 recapitulates the mainly negative results that precede it concerning the role of profits in helping to ensure a truly efficient allocation of resources, bearing in mind all the restrictions upon an economic system which arise because of asymmetric information.

Section 10 finally considers an entirely different case for a profit-driven economic system allowing a considerable degree of laissez-faire. This is that the direct costs of interfering in the economic system with an army of tax collectors, customs officers, inspectors, and other kinds of bureaucrat may well exceed any benefits from an improved allocation of resources. This is particularly true if we heed the natural desire of most individuals to lead their own lives without undue interference from state officialdom. This accords profits a very low moral status, however. They are only justified to the extent that we find it impossible to devise a better economic system which relies much less on profits.

Finally, a brief concluding summary appears as section 11.

2. THE FIRST EFFICIENCY THEOREM

> And so it is back to profit—that virtue in itself—and the quest for profit,
> which knows no bounds and grabs wherever there is something to be had,
> with the law of the market economy allowing crimes committed in the name
> of the profit motive to receive absolution.
>
> Günter Grass (1990)

2.1. Market Success

The efficiency theorems of welfare economics set out the logical connections between perfect competitive equilibrium allocations on the one hand, and Pareto efficient allocations on the other. Here "perfect competitive equilibrium" signifies an allocation resulting from complete markets for all the goods and services of interest to individuals. Producers take market prices as given; then they carry out production and trading plans which maximize their profits. Consumers take market prices and their shares of producers' profits as given; then they carry out consumption and trading plans which maximize their preference orderings. Also, there must be equilibrium prices which balance consumers' and producers' demands and supplies of each good. Note especially how consumers and producers must neglect whatever monopoly power they may actually have to influence market prices.

"Pareto efficient" allocations of goods and services in the economy are defined as those having the property that there is no way to make all individuals better off simultaneously. Actually, this is the weak concept of Pareto efficiency; it is more customary to use a slightly stronger definition requiring that nobody can be made better off unless somebody else is made worse off.

The first of the two efficiency theorems appears to be extremely powerful. It demonstrates that perfect competitive markets produce (at least weakly) Pareto efficient allocations in all circumstances when they achieve a general equilibrium of demand and supply. No other qualifications are needed. The result is strong because the hypothesis that markets have reached perfect competitive equilibrium is so strong. In addition, in order to guarantee that the stronger concept of Pareto efficiency is always fulfilled, it is necessary to make one assumption regarding individuals' preferences. They must be "locally nonsatiated" in the sense that, no matter what consumption bundle a consumer has, there is always a small change which takes the consumer to a preferred bundle. This powerful result is often associated with Adam Smith's notion of the "invisible hand." It also appears to justify the pursuit of nonmonopoly profits, since that is what competitive behavior on the part of firms amounts to. Moreover, there is no reason to deprive individuals who own firms from enjoying their full share of any profits the firm succeeds in making.

2.2. Market Failure

Although logically it is certainly very powerful, from an ethical point of view the first efficiency theorem by itself is neither interesting nor attractive. For suppose first that all individuals were identical and had the same wealth. Then there would certainly be no distributional concerns to worry about. Even so, the ethical acceptability of a perfect competitive market allocation would still rest on the important value judgment that individuals' preferences correspond to what it would be desirable for them to have. Denying this value judgment, of course, smacks of paternalism and suggests that suppressing individual liberties may be justified. Yet in fact most people I know could cite many instances where they thought it would be better if individuals' preferences did not have to be accepted as sovereign.

The first efficiency theorem carries even less ethical weight when it is recognized that individuals are actually quite diverse. This is because the distribution of wealth and power may be ethically inappropriate or even quite obnoxious. Bergstrom (1971), for instance, showed how perfect competitive markets with slavery can be Pareto efficient. The same is true of a dictatorship, or of a distribution of wealth so unequal that most individuals are unable to survive for more than a short period (see Coles and Hammond 1991). Not even perfect markets can remedy distributive injustice by themselves.

So far, nothing specific has been said about public goods and externalities. These are commonly described as "market failures" because perfect competitive markets need not bring about an efficient allocation when they are present.

It is true that in theory markets could be supplemented by similar Lindahl pricing schemes for determining the quality of the environment, including the provision of public goods. Rather more plausibly, there could also be Pigovian taxes and transfers to determine the extent to which each producer and consumer is allowed to affect the quality of the environment, either adversely or beneficially. In a sense, such arrangements amount to making sure that markets really are complete. Pigovian taxes amount to charges for the right to create pollution or to behave in other ways that affect other people adversely. Lindahl prices amount to specific charges for all individuals according to what they are willing to pay at the margin for the public goods from which they benefit. Measures of profit, and dividends paid out, should be decreased to allow for such charges, or increased to account for any benefits the firm may create. In this way the economy will function as if there were perfect markets even for public goods and externalities, so Pareto efficiency is restored.

Another kind of market failure arises in connection with monopoly. This creates inefficiency in two ways. One, which has been well understood for many years, is that monopolists who seek higher profits can do so by restricting their output in order to drive up the prices of their products. Such inefficiencies can be overcome by encouraging effective competition, or by putting ceilings on monopoly prices so that the price is lowered and the output increased to that which would occur in a competitive market, or even by *subsidizing* the monopolist's output in a way that encourages it to produce the competitive output. A second source of inefficiency, however, may be more important. Because monopoly power brings in additional profits, firms and individuals are encouraged to devote resources to establishing or maintaining their monopoly power. These resources are worse than merely wasted, since they are used up in a way that actually worsens the allocation of the goods and services that remain. Obvious examples include much advertising expenditure, and some research and development that is designed not to improve the firm's product so much as to make it more difficult for other firms to compete. Less obvious but equally important examples include some barriers to entry into professions protected by various forms of legislation—for example, the need to qualify by passing examinations based on knowledge which will probably never be used. Really these inefficiencies arise from "rent-seeking" behavior such as that described by Tullock (1967), Krueger (1974), and Bhagwati (1982).

Notice that the monopoly profits themselves do not create inefficiencies. Rather, the waste arises from the way in which monopoly power leads to distorted markets and "directly unproductive" or wasteful behavior. Monopoly profits often add to distributive injustice, of course, but need not always do so. Many companies with monopoly power are actually largely owned by pension funds, with many beneficiaries who are not especially well off.

Some profits from externalities and monopolies, however, are so monstrous that they can surely be described quite properly as "obscene." In the quotation above, Günter Grass was describing as "crimes" the profits earned by some (erstwhile West) German firms from selling equipment for producing poison gas to Saddam Hussein's regime in Iraq. Indeed, companies all over the world continue to make profits from selling arms used to terrorize populations or wage totally immoral wars. Others grossly mistreat their workers. Another extreme example concerns the "calculation table for value in terms of profitability of concentration camp slaves, which 'assuming an average life-span of nine months,' gave a profit of '270 × 5.30 Reichsmarks, a profit increased by rational utilisation of the corpses.' "[1]

3. The Second Efficiency Theorem

3.1. Market Success

From an ethical point of view, the second efficiency theorem appears much more interesting. It assures us that (almost) *any* Pareto efficient allocation can be achieved through perfect competitive markets—*provided* that wealth is redistributed suitably by "lump-sum" transfers which are, by definition, entirely independent of individuals' market transactions or other decisions. In particular, an ethically optimal allocation that combines efficiency with distributive justice may well be achievable in this way. Moreover, this second efficiency theorem is what really lies behind the view of many economists that efficiency and distributive justice can be separated and even pursued with quite different policy instruments. General policy tools can be used to promote efficiency; lump-sum transfers can be used to promote distributive justice.

Actually, unlike the first efficiency theorem, the second is only true under some rather stringent technical conditions which ought to be discussed carefully. I shall not do so here, however, but ask the interested reader to consult one of the many technical works which set out the assumptions under which the result is true. Very briefly, the additional conditions require local nonsatiation, continuity and convexity of preferences, and also convexity of production possibilities. Even then, some extra assumptions are needed to rule out prob-

---

1. Quoted from Veronica Horwell's review of Potts (1990) in the *(Manchester) Guardian Weekly,* February 3, 1991. See p. 139 of Potts's book (1988 and 1990) which is based on Kogon's (1948, pp. 349ff.) description of Nazi policy and which makes clear that such calculations were explicitly made by those responsible for administering the camps, whose purpose was "extermination through work" (p. 140).

lematic examples in which some consumers are on the boundaries of their feasible sets (see Arrow 1951 and the many later discussions of what has come to be known as "Arrow's exceptional case," including Hammond 1993b).

3.2. The Benefits of Profits . . .

Where the second efficiency theorem is valid, it clearly allows us still to justify competitive profit maximization as the proper goal of a firm, since that is part of what lies behind a competitive equilibrium. A direct argument is also possible, in some cases at least. Suppose that the economy has reached an allocation resulting from an equilibrium of demand and supply in which one or more firms are not maximizing their profits, taking prices as given. Then, in the absence of public goods, it would be possible to arrange a Pareto improvement as follows.

First, improve the "supply side" of the economy by having firms announce new demand and supply functions of prices for which the resulting profit is never lower than what they could earn by sticking to their original production plan, and in some cases is actually higher. Assume in fact that no matter what the price vector may be, there is always at least one firm making more profit than at the original allocation. This is true at the equilibrium prices because of the assumption that, originally at least, one firm was not maximizing its profits at those prices. At other prices, however, it is not automatically true, so there is an additional assumption here.

Second, specify a lump-sum transfer to each consumer as a function of prices so that, together with any profits received from firms, every consumer always has more income than is needed to purchase what he was previously consuming. This is also possible, given that firms must be earning more profits in the aggregate.

Third, have consumers announce their preference-maximizing demands and supplies as functions of prices, taking these transfer functions as given.

Finally, find new equilibrium prices, assuming they exist, and then allow firms and consumers to carry out their announced demands and supplies at these prices. Because of the way the transfer functions have been constructed, at any price vector all consumers can afford something they strictly prefer to the original allocation, and so the resulting equilibrium allocation makes all consumers better off.

This argument is very similar to one Grandmont and McFadden (1972) used to establish rigorously for the first time the validity of the classical propositions concerning the gains from international trade. The existence issue is taken care of by the standard technical assumptions. For the issues being discussed in this chapter, the most crucial part of the argument is the second step. Consumers must be compensated so that nobody is made worse off from the comparative static effects of having producers increase their profits. The benefits of more profitable production cannot be assumed to "trickle down" automatically in the absence of some such compensation. The Luddites may not have been justified in trying to resist the Industrial Revolution in England, but they surely had some legitimate grievances. Too many economists in the past have been willing to consider only "potential" Pareto improvements, which occur when there are potential lump-sum transfers by which the gainers could compensate the losers. This is in contrast with the much stricter test of an *actual* Pareto improvement involving *actual* lump-sum transfers.

Notice the need to consider new demand and supply *functions* for all producers and transfer *functions* for all individuals. This is because compensating consumers for price changes affects the income distribution and so typically alters equilibrium prices even further. Seeing this, as well as the need to consider whether there would exist a new equilibrium the economy could reach after the change, was really the main contribution of Grandmont and McFadden's work on the gains from international trade.

3.3. . . . to Society as a Whole

As in section 2, competitive profit maximization, therefore, remains a desirable goal. The difference from section 2 is that the owners of a firm are no longer necessarily entitled to its profits. Suitable lump-sum redistribution may well involve taking away most of these profits and giving them to those most in need. In addition, public goods may well have to be financed by levies on all individuals, including the owners of profitable corporations. Now that efficiency and distributional issues have been so successfully separated, there is no particular reason to allow shareholders to keep their dividend income. Nor is there any reason either why workers will keep the full fruits of their labor, or resource owners the full value of what they own. Indeed, there is no reason to respect any form of private property; adapting a famous quotation from Karl Marx, it is as though private income is first collected from each according to their ability to pay, and then given out to each according to their needs.

4. PRIVATE INFORMATION AND INCENTIVE CONSTRAINTS

Although the second efficiency theorem can only be proved under rather restrictive assumptions, this is not the main problem with it. Rather, the trouble arises from the crucial proviso that wealth should be suitably redistributed by means of lump-sum transfers. This is obviously essential if the second efficiency theorem is to have more ethical significance than the first. Yet the requisite transfers should typically be from those who have sufficient skill and good fortune to prosper on their own, toward those for whom life in the absence of transfer payments would be at best a miserable struggle. This creates obvious grave problems when individuals' true needs and abilities are unknown, because then the transfer payments could only depend on appearances of need or of skill. Individuals who understand this would be provided with every incentive to manipulate the transfer system by altering their apparent needs or skills. There would be little incentive to work hard, acquire useful skills, or be productive, but every incentive to appear needy.

Another problem when there is private information arises in connection with the environment, including public goods. In order to determine how clean the air should be, or what level of public schooling or health care facilities to provide, the relevant preferences of different individuals have to be discovered. So do the true costs of keeping the air cleaner, or of providing the chosen outputs of public goods. As Samuelson (1954, 1955) was probably the first to point out, the standard Lindahl pricing scheme is unlikely to work well because it charges people their stated marginal willingness to pay. This provides an obvious incentive for individuals to "free-ride" by understanding how much they value public goods. Indeed, at any equilibrium of the usual Lindahl pricing scheme, one individual offering to pay one dollar less toward the cost of a public good would save himself a dollar, but the *total* loss to *all* individuals from a reduction in the public good would be only one dollar. This leaves the individual who pays one dollar less with a very much smaller loss from the reduced provision of the public good, and so a net benefit not much less than a whole dollar.

Previously it was often assumed, at least implicitly, that an economic system would have to respect only the physical feasibility constraints concerning both what individuals and firms can supply or produce and the need to balance demand and supply. Now it can be seen that there are additional and equally important "incentive constraints" due to ignorance concerning the relevant characteristics of consumers and producers in the economy. The latter constraints require that, whenever an individual has some private information which is not monitored directly, the economic system must function in a way that does not encourage the individual to conceal or misrepresent it. No matter what economic system we think we may be designing, it turns out that, by the time individuals have manipulated it as they wish, the final result must inevitably be a system that respects these incentive constraints. This fundamental property of mechanisms which work in the presence of incomplete information has come to be known as the "revelation principle"; the economy must function as it would if individuals were revealing their private information willingly because they had no disincentive to do so.

Taking these incentive constraints into account, the second efficiency theorem fails spectacularly. It must be admitted that the relevant incentive constraints may be satisfied by some very particular Pareto efficient allocations— namely, those which could result from perfect competitive markets if no attempt whatsoever were made to redress distributive injustice, and if public goods were entirely financed by means of uniform poll taxes which were not so high that some individuals would lack the means to pay them (Hammond 1979). Otherwise, all other "incentive constrained" Pareto efficient allocations require interference in and "distortions" of markets in order to achieve even a limited amount of redistribution of resources, or some more acceptable source of public finance than a pure poll tax. With very rare exceptions likely to be met only in theoretical writings, incentive constraints really do bind.

5. MARKETS AS CONSTRAINTS

The previous section considered incentive constraints due to private information concerning needs, abilities, and willingness to pay for public goods. In the insurance literature, such private information is often known as "adverse selection." As Akerlof (1970) pointed out, "lemons" are likely to feature more prominently among second-hand cars offered for sale than they do among those on the roads. The old, infirm, and people with parental responsibilities are more ready to buy private health insurance (if they can afford it) than the young, healthy, and childless. Bankers are more willing to lend to those who already have plenty of liquid assets. Cities, states, and nations which are generous in providing public goods and public assistance to the poor will tend to attract those most in need of such assistance.

Such incentive constraints, however, are by no means the only ones. Others can arise because of "moral hazard" or "hidden action." Lenders may find it difficult to get their borrowers to repay, and so they demand collateral. Fire insurance companies must worry not only about negligence but also arson. Tax inspectors face evasion. And deposit insurance corporations are facing the consequences of having insured excessively risky lending practices during the last decade.

When we consider general economic systems, a particular form of moral hazard arises. If market transactions could be perfectly monitored and controlled, an incentive constrained Pareto efficient economic system would typically involve nonlinear taxation and pricing, possibly some forms of rationing, and a large range of similar forms of intervention in the allocation process. In practice, however, market transactions can only be monitored and controlled very imperfectly. Rationing schemes usually lead to black markets, income taxes to evasion, customs duties to smuggling, excessive regulation to corruption. Market forces are powerful, and suppressing them is difficult. Accordingly, any description of an economic system remains seriously incomplete until it spells out how rationing schemes and other kinds of regulation will be enforced, how taxes and duties will be collected, and what will happen to defaulters, evaders, and nonpayers. The almost inevitable failure of markets to achieve distributive justice or to determine a proper quality of the environment or allocation of public goods creates a need for nonmarket remedies; these imply that markets can make things worse rather than better by adding to the incentive constraints that need to be respected. Markets emerge as constraints upon the economic system rather than as desirable instruments for achieving Pareto efficiency.

6. PROFITS AS CONSTRAINTS?

6.1. The Second-Best Case for Profits . . .

Despite all these limitations upon markets as efficient allocators of resources when there is private information, there are still cases when it is useful to ask producers to maximize profits taking as given some particular "producer" prices. Of course, these will typically not be the same prices as consumers face. As in real mixed economies, for goods which producers sell to consumers, producer prices will be net of tax, while consumer prices will include taxes. For goods like labor which consumers sell to producers, it is the other way around—producers have to pay wages which include taxes, but workers only receive wages after tax. Anyway, the issue is whether there exists a single vector of producer prices which all firms should be asked to use in valuing their inputs and outputs and then to maximize profits. And, as pointed out in the Introduction to this chapter, if such uniform producer prices are to exist at all, then it must be desirable to have the production sector as a whole produce efficiently. Indeed, the desirability of aggregate production efficiency is not only necessary; at least when the aggregate production possibility set is convex, being at a point of its efficiency frontier is also sufficient for the existence of a "supporting hyperplane" at that point, and then the (geometric) normal to that hyperplane will be a price vector having components that are appropriate producer prices for all firms to use. This is merely a generalization of the "marginal rates of transformation" to be found in most elementary economics textbooks.

So—Is aggregate production efficiency in fact desirable? Suppose that the economy finds itself with an allocation which is not on the efficiency frontier of the aggregate production possibility set but actually in the interior of this set. Can some Pareto improvement be arranged? To see whether it can, try adapting the argument for profit maximization presented in section 3 above. Start by assigning all firms new demand and supply vectors so that the aggregate net output of every good is higher than it was for the original production plan. This must be possible because of the assumption that the original production plan is in the interior of the aggregate production possibility set. This first step of the improvement process is actually simpler than before, since no demand or supply functions have to be specified for firms. The reason is the stronger hypothesis that one can produce more of every good in aggregate rather than just make more profit overall.

The other steps of the process are not nearly as simple, and there will be many cases where they do not work at all. In fact, before the remaining steps can be described, it is first necessary to specify what prices or alternative market signals will be used to overcome any imbalances between demand and supply. Notice that this is *not* presuming any equilibrating process in the usual sense; in order to reach a feasible allocation, every economic system must ultimately balance demand and supply, if only by an unsystematic rationing scheme that leaves many economic agents frustrated. What I have in mind here are rather general signaling schemes like those described by Drèze and Stern (1987, 1990). So I will speak of demands and supplies as being functions of *market signals;* indeed, I will even have to do the same for tax rates and other policy instruments.

Then the second step of the move toward a Pareto improvement requires that compensating policy instruments should be specified as functions of market signals, ensuring that any change in market signals needed to reestablish balance between demands and supplies never makes any consumer worse off. In section 3 these policy instruments were lump-sum transfers as functions of market prices. In Diamond and Mirrlees (1971), Mirrlees (1972), and Hahn (1973), as well as in later work on the gains from trade and from customs unions by Dixit and Norman (1980, 1986) and Dixit (1987), the market signals were both producer and consumer prices. These differed from each other because of commodity taxes, which served as the policy instruments. As no restrictions were placed on the rates of commodity taxation for different goods, a possible compensating policy would adjust these rates in order to hold consumer prices constant, even while producer prices were varying. This is equivalent to putting a total freeze on consumer prices and wage rates but then setting taxes and subsidies in order to clear markets. It has the effect of leaving each consumer with exactly the same budget constraint as originally, so there is no way any consumer could become worse off.

The third step of the adjustment process involves making some small change to the functions determining how those policy instruments which directly affect consumers depend upon market signals, doing so in a way which guarantees a Pareto improvement. One can virtually always find an instrument which will work, such as a uniform poll subsidy paid to all consumers. One alternative would be reduced taxes which lower the consumer prices of some goods which everybody consumes; another would be reduced taxes which *raise* the consumer prices of some goods such as different types of labor that everybody supplies. After Diamond and Mirrlees (1971), a more thorough investigation of the possibilities for Pareto improving tax changes can be found in Weymark (1978). Or, instead of tax changes, it may be possible to use the increased outputs of the production sector in order to expand the provision of some public good which benefits everybody.

Of course, after all these three prior steps, there is still market balance to worry about. One possibility is that market signals can be relied upon to remove all imbalances, as in section 3 and as assumed by Diamond, Hahn, and Mirrlees in the articles cited above. But even if not, provided that aggregate demand for each commodity is a continuous function of market signals, then a small enough change in policy instruments will produce a change in aggregate demand small enough to ensure that the extra output of every commodity, arranged in step one described above, does not get exhausted. The surplus of any good can then be disposed of, if necessary, by giving it away to some people who value it.

6.2. . . . and Its Limitations

Although it is certainly a very powerful generalization of the "managed trickle down" argument of section 3, there are many cases where it will not work. The second step can create severe difficulties. Obviously, the set of policy instruments may not be powerful enough to allow *every* consumer to be fully compensated for any damage suffered because the aggregate efficiency of production has been improved. The model of Diamond and Mirrlees (1971) allows different taxes to be levied on any pair of different commodities. Bearing in mind that commodities should be distinguished by location, this implies that tax rates are allowed to be entirely different in different localities. Yet most fiscal systems allow very few different rates of sales or value-added tax on different consumption goods. The European Union, after virtually outlawing tax discrimination between different regions of the same nation, has been strenuously seeking to "harmonize" value-added tax rates by abolishing many of those international differentials that had been allowed to remain. As the Regional Program expands, perhaps its direction of specific community expenditure toward poorer areas is becoming more of an acceptable substitute.

Even in the Diamond-Mirrlees model with unrestricted commodity taxation, however, there is still a difficulty in arranging suitable compensation at step two. So far nothing has been said about what happens to the increased profits firms will make from being more efficient. In the original Diamond-Mirrlees model there were constant returns to scale in private production, implying that there were no profits anyway. As an alternative, it could be assumed that profits would be taxed away at a rate of 100%. In reality, however, some profits at least typically pass into the hands of shareholders, even after the company has paid corporation tax, and possibly special taxes on distributed profits, while each shareholder has also paid income tax on dividends received. As Mirrlees (1972) showed by means of a simple example, these additional profits could make it impossible to generate a Pareto improvement after all. What can happen is that those who receive the extra profits then bid up the price of some commodity that absorbs a large share of some poor individuals' budgets, and there may not be enough tax instruments to compensate them. It would seem that there also has to be unrestricted profits taxation—with different rates on different firms, moreover, unless the common rate is 100%. In this case there is the paradox that profits can only be justified as a desirable target for a firm if those who cause them to increase are not allowed to keep any extra!

Perhaps the Mirrlees example is somewhat far-fetched in practice. Even so, there are certainly cases when even just making production more efficient in aggregate by having more of every output and less of every input will also involve changes that disrupt the livelihoods and the lives of some individuals— for example, by abolishing their jobs. There is far too much evidence that the range of tax and other instruments that the world's governments are able and willing to use in such cases is insufficient always to provide full compensation to all. Making production more efficient may benefit most individuals, but often some inevitably lose as well. Then only interpersonal comparisons can establish whether or not the gains outweigh the losses. The same is true, a fortiori, of any change which increases producers' profits. Indeed, there are often small gains to virtually all consumers. These have to be set against the large losses of the workers, managers, and others who may have specialized in selling services to an inefficient or protected firm which is forced to close or to reorganize drastically.

Profit maximization is, therefore, much harder to justify after all when incentive constraints and other limitations on the instruments of redistributive policy are taken into account. But not quite so much harder as first thoughts might have led one to expect. Once profits have been earned, incentive constraints make it rather easier to claim that capitalists deserve at least some share of them than was the case without incentive constraints. Suppliers of capital, entrepreneurs, and inventors are all affected by incentives no less than suppliers of labor, and all have private information about their willingness to supply, their capabilities, their technical knowledge. But what the optimal incentive payment to a capitalist should be is highly complicated. There seem to be plenty of good reasons for allowing managers, workers, and even consumers to receive a significant share of a company's profits along with its owners and, as recipients of profits taxes, the tax authorities. After all, workers who share in the firm's profits have some incentive to be more productive. If consumers also have a share in those profits, they may be more willing to offer suggestions which help make the firm more responsive to their requirements. But if shareholders receive too large a proportion of the firm's profits, the firm may be at the mercy of professional investors whose only concern is with short-run returns. The firm will find it difficult to pursue in secrecy long-run projects of research and development whose costs depress earnings in the short run, but whose long-run expected benefits, to both the firm itself and to society as a whole, may be enormous. For these and for other reasons, both microeconomic and macroeconomic schemes of profit sharing have long been advocated. The works of Weitzman (1984), Drèze (1989), Wadhwani and Wall (1990), and Smith (1990) form a possibly unrepresentative sample of the fairly recent literature.

7. INTERTEMPORAL ISSUES

The last five sections have not explicitly considered either time or uncertainty about exogenous events. In principle, both can be handled by introducing sufficient contingent commodities, as in Debreu (1959). That is, the commodity space must be extended to distinguish between goods for delivery at different times or in different uncertain events or "states of the world." Not surprisingly, however, there are a number of additional complications this ingenious apparatus does not entirely resolve. For one thing, as Tesfatsion (1986) has demonstrated, there are new problems surrounding the second efficiency theorem of welfare economics that was discussed in section 3 above. Typically, in any period the optimal transfers to every individual will depend upon their different needs, which in turn depend upon their previous personal histories. Such histories, however, are affected by individuals' past decisions, such as what assets to accumulate, or what skills and habits to acquire. Understanding this, individuals will in part choose their personal histories in order to improve the transfers to which they are entitled. This being so, the transfers lose their lump-sum character and instead become taxes and subsidies on history which will typically create Pareto inefficiencies in the resulting intertemporal market allocation. Hammond (1993a) presents a specific example of this phenomenon.

Of rather more interest, perhaps, is what happens to incentive constraints in intertemporal economies. In fact, new ones emerge in connection with all kinds of loan contract, securities and futures markets, etc. The problem is that borrowers engage in contracts which pose a risk of default. Attempting to enforce such contracts requires real resources to be devoted to tracking down the assets of a defaulter. Even if this process were perfect, there would still remain some instances where the defaulter really is unable to repay. So loan contracts always include, at least implicitly, some escape clause allowing the borrower not to repay. Usually, of course, the default option is made sufficiently unattractive to prevent it being used, but plenty of defaults do actually occur. The need for loan contracts to take such default possibilities into account imposes yet more incentive constraints upon a feasible economic system, as I explain more fully in Hammond (1992).

But what of the desirability of profit maximization, or even of production efficiency? And of the desirability of having a firm's owners keep a significant share of any profit? The rather vague conclusions of section 6 for static economies are likely to hold a fortiori for intertemporal economies. There are additional reasons for lump-sum redistribution to be infeasible and additional incentive constraints to take into account.

Yet more problematic are the extra difficulties in even defining profits for a firm in an intertemporal economy. Economists have become used to considering the total present discounted value of an entire stream of future profits. What rate of discount to use, however, is not always a question with a straightforward answer. Even if it were, there would still be the issue of how to allow for uncertainty. This reflects the fact that profits are not well defined, in general, unless there is a market price or rate of discount attached to the future returns of the firm at each future date and for each future event or contingency. There would be such prices if there were "complete markets" in the sense which has become familiar to many economists following the important work of Arrow (1953, 1964) and Debreu (1959). When markets fail to be complete in this way, however, each firm has to decide how to trade off its profits at different dates and in different possible contingencies without clear market signals concerning how to do so. It is true that the stock market's valuation of the firm's prospects could, in theory, provide some useful indication of how its shareholders are willing to make this trade-off. Accordingly, the firm may try to set itself the goal of maximizing its stock-market valuation. Yet there are rather obvious problems with this because the firm is very likely to have considerable influence over the relative implicit prices of its profits at different dates and in different contingencies. In other words, the usual competitive price-taking hypothesis makes little sense unless there are very many firms producing similar patterns of financial returns in different times and in different states of the world. This is the implicit hypothesis, it seems, behind Diamond's (1967) pioneering article and Makowski's (1983) particularly interesting contribution. But by now there is an extensive literature on this vexed topic, of which Duffie (1988, chap. 13), Drèze (1989), and DeMarzo (1993) are just a few of the most recent works which have struck me as the most important.

This and other difficulties in extending our usual theories to intertemporal economies suggest that a new and less ambitious approach may be desirable. One possibility is to follow Allais's (1943, 1947, 1953) example in treating the same individual at different dates or in different events as many different dated contingent individuals, though each inherits many of the characteristics of some remarkably similar predecessors. And also to do the same for firms. Then the intertemporal economy has essentially been reduced to a linked series of dated contingent static economies. The rather negative conclusions of section 6 would appear to retain their validity within each of these static economies; now they concern the profits which each firm makes at a single date and in a single contingency, with the associated concept of "sequential" efficiency of production and consumption in the economy as a whole.

8. Some Omitted Considerations

8.1. Disequilibrium and Austrian Economics

Those "Austrian" economists who follow the ideas of von Mises, Hayek, and others may legitimately object that the arguments presented above rely too heavily upon some kind of equilibrium analysis. In section 6, I did try to be careful not to presume anything like a standard equilibrium concept, recognizing instead that the inevitable ultimate balance between demand and supply may come about through rather unsystematic procedures. Even so, it probably is better to consider the allocation mechanism in the economy as a form of trading process in continuous time which never converges to an equilibrium. Indeed, as Fisher (1983) and others have argued, if convergence to equilibrium were to occur, it may well be because the pursuit of profit has actually played an important role in the adjustment process. But even if such convergence does eventually occur, the effects of trading at "false prices" certainly deserve the attention of welfare economists.

Nevertheless, unlike (to my knowledge) most of the "Austrians," I still think that a benevolent government may have a key role to play in redistributing income, providing public goods, controlling externalities, and combating monopoly power. In our models, government agencies should not be excluded a priori from making a positive contribution to the economic process just because in reality they inevitably lack the information needed to make the consequences of their actions fully predictable. A proper model of an economic system, it seems to me, should have the potential for both public and private agents to interact. Otherwise, of course, it becomes far too easy simply to dismiss any kind of policy intervention in the economy as at best irrelevant and generally harmful. All the earlier conclusions of section 6 regarding the moral status of profit in economies with limited information then appear to remain valid. Profit maximization can only be justified at the "right" prices, if at all. Yet such prices may never be known unless and until the economic process has converged to some kind of equilibrium or more general balance between demand and supply. One could well argue that it is better for firms to use some price information than none at all, and that the price information which they are most likely to have concerns the prices at which they can actually buy and sell. Yet this does not make these prices the right ones, nor does it even justify profit maximization at any prices. And, of course, there are still only incentive reasons for profit makers to be allowed to keep (part of) their actual profits, rather than having them all be taxed away in order to use the proceeds to benefit the population of all economic agents as a whole.

8.2. Directly Unproductive Activities

The preceding analysis also presumes that governments and their agents are both fairly benevolent and also moderately competent. If they were not, it could be argued that, even though policy intervention by federal, state, or local governments could in theory do much to promote distributive justice and enhance economic welfare, in practice it only serves to make things worse. This seems to lie behind the claims of such "conservative" writers as Gilder

(1981) and Murray (1984), which may well have influenced the Reagan administration's apparent lack of concern for the increase in poverty within the United States.

In fact, it seems to me that specifying models which assume purely self-serving and/or hopelessly incompetent bureaucrats and politicians may do us all a serious disservice by encouraging exactly that kind of contemptible behavior which they describe. And perhaps the failures in America's antipoverty programs have more to do with a lack of political will to see them working properly. Indeed, it is possible that an efficiently functioning program of poverty relief would do too much to undermine the apparent convictions of many Americans that free markets are the best way of dealing with virtually any economic problem—with the notable exceptions, that is, of immigration and drug abuse. If such attitudes were to change, one might see more sympathetic consideration given to negative income taxes or other sensible reforms such as those advocated by Ellwood (1988) and others. One might also ask whether the programs of poverty relief in the United States seem to perform so badly simply because so few resources are devoted to them in comparison with other countries, especially those in Western Europe. Esping-Anderson and Micklewright's (1990) recent comparative study is careful *not* to suggest this explicitly. Yet they cite statistics (published by the International Labour Organisation in 1988) for the total of private and public expenditure, for all income classes, on all items of social security—medical care, all kinds of benefit for sickness, invalidity, employment injury, unemployment, old-age, survivors, family, and maternity as well as public assistance. These figures point to how small a fraction (13.8%) of gross domestic product in 1983 was devoted to all forms of such expenditure in the United States compared to the former West Germany (24.3%) or Sweden (33.3%). Since private health care makes up quite a large fraction of the U.S. figure, the true discrepancy has presumably been understated by a considerable amount. One could argue, I suppose, that the U.S. economy makes many more low-wage employment opportunities open to the poor, thus making some forms of social security expenditure less necessary. Yet many obvious and well-documented gaps remain to be filled before the United States becomes anything like a "welfare state," or even one which can take any pride in the way it treats many of its poorest citizens.

In the end, however, it clearly is naive merely to assume away the corruption, rent seeking, and other forms of directly unproductive activity (Bhagwati 1982) which certainly bedevil many real polities. Such activities function like external diseconomies, in effect. While I cannot (yet) present a full analysis of their implications, one is tempted to suggest that their costs could be greatly reduced by leaving fewer profits around in uncontrolled hands, where they create both a source of temptation and also the wherewithal to finance undesirable lobbying and other political activities.

9. PROFITS: A NECESSARY EVIL?

This is about as far as I can go in discussing the role of profits in ensuring an efficient and just allocation of resources. The case for profits appears very weak indeed. My answer to question (*a*), regarding the desirability of maximizing profits, has been an extremely guarded "Yes, but really only in rather special circumstances, depending on what will happen to the profits, how they are measured, what price system is used, etc." The reservations will be fairly familiar to most economists. They are generally seen as arising because of possible divergences between social and private (marginal) costs and benefits. The divergences due to market failures such as unwarranted monopoly power or externalities are widely acknowledged and understood. But there are also important divergences due to the lack of sufficiently powerful ways to redistribute income in order to abate poverty and promote an ethically acceptable level of distributive justice. These have been much less widely recognized. Yet they also imply that an ethically appropriate measure of social profit may differ considerably from the private profit which is more likely to be the goal of actual firms.

The answer to (*b*), however, concerning whether a firm's owners are entitled to a significant share of the profits, is rather more subtle. In the unrealistic world of unlimited information which still fills too large a fraction of economics textbooks, the answer has to be, "No, not at all, except as payments for services rendered, which are really part of normal rather than supernormal profits." This was the unambiguous conclusion of section 3. Real economies, however, do have limited or asymmetric information. Then, in considering the role of profits in allocating resources efficiently, the *only* reason for firms and their owners to be allowed to keep their (supernormal) profits is precisely the need to provide incentives, especially when there is asymmetric information. Cicero's Alexandrian merchant who first reached the island of Rhodes with some urgently needed wheat probably deserves much of the high price the inhabitants are willing to pay while they still do not know whether other ships are coming (though they are surely likely to guess that they may be). But he does so only to the extent that the expectation of such a higher price encouraged him to buy and load his wheat as quickly as possible, in order to arrive in Rhodes before anybody else. Even then, he should share his profits with the crew who have no doubt made exceptional efforts to speed his voyage. As for

Cicero's house seller, if he could get away with selling at full price a house whose maintenance he has neglected, not only is he being dishonest, but perhaps even worse, the reward he reaps for his dishonesty provides all sorts of inappropriate incentives for other people who hold and eventually plan to sell their houses.

At this point, the reader may be willing to concede much of the above argument but still question whether the issue is quantitatively important. Specifically—Are there really significant welfare gains to be had from redistributing profit income? Especially as Sah's work (1983) suggests that using feasible redistributive instruments like commodity taxes will generate rather small gains in distributive justice, even when tailored to suit the worst off participants in an economy? A full answer to this question would obviously involve a huge empirical study which I do not have either the qualifications, the resources, or the time to carry out. So I can only report on some work which bears on the question but without providing anything like a complete answer.

First, Sah's paper actually has a rather serious limitation. An obvious way of improving the lot of the worst off would be to institute some kind of "unconditional basic income" such as that suggested by Meade (1989) and van Parijs (1991). Somewhat similar is the "negative income tax" considered some years ago by Friedman, Tobin, and others. Yet Sah's paper allows *only* commodity taxes and subsidies which thereby relate subsidies to the quantities of subsidized goods that are consumed. So somebody whose income is zero and who spends nothing at all receives a zero subsidy. Accordingly, Sah excludes what may be the most powerful redistributive tool available.

Second, even if first best optimal redistribution of income were feasible, one may argue whether it could have a sizable effect on welfare. Obviously, this depends on value judgments concerning what may be expressed in rather crude terms as the trade-off between equality and total wealth. At one extreme, if there is no willingness at all to exchange any total wealth in order to enhance equality, then first best redistribution would make no difference to total wealth, and attempts to redistribute by feasible taxation schemes could only lower it. At another extreme, one may make assumptions like those in Jorgenson's (1990) 1987 presidential address to the Econometric Society. There he argues (pp. 1031–32) that, while real consumption per head in the United States grew at an average rate of 2.51% *per annum* for the period 1947–85, an equity corrected welfare-based measure of the standard of living in the United States grew at 2.92% over the same period. In other words, it can be argued that even the rather limited measures that various governments in the United States have undertaken to enhance distributive justice have succeeded in adding

0.41% to the annual average growth rate of equity adjusted consumption per head over a period of almost forty years. In fact, consumption expenditure per capita, in 1982 dollars, rose from $3750.81 in 1947 to $9724.02 in 1985, or by a factor of 259%. Jorgenson's equity index, however, also rose from 0.5800 to 0.6782 (where 1.00 would indicate a fully equitable distribution). This equity index is defined so that the welfare-based measure of the standard of living is obtained by multiplying real consumption expenditure per capita by the equity index. Accordingly, this standard of living, again measured in 1982 dollars, rose from $2175.62 in 1947 to $6594.94 in 1985, or by a factor of 303%. It may be worth noting finally that almost all the increase in Jorgenson's equity index occurred in the period 1958–78, during which time it rose from 0.5678 in 1957 to 0.6737 in 1978.

While there are very many special and even highly implausible assumptions that lie behind these calculations by Jorgenson, they do make the point that the effect of good redistributive policies on welfare could turn out to be significant. After all, there are ways of doing the calculations which show that the welfare effects of actual redistributive policies are equivalent to an increase in the annual growth rate from 2.51% to 2.92% sustained over a period of four decades.

10. LIBERTY AS AN OBJECTIVE

> Humanity has not yet developed anything more efficient than a market economy . . . The prerequisite to ensure the effective functioning of the market [includes] de jure equality of all types of property, including private property . . . revenue from property should be recognised as lawful profit.
>
> From the Shatalin Plan for reforming the (ex-)Soviet economy, quoted in *The Economist,* September 15, 1990.

Shatalin may have been right. Democracy has been described as the least bad political system yet devised. So might a market economy yet be the least bad economic system, despite its many faults described in this chapter. Economists of Eastern Europe especially have seemed eager to assign profits a very much larger role in their economic systems. When it is suggested that markets have also many disadvantages, they may display some impatience with which one can well sympathize. It seems that they are looking for freedom and have come to associate economic controls with other kinds of interference with personal liberties, many of which may be much less justifiable. They want to try market economies, at least, and to enjoy even the freedom to learn from being wrong—if that is how things turn out.

So far, my discussion has not paid special attention to individual freedom as a value in itself. In line with the work of virtually all economists, I have concentrated solely on the allocation of resources. This may be leaving out some things which are very important. For one thing, much of what is best in life cannot easily be bought and sold, or is devalued by being traded. A specific example of this which aroused some interest twenty years ago was blood donation (see Titmuss's 1970 book and Arrow's 1972 review article). In addition, Hahn (1982) points out that it may not be legitimate to judge economic systems only on the basis of the allocations they produce. Earlier, Rowley and Peacock (1975) provided an extensive discussion of the implications for welfare economics of valuing freedom for its own sake. Similar ideas are discussed in Sen (1987, esp. p. 50 n.22 and pp. 60–65) and also emerge in the group of papers presented to the 1987 Conference of the European Economic Association by Kornai (1988), Lindbeck (1988), and Sen (1988). Earlier Sen tended to think of such concern for rights as "nonwelfarist" ethics, but I would disagree and prefer to speak instead of "extended welfarism." Otherwise, we would be in danger of joining those libertarians who always want all individuals' rights to be valued positively, even in a society where it was demonstrably better for individuals to have some of their liberty limited. It seems to me that we should value liberty to the extent that individuals themselves value it and are also made better off when they experience it. For this reason, I prefer to regard desirable liberties as components of individual welfare, along with the commodities needed for a good life and also any ethically relevant concept of desert, etc.

If liberty is an important part of individual welfare, this makes a considerable difference to the way we think of profits. Indeed, suppose that we follow the extreme libertarians, or even Rawls, in making liberty a primary value, "lexically prior" to a good allocation of resources in our scale of priorities. In this case, on one popular interpretation of liberty, a laissez-faire economic system becomes an end in itself. Profits become justified as an essential part of such a system, with those who earn them being entitled to keep them. This, however, seems to me a strange sort of morality. Many thoughtful moral philosophers and economists may be willing to give considerable weight to individual liberty in a social welfare function, but surely not to pursue liberty at all costs regardless of how much distributive injustice there is in the economic allocation which results. If there is a trade-off between liberty and distributive justice, the objections to profits raised above may be significantly weakened but not entirely removed.[2] Moreover, other concepts of liberty may be much

2. Steven Lukes (1990) argues that one cannot really talk about such a trade-off. But his argument does not totally exclude the possibility that there are some policies which promote some

more inimical to profit. Did Robin Hood have the right, or even the duty, to help the poor by robbing those whose wealth resulted from undeserved profits?

Indeed, incentive constraints imply that some respect has to be given to individual rights anyway. Limiting the extent of tax evasion, black marketeering, and other illegal activities in the economy requires a costly tax inspectorate, police force, etc. If official controls are too tight, they will either fall into disuse or will have to be backed up by an expensive, intrusive, and objectionable bureaucracy. Such constraints are already covered, at least implicitly, in our earlier discussion based upon the allocation of resources. Nevertheless, I am willing to concede that liberty can be a value in its own right, so that the earlier objections to profit may be somewhat overstated. In the end, therefore, another reason for firms and their owners to be allowed to keep at least some of their (supernormal) profits is the desire to promote freedom from interference *for its own sake* rather than because such freedom improves the allocations of resources, or because of the more plausible concern to reduce the costs of collecting taxes, etc. The case, however, should certainly not be overstated.

11. CONCLUSIONS

There are perhaps two kinds of freedom. Libertarians emphasize one kind, which is freedom to choose, without interference by tax gatherers, police officers, etc. Others may want to emphasize a different kind of freedom— freedom from poverty, hunger, disease, ignorance, homelessness—in other words, the freedom to have the basic necessities of modern life. Such freedom is enhanced by a proper allocation of resources, both privately and publicly provided. Studying such allocations is the subject of economic science, in general, and of welfare economics in particular. And greater freedom to choose has to be set against possible—even likely—decreases in people's freedom to have their basic needs for food, shelter, clothing, health care, etc., all met.

This chapter has examined the role of profits and similar rewards in helping to bring about an acceptable allocation of resources. It has argued that this role is very much weaker than most economists have claimed in the past. Indeed, most of their earlier arguments turn out to be hopelessly inadequate in the face of realistic considerations like private information and the consequent need to provide adequate incentives to workers and capitalists. It is no wonder that most ordinary people know better than to trust what most econo-

---

meaningful concept of liberty, and that some of these are also incompatible with other policies that would help promote distributive justice.

mists have been telling them. And no wonder that many thoughtful people I know regard the profit motive as at best suspicious and at worst even obscene.

On grounds of economic efficiency alone, and bearing in mind incentive constraints caused by asymmetric information, the best that can be said about profit-seeking behavior is that it may provide benefits which trickle down to the general population. Such trickling down, however, is by no means assured. Increasing profits often means shutting down inefficient enterprises, throwing people out of work, and causing real hardship. In theory it may be possible to compensate those who are adversely effected, but this will generally require a great deal of intervention in the economic system. In any case, after the necessary incentives for managers, workers, and financiers have been provided, there is no good reason why they should be allowed to retain any additional surplus profit.

In anything like a well-functioning economic system, therefore, the ethical case for pure profit, as opposed to incentive payments, seems to be exceedingly weak. Of course, libertarians may object that I am judging economic systems only by the allocations of goods and services which they generate, with no special consideration for individual rights. Yet only the most extreme libertarians can claim that my arguments have no relevance.

Others may argue that some economic systems have been misperforming so abysmally that almost any move toward a laissez-faire system would be an improvement, even though it may create widespread suffering for those who are already poor. Yet this seems like a counsel of despair, and it is time that those designing economic reforms came up with some less obnoxious recommendations. I also suspect that even they would want to emphasize the role of incentive payments rather than of profits.

ACKNOWLEDGMENTS

For comments on previous versions of this chapter I am much indebted to the conference organizers and participants for the high quality of the discussion—but especially to Mario Rizzo, Jan Narveson, Dan McCloskey, and Michael Bratman for particularly valuable suggestions which have caused me to make various improvements. My apologies also to the other participants whose interesting observations could not be dealt with in the limited time and space which was available. At the European University Institute, my industrial economist colleagues Stephen Martin and Louis Phlips have had some interesting points to make, as have Alessandro Pizzorno and Philippe van Parijs on the occasion of a later seminar presentation. In addition, Marcello de Cecco was kind enough not only to inform me of Cicero's discussion of asymmetric information but also to provide me with his own English translation to accompany the Latin original. I hope he forgives me for using a published translation. Jan Narveson's prompting at the conference led me to look for recent discussions of the ineffectiveness of welfare programs in the United States (and elsewhere), and my (necessarily brief) search has been much assisted by Gøsta Esping-Andersen. Kanaklata Patel kindly introduced me to Griffith's provocative book, which raises far more problems than economists are usually aware of in trying to define profits. None of these is responsible for the many inadequacies which remain.

REFERENCES

Akerlof, George. 1970. "The Market for Lemons: Qualitative Uncertainty and the Market Mechanism." *Quarterly Journal of Economics* 84:488–500.

Allais, Maurice. [1943] 1952. *A la recherche d'une discipline économique.* 2d ed. Published as *Traité d'economie pure.* Paris: Ateliers Industria; and Imprimerie Nationale.

———. 1947. *Economie et intérêt.* Paris: Imprimerie Nationale.

———. 1953. "La généralisation des théories de l'équilibre économique et du rendement social au cas du risque." Pp. 81–120 in *Econométrie.* Paris: Centre National de la Recherche Scientifique.

Arrow, Kenneth J. 1951. "An Extension of the Basic Theorems of Classical Welfare Economics." Pp. 507–532 in *Proceedings of the Second Berkeley Symposium on Mathematical Statistics and Probability,* ed. Jerzy Neyman. Berkeley: University of California Press.

———. 1953, 1964. "Le rôle des valeurs boursières pour la repartition la meilleure des risques." *Econometrie.* (Colloque International, CNRS Paris) (1953), 40:41–47; translation of "The Role of Securities in the Optimal Allocation of Risk Bearing." *Review of Economic Studies* (1964), 31:91–96.

———. 1972. "Gifts and Exchanges." *Philosophy and Public Affairs* 1:343–62.

Bergstrom, Theodore. 1971. "On the Existence and Optimality of Competitive Equilibrium for a Slave Economy." *Review of Economic Studies* 38:23–36.

Bhagwati, Jagdish. 1982. "Directly Unproductive Profit-Seeking Activities." *Journal of Political Economy* 90:988–1002.

Coles, Jeffrey L., and Peter J. Hammond. 1991. "Walrasian Equilibrium without Survival: Existence, Efficiency, and Remedial Policy." European University Institute, Working Paper ECO no. 91/50; revised version to appear in *Development, Welfare and Ethics: A Festschrift for Amartya Sen,* ed. Kaushik Basu, Prasanta K. Pattanaik, and Kotaro Suzumura. Oxford: Oxford University Press.

Debreu, Gérard. 1959. *Theory of Value: An Axiomatic Approach to General Equilibrium Theory.* New York: John Wiley.

DeMarzo, Peter M. 1993. "Majority Voting and Corporate Control: The Rule of the Dominant Shareholder." *Review of Economic Studies* 60:713–34.

Diamond, Peter A. 1967. "The Role of a Stock Market in a General Equilibrium Model with Technological Uncertainty." *American Economic Review* 57:757–76.

Diamond, Peter A., and James A. Mirrlees. 1971. "Optimal Taxation and Public Production, I and II." *American Economic Review* 61:8–27 and 261–78.

Dixit, Avinash K. 1987. "Tax Policy in Open Economies." Pp. 313–74 in *Handbook of Public Economics, Vol. 1,* ed. Alan J. Auerbach and Martin Feldstein. Amsterdam: North-Holland.

Dixit, Avinash K., and Victor Norman. 1980. *Theory of International Trade.* Welwyn: James Nisbet.

———. 1986. "Gains from Trade without Lump-Sum Compensation." *Journal of International Economics* 21:99–110.

Drèze, Jacques H. 1989. *Labour Management, Contracts and Capital Markets.* Oxford: Basil Blackwell.

Drèze, Jean P., and Nicholas H. Stern. 1987. "The Theory of Cost-Benefit Analysis." Pp. 909–89 in *Handbook of Public Economics, Vol. II,* ed. Alan J. Auerbach and Martin Feldstein. Amsterdam: North-Holland.

———. 1990. "Policy Reform, Shadow Prices and Market Prices." *Journal of Public Economics* 42:1–45.

Duffie, Darrell. 1988. *Security Markets: Stochastic Models.* San Diego: Academic Press.

Ellwood, David T. 1988. *Poor Support: Poverty in the American Family.* New York: Basic Books.

Esping-Anderson, Gøsta, and John Micklewright. 1990. "Welfare State Models in OECD Countries: An Analysis for the Debate in Eastern Europe." Paper delivered to the UNICEF Conference, Warsaw, October 16–18.

Fisher, Franklin M. 1983. *Disequilibrium Foundations of Equilibrium Economics.* Cambridge: Cambridge University Press.

Gilder, George. 1981. *Wealth and Poverty.* New York: Basic Books.

Grandmont, Jean-Michel, and Daniel McFadden. 1972. "A Technical Note on Classical Gains from Trade." *Journal of International Economics* 2:109–25.

Grass, Günter. 1990. "The West German Business Blitzkrieg." *(Manchester) Guardian Weekly,* November 11.

Griffiths, Ian. 1986. *Creative Accounting: How to Make Your Profits What You Want Them to Be.* London: Unwin Paperbacks.

Hahn, Frank H. 1973. "On Optimum Taxation." *Journal of Economic Theory* 6:96–106.

————. 1982. "On Some Difficulties of the Utilitarian Economist." Pp. 187–98 in *Utilitarianism and Beyond,* ed. Amartya K. Sen and Bernard Williams (Cambridge: Cambridge University Press.

Hammond, Peter J. 1979. "Straightforward Individual Incentive Compatibility in Large Economies." *Review of Economic Studies* 46:263–82.

————. 1985. "Welfare Economics." Pp. 405–34 in *Issues in Contemporary Microeconomics and Welfare,* ed. George R. Feiwel. London: Macmillan.

————. 1987. "Markets as Constraints: Multilateral Incentive Compatibility in Continnum Economies." *Review of Economic Studies* 54:399–412.

————. 1989. "Some Assumptions of Contemporary Neoclassical Economic Theology." Pp. 186–257 in *Joan Robinson and Modern Economic Theory,* ed. George R. Feiwel. London: Macmillan; and New York: New York University Press.

————. 1990a. "Incentives and Allocation Mechanisms." Pp. 213–48 in *Advanced Lectures in Quantitative Economics,* ed. Rick van der Ploeg. New York: Academic Press, 1990.

————. 1990b. "Theoretical Progress in Public Economics: A Provocative Assessment." *Oxford Economic Papers (special issue on public economics)* 42:6–33.

————. 1990c. "The Role of Information in Economics." Pp. 177–93 of *L'informazione nell'economia e nel diritto.* Milan: CARIPLO, 1990.

————. 1992. "On the Impossibility of Perfect Capital Markets." Pp. 527–60 in *Economic Analysis of Markets and Games: Essays in Honor of Frank Hahn,* ed. Partha S. Dasgupta, Douglas Gale, Oliver Hart, and Eric Maskin. Cambridge, Mass.: M.I.T. Press.

————. 1993a. "History as a Widespread Externality in Some Arrow-Debreu Market Games." University of Bristol, Department of Economics Discussion Paper no. 93/356; revised for inclusion in *The Formulation of Economic Theory and Other Essays in Honor of Kenneth Arrow,* ed. Graciela Chichilnisky. Cambridge: Cambridge University Press. In preparation.

————. 1993b. "Irreducibility, Resource Relatedness, and Survival with Individual Non-Convexities." Pp. 73–115 in *General Equilibrium, Growth and Trade, II: The Legacy of Lionel W. McKenzie,* ed. Robert Becker, Michele Boldrin, Ronald Jones, and William Thomson. New York: Academic Press.

Jorgenson, Dale W. 1990. "Aggregate Consumer Behaviour and the Measurement of Social Welfare." *Econometrica* 58:1007–40.

Kogon, Eugen. 1948. *Der SS-Staat.* Munich.

Kornai, Janos. 1988. "Individual Freedom and Reform of the Socialist Economy." *European Economic Review* 32:233–67.

Krueger, Anne O. 1974. "The Political Economy of the Rent-Seeking Society." *American Economic Review* 64:291–303.

Lindbeck, Assar. 1988. "Individual Freedom and Welfare State Policy." *European Economic Review* 32:295–318.

Lipsey, Richard G., and Kelvin J. Lancaster. 1956. "The General Theory of the Second-Best." *Review of Economic Studies* 24:11–32.

Little, Ian M. D. 1957. *A Critique of Welfare Economics.* 2d ed. Oxford: Oxford University Press.

Lukes, Steven. 1990. "Equality and Liberty: Must they Conflict?" European University Institute. Mimeo.

Makowski, Louis. 1983. "Competitive Stock Markets." *Review of Economic Studies* 50:305–30.

Meade, James E. 1989. *Agathotopia: The Economics of Partnership.* Aberdeen: Aberdeen University Press.

Mirrlees, James A. 1972. "On Producer Taxation." *Review of Economic Studies* 39: 105–11.

Murray, Charles. 1984. *Losing Ground: American Social Policy, 1950–1980.* New York: Basic Books.

Potts, Lydia. 1988 and 1990. *Weltmarkt für Arbeitskraft: Von der Kolonisation Amerikas bis zu den Migrationen der Gegenwart.* Hamburg: Junius Verlag GmbH, 1988. Translated as *The World Labour Market: A History of Migration.* London: Zed Books, 1990.

Rowley, Charles K., and Alan T. Peacock. 1975. *Welfare Economics: A Liberal Restatement.* London: Martin Robertson.

Sah, Raaj. 1983. "How Much Redistribution Is Possible through Commodity Taxes?" *Journal of Public Economics* 20:89–100.

Samuelson, Paul A. 1954. "The Pure Theory of Public Expenditure." *Review of Economics and Statistics* 36:387–89.

———. 1955. "Diagrammatic Exposition of a Theory of Public Expenditure." *Review of Economics and Statistics* 37:350–56.

Sen, Amartya K. 1987. *On Ethics and Economics.* Oxford: Basil Blackwell.

———. 1988. "Freedom of Choice: Concept and Content." *European Economic Review* 32:269–94.

Smith, Stephen C. 1990. "On the Economic Rationale for Codetermination Law." European University Institute, Working Paper ECO no. 90/12.

Tesfatsion, Leigh. 1986. "Time-Inconsistency of Benevolent Government Economies." *Journal of Public Economics* 31:25–52.

Titmuss, Richard M. 1970. *The Gift Relationship: From Human Blood to Social Policy.* London: Allen & Unwin.

Tullock, Gordon. 1967. "The Welfare Cost of Tariffs, Monopolies and Theft." *Western Economic Journal* 5:224–32.

Van Parijs, Philippe. 1991. "Why Surfers Should Be Fed: The Liberal Case for an Unconditional Basic Income." *Philosophy and Public Affairs* 20:101–31.

Wadhwani, Sushil, and Martin Wall. 1990. "The Effects of Profit-Sharing on Employment, Wages, Stock Returns and Productivity: Evidence from Micro-Data.'' *Economic Journal* 100:1–17.

Weitzman, Martin. 1984. *The Share Economy*. Cambridge, Mass.: Harvard University Press.

Weymark, John. 1978. ''On Pareto Improving Price Changes.'' *Journal of Economic Theory* 19:338–46.

5 Rights to Natural Talents and Pure Profits: A Critique of Gauthier on Rights and Economic Rent

Eric Mack

David Gauthier's *Morals by Agreement*,[1] is an impressive, indeed daunting, exercise in contractarian moral and political philosophy. The primary purpose of his treatise is to provide an explication of practical rationality as constrained maximization and of morality as compliance with these constraints. Gauthier offers an account of which constraints on straightforward utility maximization each rational individual will be prepared to accept and to comply with on the condition that other individuals also will accept and comply with them, and an explanation of why compliance with those constraints counts as morality. However, although *Morals by Agreement* is in the great tradition of Hobbesian moral and political theorizing, Gauthier's morality by agreement does not begin with the Hobbesian state of nature. Gauthier does not start by envisioning a Hobbesian war of all upon all, which has been generated by rational individuals each pursuing his own maximum utility, and then providing an account of what interpersonal constraints would, if generally abided by, lift us out of the sorry Hobbesian condition.[2] Rather, Gauthier takes the primary domain of morality by agreement to be that which is characteristically addressed within theories of distributive justice. His primary question is, What principles of division will it be rational for all utility maximizing individuals to adopt, when mutually advantageous cooperation is possible but only on the condition of general compliance with some principles for the division of the benefits of cooperation? It is, according to Gauthier, precisely because such

---

This chapter is a slightly revised version of "Gauthier on Rights and Economic Rent," by Eric Mack, published in *Social Philosophy and Policy* 9, no. 1 (Autumn 1992): 171–200. © Cambridge University Press. Reprinted with the permission of Cambridge University Press.

1. David Gauthier, *Morals by Agreement* (Oxford: Clarendon Press, 1986). All bracketed citations in the text are to *Morals by Agreement*.

2. This is the strategy of Jan Narveson's *The Libertarian Idea* (Philadelphia: Temple University Press, 1988).

> Left absolutely to their own devices . . . people will perform actions that lead to a [Hobbesian] condition that will make their lives immeasurably worse than if they were instead subject to restrictions: namely, restrictions on just the sort of actions that have that effect. [136]

principles are not needed in the "perfect market" that "the perfect market . . . would constitute a morally free zone, a zone within which the constraints of morality would have no place" [84].[3]

Gauthier, however, is not silent about the principles that seem most conspicuously absent in the Hobbesian state of nature and most conspicuously needed for the existence of a market order, namely, rights to one's person, one's powers, to the products of one's labors, and to the receipts of one's trades. According to Gauthier, these rights are presupposed by any rational agreement giving rise to morality. Rational bargainers will not agree to, will not comply with, and will not expect others' compliance with bargains that preserve past predations or free rides or prospectively tolerate any such advantage taking. The victims of predations or free rides will insist, and their beneficiaries will concede (out of fear of losing the potential gains from interaction) that their joint initial bargaining position be adjusted to negate these past forms of advantage taking. The bargainers lift themselves out of the Hobbesian condition of unlimited blameless liberty, they accept retrospectively (and prospectively) a ban on advantage taking, so that they can securely capture the gains of subsequent cooperation.

> . . . all effects of taking advantage must be removed from the initial
> bargaining position. . . . This constraint is part of morals by agreement,
> not in being the object of an agreement among rational individuals, but
> in being a precondition to such agreement. [192]

This constraint on advantage taking, that is, on bettering one's position by way of worsening the condition of others, is expressed by Gauthier in the form of a Lockean Proviso, a proviso which throughout this essay shall be referred to as "Gauthier's Proviso."[4] The rights derived from this proviso are supposed to constitute the basic (Lockean) moral structure upon which the superstructure of market interaction and nonmarket cooperation is to rest. Through the defense of his proviso and his derivation of rights from it, Gauthier attempts a backward Lockeanizing of his (otherwise) Hobbesian state of nature. In this respect, Gauthier's Proviso is intended to do much more than any normal Lockean

---

3. Gauthier persists in this way of speaking despite recognizing that Smith's "obvious and simple system of natural liberty" requires that each "not violate the laws of justice" [83, 85].

4. The term "Lockean Proviso" is introduced by Nozick to refer, in the tradition of Locke's requirement that private acquisition from nature leave "enough and as good" for others, to a moral restraint on people's private acquisitions and subsequent holdings to insure that, in some specified way, the institution of private property does not worsen any individual's circumstances relative to his situation in a preproperty state of nature. See Robert Nozick, *Anarchy, State and Utopia* (New York, Basic Books, 1974), pp. 174–82.

Proviso. For rather than being merely a constraint on the permissible exercise of certain independently identified rights, for example, rights of acquisition and transfer, it is supposed to serve as a scheme for the generation of people's most basic rights.[5]

This chapter does not directly address Gauthier's contention that a ban on advantage taking would arise as a by-product of an agreement by rational individuals about the division of the benefits of their social cooperation. Instead, it focuses on questions about what Gauthier's Proviso implies, or fails to imply, about individuals' rights—and more specifically about people's economic rights to rents and people's basic (Lockean) rights to their own natural endowments. In section 1 of this inquiry, I focus on Gauthier's endorsement in principle of the confiscation of economic rent—with the proceeds of that confiscation to be distributed across all members of society in accordance with his principle of minimax relative concession.[6] I draw out certain features or implications of Gauthier's views about economic rent that are odd in themselves or coexist most uncomfortably with other aspects or aspirations of Gauthier's doctrine. In section 2, I deal briefly with Gauthier's positive argument

---

5. The constraints of Gauthier's Proviso only apply among individuals who stand to benefit from cooperation. Gauthier often writes as though *whatever* ban there is on the initiation of force derives from the need for such a ban as a condition for positive cooperation.

> . . . it is rational for utility-maximizers to accept the proviso as constraining their natural interaction and their individual endowments, in so far as they anticipate beneficial social interaction with their fellows. . . . Without the prospect of agreement and society, there would be no morality, and the proviso would have no rationale. [193]

This suggests that there would be no rationale for the proviso among two individuals between whom a nonaggression pact would be mutually advantageous but for whom there are no other potential benefits from interaction or cooperation. Hence, there would be no ban on aggression between these individuals. But, elsewhere [115, 132] Gauthier indicates that a nonaggression pact among these two individuals would itself count as a bit of cooperation ''in order to avoid mutually destructive conflict.'' Thus, there is a rational basis for a ban on aggression even in this case. But note that here the ban *is* ''the product of rational agreement'' and not, as the ban within the proviso is supposed to be, ''a condition that must be accepted by each person for such agreement [on positive cooperation] to be possible'' [16].

6. Strictly speaking, that individuals have no right to noncoercively derived rents is a feature of the state of nature theory that is generated by Gauthier's Proviso while the positive prescription of the distribution of rents according with minimax relative concession is the object of rational agreement.

The principle of minimax relative concession requires that the cooperative surplus be divided so that the greatest relative concession experienced by anyone of the cooperating parties be less than that relative concession would be under any alternative division of the surplus. An agent's relative concession is the degree to which his actual allotment from the surplus represents a concession from his demand for as much of the surplus as it is possible for him to receive (without driving others away). See Gauthier [136–46].

for treating rents as part of the cooperative "surplus" and, hence, as subject to redistribution in accord with minimax relative concession.[7] In section 3, I turn to Gauthier's endorsement, as an implication of his proviso, of people's rights over their respective natural endowments. Gauthier contends that the right of individuals to their respective natural endowments does not imply a right to the rents noncoercively derived from the sale of their services. Hence, he maintains, his denial of rights to rent does not conflict with his assertion of rights to natural endowments. I question these contentions, suggesting that Gauthier's conclusions about economic rent do reflect a failure of philosophical commitment to robust rights to natural endowments. In addition, I challenge Gauthier's claim that his proviso can generate rights of persons to their own natural endowments and, hence, to their own powers. In addition, I contend that, in practice, a no-rent policy would require the institution of forced labor and that nothing within Gauthier's doctrine of persons' rights over their own powers would forbid this development. I argue that the proviso's incapacity to yield robust rights is due to Gauthier's implicit and flawed conception of rights as claims to specified utility levels.

Economic rents are pure profits. Economic rents acquired through the exercise of one's own distinctive talents (or knowledge) constitute a significant subclass of pure profits. It is the subclass of pure profits that is most intuitively legitimate since these pure profits derive from the exercise of our most intuitively legitimate entitlements—entitlements over our respective talents (and insights).[8] Thus, Gauthier's denial of the legitimacy of economic rents that arise through the exercise of one's own talents (or insights) amounts to a denial of the legitimacy of the most intuitively legitimate subclass of profits. Hence, to demolish Gauthier's case for the confiscation of economic rents that arise through exercise of people's natural endowments is to rebut an important argument against these most intuitively legitimate pure profits. Furthermore, to show that Gauthier's opposition to this category of economic rent does reflect

7. The term "surplus" is not normatively neutral. When part of someone's holdings is described as a surplus, there is a strong suggestion that there is no significant moral barrier to the redistribution of that holding and, furthermore, that there is some good reason in support of that redistribution. Nevertheless, the term is ubiquitous. It cannot be avoided readily. Occasionally I allow myself to mark the nonneutrality of the term by the use of scare quotes.

8. For an account of pure entrepreneurial profits as a product of the entrepreneur's distinctive insight see Israel Kirzner's *Competition and Entrepreneurship* (Chicago: University of Chicago Press, 1973), especially chaps. 2 and 3. The subclass of pure profits I focus on is more inclusive than Kirzner's entrepreneural profits. For, in some cases, it is not the talent holder's distinctive *awareness* of his talent or desire of others for its exercise that accounts for his receipt of payments in "excess" of a perfectly competitive return. I am, in effect, proposing that Kirznerian entrepreneurial profits can be seen as rents accruing to the entrepreneur on the basis of his scarce insight.

a lack of commitment on Gauthier's part to persons possessing robust rights over their own natural endowments and that a practical implementation of a no-rent policy would require instituting forced labor is to provide strong support for a significant claim on behalf of profits. That claim is that if one endorses persons possessing robust rights over themselves—rights robust enough morally to preclude forced labor—one must also endorse the legitimacy of the pure profits that arise through persons exercising their respective natural endowments.

1. GAUTHIER ON ECONOMIC RENT

Gauthier characterizes economic rent as follows:

> The recipient of rent benefits from the scarcity of the factors she controls—a scarcity which is of course entirely accidental from her standpoint, since it depends, not on the intrinsic nature of the factors, but on the relation between them and the factors controlled by others. She receives more than is needed to induce her to bring her factors to the market; rent is by definition a return over and above the cost of supply. [98][9]

Gauthier's discussion focuses on rents derived from the exercise of talents and, in particular, on the rents derived by hockey player Wayne Gretzky and basketball player Wilt Chamberlain.[10] Let us focus on the latter since we already have from Robert Nozick a hypothesized figure for the annual income of Chamberlain generated in the nonperfect market for his services, namely, $250,000 (in 1974 dollars!).[11]

9. There seem to be two distinct albeit closely related conceptions of rent at work in this passage. First, there is economic rent as ''by definition a return over and above the cost of supply.'' Second, there is economic rent as return over cost of supply *in virtue of* the scarcity of the factors controlled by the recipient. Thus, later in *Morals by Agreement,* Gauthier declares, ''Rent is determined by factor scarcity; it is the premium certain factor services command, over and above the full cost of supply, because there is no alternative to meet the demand'' [272]. It seems that the two notions need not be extensionally equivalent. For something other than the scarcity of the item brought to market may account for a seller's returns exceeding the costs of supply. For instance, the seller may receive rent because buyers are ignorant of how little this seller and his competitors would be willing to accept.

10. ·Gauthier, of course, recognizes that among the payments needed to bring certain skills to market, for example, Wilt's basketball skills, are the payments needed to induce individuals with various natural talents to identify and cultivate those native capacities. The payments necessary to motivate individuals to develop their respective skills do not count as rent. Yet (as Ellen Paul has suggested to me), does not the very recognition that individuals develop their respective skills, that they chose to cultivate this or that natural talent—sometimes precisely because of the anticipated scarcity of the resulting skill—cast doubt on Gauthier's idea that the scarcity of an agent's skill will (always) be ''entirely accidental from her standpoint''?

11. Nozick (1974), pp. 160–64.

According to Gauthier, whatever segment of this $250,000 exceeds the minimum that would induce Wilt to play basketball were Wilt to be certain that no higher offer would ever be forthcoming represents factor rent on Wilt's scarce natural endowments.[12] Gauthier favors (at least in principle) confiscatory taxation of that entire segment. Such a tax, Gauthier tells us, would have no affect on the supply of factor services. For, by hypothesis, Wilt would still be motivated—albeit only minimally motivated—to apply his talents to basketball. Nor, according to Gauthier, would such a confiscation constitute any infringement upon Wilt's employment freedom. For Wilt remains free to choose among occupations. He is not being required to play (or not to play) basketball.

> [Wilt's] right to use his [basketball] skills as he pleases is not affected by the distribution of rent; we have just seen that a confiscatory tax on rent would not, and could not, affect his willingness to play [basketball]. Each person's right to his basic endowment is a right to the exclusive use of that endowment in market and cooperative interaction. But market interaction is not affected by the distribution of the surplus represented by rent; each person's exclusive use of his capacities in market interaction is left untouched if rent is confiscated. [273–74]

Furthermore, according to Gauthier, Wilt's natural freedom is not infringed upon by forbidding his receipt of the full $250,000.

> Certainly the principle [i.e., of minimax relative concession applied to the distribution of Wilt's rent income] does interfere with a particular liberty—specifically, the freedom to collect factor rent. But this is no part of the freedom of a solitary being; the surplus represented by rent arises only through interaction. And so it is not a necessary part of market freedom conceived as an extension of the natural freedom enjoyed by Robinson Crusoe. [276][13]

12. More precisely, the rent is not the difference between the payment that *now* would induce Wilt to play and the $250,000. Rather it is the difference between the amount needed both to elicit Wilt's development of his skills (in light of his uncertainty about whether he will really "make it") and to draw forth his current supply of those developed skills and the $250,000.

13. Unfortunately, as Jeffrey Paul has pointed out to me, Gauthier's discussion ignores the allocative function of rents. Wilt will play basketball for anyone for $30,001 if no greater payment is possible. But, especially at that price, *lots* of coalitions of fans are eager to purchase his services. How is he to determine whether to play for the fans in L.A., in Philadelphia, or in Shreveport—each coalition of which *easily* comes up with an offer of $30,001? Should Los Angeles be allowed to tempt Wilt away from Shreveport with its beachfront communities, or should Shreveport be allowed to add a special hardship component to its salary offer? Is the ultimate choice of employer even Wilt's choice to make? If we allow equalization of bids by allowing, for example, Shreveport to add some extra monetary payment to compensate for the charms of Shreveport and do not allow competitive bidding among the aspiring employers, we

This argument is puzzling. Clearly, "market freedom conceived of as an extension of . . . natural freedom" includes some freedoms *not* enjoyed by "solitary beings." It certainly includes the freedom to benefit from the perfectly competitive sale of one's services. Why does it not also include the freedom to benefit from the nonperfectly competitive sale of one's services?

Market freedom does not include this because Gauthier's discussion is deeply and pervasively colored by the "perfect competition" model. Within a perfectly competitive market, any prospective sale of some good or service for more than the seller's cost of bringing that good or service to market is instantaneously met by competing sellers increasing the amount of that good or service offered and decreasing their selling price, with the effect of driving the selling price down to the cost of supply—thus eliminating any prospective "economic rent." Thus, in a perfectly competitive market, there are no gains to be had from the relative scarcity of one's productive factors or from one's special insights.[14]

For Gauthier, this perfect competition model functions not merely as an analytic device, but also as a norm that morally marks off gains obtained in perfectly competitive markets from gains attributable to departures from perfect competition. It is, unfortunately, not needless to say that this "idealization" of the market completely abstracts from a standard feature of actual market exchanges and the dynamic virtues of real competitive markets. The standard feature of actual exchanges is that both parties gain, and more than minimally, from them. Both parties receive more than covers their costs in bringing their supply (of, e.g., hockey sticks or money) to the exchange; both parties receive more than their costs plus that smidgen of return which would move them to make the exchange were they assured that no greater payment (in money or hockey sticks) were possible. In standard actual exchanges each payment (e.g.,

fully eliminate net return to Wilt as an allocative device and, in the (intentionally?) ominous words of one economic text, ". . . some other technique would have to serve this function" (A. Alchian and W. Allen, *University Economics,* 2d ed. [Belmont, Calif.: Wadsworth, 1967), p. 99]). Whether or not this shows that a blanket prohibition on rent infringes upon Wilt's market freedom, it certainly seems to show that it infringes upon the market freedom of would-be competitors for Wilt's services. And, in light of the rationing function of rents, it is certainly false that "market interaction is not affected by the distribution of the surplus represented by rent" [273].

14. I am told that if perfect competition is defined in terms of all sellers being pricetakers (i.e., are unable by any bargaining to affect their selling price), then profit (and rent?) are possible under perfectly competitive conditions. It is not clear to me (unversed in these matters as I am) that this is so. For it is not clear to me how, if the conditions for sellers not being pricetakers to any extent are satisfied, sellers will be able to elicit more for their goods or services than the cost of their supply (plus the smidgen needed to induce them to bring those goods or services to market). In any case, Gauthier does not characterize perfect competition in terms of all sellers being pricetakers.

money for hockey sticks, hockey sticks of such-and-such quantity for money) is wasteful or inefficient in the sense that some lesser payment would have called forth the same supply had the supplier known that this lesser payment was the maximum possible payment to him. But, of course, the total "surplus" from each exchange, which is divided among the traders in accord with the terms they have agreed to, is not "socially" lost. What is lost to the purchaser of hockey sticks is found in the seller's greater than minimal return, and what is lost to the seller of hockey sticks (in the form of having provided more or better sticks than he might have had to for the money received) is found in the purchaser's greater than minimal return. Those who invoke the model of perfect competition recognize, of course, that it is an "idealization." Nevertheless, the invocation characteristically suggests that there is something fishy about gains that exceed those that would exist, if any would, under the conditions of perfect competition.

The suggestion that there is something suspicious about more than perfectly competitive returns is strongly reinforced by the idea that the competition that enhances efficiency and that is appropriately envisioned in the economic justification of the competitive market is one which steadily and incrementally reduces suppliers' more than perfectly competitive returns. The more competitive the world is, the more potential competitors will sense any gap between the return to the hockey stick provider and his costs and will rush in to bid down the price of these implements. At least the *tendency* of unrestricted competition will be to reduce returns to the cost of supply. In actual competitive economies, however, insightful entrepreneurs will not imitatively ape the production and marketing of others. Rather they search out new ways of producing for new, or as yet unexploited, markets. The entrepreneur does not replicate the efforts of the existing supplier except for the hope of marginally undercutting his prices. She hopes instead to create a new market or a new way of producing for an existing market such that the gap between her costs and the value that her potential customers see in her product will be *greater* than the gap between the present supplier and his customers. She seeks not less but more in the way of imperfectly competitive returns. If she succeeds, she renders her competitor not so much undercut as obsolete.[15] Even the entre-

15. Such actual, entrepreneurial, competition is, therefore, much more like the competition between diverse cultures with different perceptions of the world and different technologies, as this larger-scale competition is described by Gauthier himself. The "old ways" of the North American natives "were highly effective adaptions to an environment that the native inhabitants were unable to transform." The Europeans did not engage in incrementally better versions of those adaptions. Rather,

    . . . European technology rendered these adaptions obsolete. The problems with

preneur who merely (!) finds a better, more cost-effective, way of providing a good or service identical to her competitor's may achieve a greater net return than the competitor while undercutting his price. This actual competition is the source of the innovative and dynamic quality of market economies—a quality which is both needed to keep pace with a world of changing technology, resource availability, information, and consumption preferences and which contributes to market societies being such worlds.[16] This is competition as a "discovery procedure," through which portions of the knowledge that the perfect competitive model assumes to exist in superabundance first become available to economic agents.[17] The perfectly competitive market idealization draws our attention away from the way in which actual competition enhances value and knowledge in society through a process whose participants aim at, and sometimes achieve, higher than normal imperfectly competitive returns.

The point of the last couple of paragraphs is not that, since profits and rents are essential to actual innovative competitive processes and since these competitive processes are good, individuals (typically) have a right to their entrepreneurial profits and noncoercively derived rents—although that would not be too bad an argument. Instead, the argument is that it is only the pervasiveness of the perfect competition idealization in *Morals by Agreement* that gives any initial plausibility to a distinction between, on the one hand, economic rents (i.e., pure profits) and, on the other hand, the smidgen of gain, that minimally motivates trades and the benefits that derive from the division of labor. It is only this faulty idealization that suggests that economic rents (i.e., pure profits) are any less likely candidates for membership in the system of natural liberty.

Let us proceed to Gauthier's core claim that all rent should in principle be

---

which the natives grappled were dissolved by that technology—to be replaced, to be sure, by new and different problems, but related to a more advanced level of human development. . . . The effect of the European incursion was to turn cultural practices that had been necessary to survival into a form of play. [296]

16. The classic reference, of course, is to Joseph Schumpeter's discussion of the "creative destructiveness" of market economies. See *Capitalism, Socialism, and Democracy,* 3d ed. (New York: Harper and Row, 1950), chap. 7. Schumpeter's own weary sense that the rate of technological, informational, and preference change was diminishing contributes to his conclusion that in the future a bureaucratic structure that simulated the actions of a perfectly competitive market would be feasible and adequate to that more static world. See Schumpeter, chaps. 16 and 17.

17. See F. A. Hayek's "Competition as a Discovery Procedure," in his *New Studies in Philosophy, Politics, Economics and the History of Ideas* (Chicago: University of Chicago Press, 1978), 179–90; and, more important, "The Meaning of Competition," in his *Individualism and Economic Order* (Chicago: University of Chicago Press, 1948), pp. 92–106. Israel Kirzner is preeminent among those currently developing the Hayekian insights. See, for example, his *Discovery and the Capitalist Process* (Chicago: University of Chicago Press, 1985), chaps. 1–4.

confiscated and what this portends for the program of treating individuals as bearers of entitlements to their respective natural endowments. For illustrative purposes, let us return to Wilt Chamberlain and his annual payment (in 1974 dollars) of $250,000 in the imperfect market for B-Ball services. And let us make the assumption (for now) that Chamberlain is indifferent among various occupations; he chooses among them entirely on the basis of financial remuneration. At first blush, it would seem that to identify Chamberlain's nonrent B-Ball income we need only identify his next best employment alternative and add a dollar to that alternative to motivate Wilt to choose B-Ball. So, if his next-best alternative is serving as the stand-in for the Incredible Hulk at $100,000, then his nonrent income from B-Ball is $100,001. Were Wilt forbidden to receive anything over $100,001, he would still be motivated to pursue B-Ball; he would still "freely" pursue his socially most highly valued activity. The proposal that Chamberlain's economic rent be confiscated seems, then, to require the confiscation of all his proceeds in excess of $100,001.

Our question, however, is whether $100,001 is really needed to induce Wilt to choose B-Ball. It is *if and only if* Wilt would be permitted to keep all the $100,000 that he would receive as the stand-in for the Incredible Hulk. And, of course, he would be permitted to keep that $100,000 *if and only if* all of *that* remuneration would be nonrent income. But surely it would only be because of the scarcity of his Hulk-like qualities that Chamberlain would be able to solicit an offer of $100,000 for being the Hulk's stand-in. In such a case, we have to ask the further question: How much of that $100,000 would represent economic rent? And, to answer that question, we would have turn to Chamberlain's next best offer, for example, $40,000 annually for service as a sanitation engineer, and reason that any remuneration in excess of $40,001 is economic rent because Wilt would choose to play B-Ball (or serve as the Hulk's stand-in) for $40,001 if it were not for the scarcity of his B-ball playing (or Hunking) qualities—a scarcity that allows him to extract extracompetitive remuneration from B-Ball (or Incredible Hulk) fans. But, then, of course, we would have to ask about what portion of Chamberlain's prospection remuneration as a sanitation engineer would itself be economic rent. For surely Wilt's possession of certain far-from-universal capacities, for example, a knack for hitting the center of a driveway with a garbage can from thirty feet, indicates that a portion of the salary he would be able to negotiate for sanitary engineering would consist in economic rent.

Where, then, must the line of inquiry end? To determine the full economic rent component of Chamberlain's $250,000 payment, we have to identify what remuneration for services Chamberlain would receive were there to be no "barriers" to entering into perfect competition with Chamberlain in the labor market. In other words, we have to identify what payment Chamberlain would receive were he only to offer for sale pure, undifferentiated universal labor. If the payment for the sale of universal labor power would be $30,000, then Chamberlain would "freely" choose to play B-Ball (or serve as the Incredible Hulk or a sanitation engineer) were he offered $30,001 for that service while no other offer over $30,000 was allowed. That $30,001 is what Wilt would receive for his performance on the court were his skills not at all scarce, for example, were there several thousand proto-Wilts. It is what he would receive were there A RESERVE INDUSTRIAL ARMY OF WILTS!

Thus, like all those who step forward from any reserve industrial army, Wilt is to receive on net nothing more than the costs of his own production as a socially useful worker—which costs equal his opportunity costs plus that one dollar needed to secure Wilt's "free" choice of the form of the employment of his talents that others most prefer. Everything above that is morally tainted rent, that is, is payment that "is determined by factor scarcity; it is the premium certain factor services command, over and above the full cost of supply, because there is no alternative to meet the demand [272]." Thus, an ironic implication of Gauthier's proposal is that sellers of services *should* be treated precisely as Marx *charges* that sellers of labor are treated under capitalism!

In what sense, if any, is Wilt left with a right to an unequal return from the market provision of his distinctive talents and powers? It seems that, with the minor addition of the minimal add-on that would motivate Wilt "freely" to opt for the socially most highly valued use of his natural assets, Wilt can only have a right to the going perfectly competitive market *rate* for the amount of universal labor he supplies. Only by limiting what he receives for the exercise of his talents to that rate can it be assured that he will not "extract" factor rent from society. Thus, if Wilt rightfully receives a greater than equal income, it must be because he supplies greater than equal *quantity* of universal labor. If Wilt's legitimate earnings exceed that of the average person, it must be because he works longer hours than the average or because somehow he produces more minutes of labor service per working minute than other workers do in the course of their work.[18] So, neither Wilt's nor anyone else's just earnings can ever be based upon or represent return upon that person's qualitatively distinctive or even relatively rare talents and powers. To receive payment for what is special about oneself, for one's relatively distinct ways of

18. Although it is certain that, for Gauthier, this is an unwelcome reading of his position, it accords with his statement: "Those who are able to supply *more factor services* to the market may expect to enjoy a preferred share of the private goods" [270; emphasis added].

doing things, must always amount to the unjust extraction of resources from others.

I want now to turn to several other questionable features of Gauthier's views on the just distribution of economic rent. It seems odd, at least as a matter of principle, that the economic rent that accrues to Wilt should be distributed across all members of Wilt's society. If anything, a more finely tuned distribution of the seized funds would be appropriate, namely, one which allotted these funds precisely to those whose economic demand for Wilt's performances added up to an offer of more than would minimally motivate Wilt. It certainly seems odd that someone whose only interest in sports is an inexplicable obsession with ice hockey should have a claim in justice on an equal societal share of the rents Wilt "extracts" from his fervent basketball fans.

But what exactly is the complaint that Wilt's fans have against him that would justify seizure of his rent income on their behalf? Chamberlain's play is worth (*at least*) $250,000 to them. Why, then, should they not be satisfied with enjoying that valued display—granted, not gratis, but for a price that each of them is quite willing, with no hint of any background coercion, to pay? We can recognize that these fans could get what they value at (at least) $250,000 for less were someone empowered to prohibit Wilt from receiving or retaining that $250,000 without being at all moved to the conclusion that they ought to get Wilt's services for less or that anyone ought to be so empowered.

If the fans who jointly pay $250,000 to see Wilt play when $30,001 would have minimally motivated Wilt can legitimately complain that Wilt has extracted rents from them, then Wilt himself will almost certainly be able to press a similar charge against his fans. For, almost certainly there is some greater sum, for example, $300,000, that Wilt's fans would have paid to see Wilt play had it been impossible for them to pay less. The difference, the $50,000 of consumer surplus, is rent extracted by the fans. The fans get $300,000 worth of pleasure and excitement from Wilt's play and slyly pay him only $250,000. This complaint against the fans on Wilt's behalf is as reasonable as their complaint against Wilt. And who can most coherently make *both* complaints? Neither Wilt, nor the fans, but SOCIETY. Society declares that each "receives more than is needed to induce [them] to bring [their respective] factors to the market"; each receives "rent [which] is by definition a return over and above the cost of supply" [98]. It is Gauthier's position that, to counteract this act of insidious mutual exploitation, the gains of each party that exceed what would have minimally motivated that party to supply his factors are to be confiscated and distributed across society.

We have been proceeding with the implausible assumption that Chamberlain is indifferently disposed toward the various occupations available to him. Suppose we adopt the more plausible assumption that Wilt would rather play basketball than engage in universal labor—and by a considerable degree. Let us assume that Wilt will engage in a season of universal labor for $30,000, but would play B-Ball for the season for $25,000. If this is so, then the rent component of Wilt's gross basketball earnings is $225,000. A policy of social confiscation of Wilt's economic rent would, then, leave Wilt with less (net dollar income) than he would receive were he only capable of supplying universal labor. This is an odd consequence for Gauthier who explicates and explicitly rejects John Rawls's view that "[n]o one has any entitlement based on being the particular person he is . . . ." [250], and who argues,

> One's natural capacities are what one brings to society, to market and cooperative interaction. Why should they not determine, or contribute to determining, what one gets in society? [220]

2. RENT AS COOPERATIVE "SURPLUS"

I have been focusing on problematic assumptions within and resulting puzzles about Gauthier's denial of rights to rents and, hence, to pure profits. But something must be said about Gauthier's positive case for treating all rents as subject to redistribution under the principle of minimax relative concession.[19] Since rents are a product of—indeed, I have argued, an ineliminable feature of—market interaction, it is surprising that they are supposed to be apportioned in accordance with minimax relative concession. For this principle is not a norm of market interaction but rather of nonmarket cooperation. Gauthier does, however, offer a reason for applying minimax relative concession to rents, and this reason consists in his construal of rents as *cooperative* surpluses which are, therefore, subject to apportionment under this rule of nonmarket cooperation.

> Society may be considered as a single co-operative enterprise. The benefit represented by factor rent is part of the surplus afforded by that enterprise, for it arises only in social interaction. But then that benefit is to be distributed among the members of society on the terms established by minimax relative concession. Each person, as a contributor to social interaction, shares in the production of the benefit represented by factor rent. [274]

19. The need for this further discussion was pressed on me by Ken Cust.

In this passage and those in support of it, Gauthier is no longer maintaining
the largely negative thesis that, since rent plays no useful function in the
operation of the free and perfectly competitive market, denying a right to rent
does not clash with the operation of the market or with people's market freedom. Rather, we have here a positive doctrine reminiscent of many nineteenth-
century social theorists who argued for the social confiscation of rents—though
they especially had land rents in mind—on the grounds that the scarcity of the
rent-generating good or service and, hence, the value of that good or service,
was a product of "society." And, as the product of society, it (the good or
service or its value) rightfully belonged to society.[20]

This sort of argument seems to rely upon a strange mixing of cost of
production and subjective theories of economic value. It conflates two different
senses of "contribution" to something's economic value and detaches the
plausible claim to entitlement associated with one sort of contribution and
misleadingly attaches that entitlement claim to contribution of the other sort.
Cost of production theories of economic value are push theories; economic
value gets pushed into objects or activities possessing it by their production
out of factors which themselves already possess economic value. There are
one or more basic factors which intrinsically possess economic value—labor
is the only such basic factor in that simplest of cost of production theories,
namely, the labor theory of value. Clearly, *no* explanation can be given for
this fundamental and intrinsic possession of economic value. In contrast, the
subjectivist theory of economic value is a pull theory. People's demand for
goods and services, reflecting their various preferences, values, and judgments,
confer economic value on those goods and services—though the value resides
in people's evaluations of those goods and services, not in those objects and
activities as such. Factors for the production of those goods and services, in
turn, acquire value through the demand for them on the part of those prepared
to use these factors in the production of those goods and services. The value
of those factors of production resides not in those factors as such but in the
preferences, values, and judgments of those seeking those factors for uses that

20. See L. T. Hobhouse's approving report of the following view:
[Site] value the land nationalizer contends is not created by the owners. It is created
by society. . . . Directly or indirectly, the community creates the site value. . . .
The land nationalizer . . . denies the justice of this [private ownership] arrangement,
and he sees no solution except this—that the monopoly value should pass back to
the community which creates it. Accordingly, he favors the taxation of site value
to its full amount. [See *Liberalism* (Oxford: Oxford University Press, 1964),
p. 53].

they believe are or will be valued. On the subjectivist view, nothing has intrinsic economic value—least of all, the most basic factors of production (assuming anything can be identified as being among the most basic factors).

Now, if economic value is conceived on the cost of production model, it is quite natural and plausible to think that he who contributes some rightfully held factor toward the production of a good or service, the value of which is received from the value of its factors of production, has, thereby, some claim on that product and its value. It will be quite natural and plausible to think that the overall entitlement to that product and its value is shared among the contributors of its value-imbuing factors. Indeed, since on this model the value of the product can never be greater than the value of its factors of production, for the contributors to receive less than a full claim to the product or its value is for those contributors to be duped and/or exploited.

On the other hand, it is not the least natural or plausible to think that one's contribution to the value of a good or service *by way of wanting it* (or by way of not oneself increasing the supply of that sort of good or service!) supports any claim to that good or service or to the value ascribed to it. The contribution that Wilt's fans make to the value of his basketball services by way of being his fans (or of Wilt's potential competitors by way of their pursuing nonathletic life plans) is quite unlike the contribution made, as a cost of production theorist sees it, by Wilt's parents, his milkman, his coaches, etc. Contributing to or creating economic value in an X by way of manifesting economic demand for an X (or by not supplying additional Xs) does not in the least indicate that some wrong is done to one if one does not receive a share of the X or a share of its economic value. The idea that contribution to a good's or service's economic value by way of demand (or by way of not oneself enhancing the supply) could establish a claim to that value requires, it seems, that we confuse this sort of contribution with the sort of contribution envisioned within cost-of-production theories.

One hesitates even to imagine that Gauthier is making this error. And yet, in Gauthier's argument, there seems to be a shift in his understanding of "contributing" toward the creation of a cooperative surplus that parallels the shift from "contributing" to economic value, in the sense of supplying productive factors to "contributing" to economic value in the sense of registering a demand. The principle of minimax relative concession is introduced as a principle governing the distribution of the difference between what is produced through the agents joint activity or joint utilization of factors of production otherwise held and used separately and what would have been produced had the agents pursued separate strategies or separate uses of their respective resources. This creation of a surplus occurs through the actual contribution and coordinated utilization of factors of production, and it is quite different from the type of "cooperative enterprise" that "creates" rents. In the latter case, there is no "production of [a] benefit" which ought "to be distributed among the members of society" [274]. Of course, the seller benefits from the exchange that ensues. The purchasers contribute to that benefit. But in doing so they are not merely receiving through purchase something which, by way of creative cooperation, they have already produced. And, although they are receiving through purchase something toward the economic value of which they have contributed, their sort of contribution to its economic value gives them no claim on the item or its value such that any payment for the good or service (above its cost of supply) wrongs the purchasers and ought to be remitted to them. Thus, if we are clear about the senses in which the market value of some X may be said to be created by social cooperation, we will not be tempted to believe that those who produce economic value merely by way of registering economic demand have, thereby, any claim upon that value.

3. GAUTHIER ON RIGHTS

We have noted that Gauthier is eager to affirm Wilt's "right to his basic endowment" which "is a right to the exclusive use of that endowment in market and cooperative interaction." This is why he insists that denying Wilt's rights to rents does not at all disparage Wilt's right "to the exclusive use of [his] endowment." I shall argue, however, that the employment of Gauthier's Proviso cannot vindicate people's possession of robust rights over their respective natural endowments. It is precisely because Gauthier does not affirm robust rights to natural endowments that he is lead to deny rights to rents; that is, to pure profits.

The core of Gauthier's Proviso is a prohibition on bettering one's situation by worsening the situation of others. About any particular use or possession by A, two questions can be asked: (1) Does A's use or possession worsen the situation of any other party? (2) Would interference with A's use or seizure of A's possession worsen A's situation? If the answer to (1) is no, A is morally at liberty to engage in that use or enjoy that holding. If, in addition, the answer to (2) is yes, then others are not at liberty (or not *unconditionally* at liberty) to interfere with that use or to seize that holding; hence, A has a right *of some sort* to that use or to that holding. Through the deployment of the proviso, Gauthier defends three successive ascriptions of rights: first, each person's "*exclusive* right *to*" his natural endowments and powers; second, each person's "right *in*" the fruits of his labor; and third, each person's "*exclusive* right *to*" the fruits of his labor and in acquired land. Throughout his discussion, Gauthier uses these two locutions to distinguish between rights in terms of the form or degree of moral immunity they provide. It is clear that the "*exclusive* rights *to,*" which Gauthier seeks to establish both with regard to natural endowments and extrapersonal holdings, are to be understand as significantly more robust than mere "rights *in.*" My main claim against Gauthier is, then, that the deployment of the proviso cannot yield rights any more robust than the relatively feeble "rights *in.*"

As the prime exhibit for my contention, we should have before us Gauthier's argument for each person's "right in" the fruits of his labors along with his explanation of why this argument does not yield an "exclusive right to" the fruits of his labors. Inspection of this argument and explanation will allow us to form some sense of what Gauthier takes these two different species of rights to be. This inspection will also reveal why, contrary to Gauthier's expectations, the application of the proviso, no matter how often repeated, will never allow us to arrive justifiably at "exclusive rights to."

After maintaining that the proviso indicates that each possesses a right to his own powers (to which contention we shall return), Gauthier redeploys the proviso to establish rights with respect to the fruits of one's own labor. First, it is pointed out that, should A cultivate some common land in the state of nature, A's benefit from the useful possession of the products of this cultivation would not be achieved through the worsening of anyone else's condition. A's cultivation and his use of those products does not violate the proviso. Second, it is asserted that B seizing A's product would benefit B through a worsening of A's position. Hence, this seizure would violate the Gauthier Proviso. Gauthier takes this nonsymmetrical relation of A and B to the proviso to "demonstrate [A's] right in the effects of [A's] labor." But he immediately *denies* that it establishes "an exclusive right to their possession." As Gauthier explains,

> For we have not shown that the proviso would be violated were someone to seize the fruits of my labor while compensating me for my effort and intended use. . . . The proviso prohibits worsening but does not require bettering another's position, in bettering one's own. It does not then require that the person who seizes the fruits of another's labour share her gains; it requires only that she compensate for costs. Thus the proviso affords a right *in* the fruits of one's labor and so to full compensation, not a right *to* those fruits and so to market compensation. [211]

To examine how the contrast between "rights in" and "exclusive rights to" might profitably be articulated, let us draw upon the distinction between "entitlements" that are protected by "liability rules" and those that are protected by "property rules."[21] Wilt's entitlement against Wayne to X is (merely) protected by a liability rule if Wayne may permissibly take X from Wilt as long as Wayne makes appropriate accompanying compensation to Wilt—where the appropriateness of the compensation is not established by Wilt's actually agreeing to it. Different liability rules will specify different levels of required compensation. The two familiar rules specify (*a*) full compensation, that is, leaving the subject indifferent to the forced exchange; and (*b*) market compensation, that is, providing the subject with what he could have received in a free (and perfectly competitive?) market exchange. In contrast, Wilt's entitlement against Wayne to X is protected by a property rule if and only if Wayne's permissible acquisition of X from Wilt requires Wilt's (prior) voluntary consent. Wayne must make Wilt an offer which Wilt voluntarily accepts. It is not permissible for Wayne to seize X along with compensating Wilt—even if Wayne compensates Wilt as much as would be required were Wayne to engage in the impermissible seizure of X. If the right to X is merely protected by a liability rule, the combined seizure and compensation leaves the (former) titleholder morally whole. In contrast, if the right to X is protected by a property rule, the seizure *wrongs* the titleholder in ways that (even) market compensation does not suffice to erase.

It is quite clear that, for Gauthier, a "right in" X is an entitlement protected by a liability rule requiring (only) full compensation. The proviso would not be violated "were someone to seize the fruits of my labor while compensating me for my effort and intended use." It is less clear whether, according to Gauthier, an "exclusive right to" X is an entitlement protected by a liability rule requiring market compensation, or is an entitlement protected by a property rule (which, if violated through the seizure of X, demands the payment of market compensation). Nevertheless, I shall generally assume that Gauthier is concerned with establishing "exclusive rights to" in the more robust, that is, property rule, sense. As we shall see, only a property rule entitlement over one's natural endowments in principle precludes forced labor. Only such an entitlement gives each a Lockean claim over "the exercise of his own powers without the hindrance from others" [210].[22]

21. Guido Calabresi and A. Douglas Melamed, "Property Rules, Liability Rules, and Inalienability: One View of the Cathedral," *Harvard Law Review* 85, no. 6 (April 1972): 1089–1128, especially 1106–10. Calabresi and Melamed cast liability rules in terms of the payment of "an objectively determined value" in contrast to an actually "agreed upon" value.

22. On the perfect competition model, the difference between full compensation and market compensation is vanishingly small. It is hard to credit that this is the only difference Gauthier means to mark with the contrast between "rights in" and "exclusive rights to."

But even if Gauthier only seeks to establish entitlements protected by market compensation liability rules, his argument falls short. For his account of why the application of the proviso that yields a right in the fruits of one's labor does not generate an exclusive right to those products is a perfectly general statement of the limits of what the proviso can provide. Recall Gauthier's remark:

> The proviso prohibits worsening but does not require bettering another's position, in bettering one's own. It does not then require that the person who seizes the fruits of another's labor share her gains; it requires only that she compensate for costs.

Thus, whether one's prospective relation to some X is that of temporary user or permanent possessor, one's only claim against others with regard to that X is that their seizure of X not on net worsen one's situation. And this claim can always be satisfied by the expropriator's providing one with full compensation. This reasoning about the severe limits of the proviso's implications points to the conclusion that no further deployment of the proviso will ever get one either to "exclusive rights to" the fruits of one's labor or to "exclusive rights to" one's natural endowments. This conclusion is supported by an examination of, first, Gauthier's transition from "rights in" the fruits of one's labor "to exclusive rights to" those fruits and to parcels of land; and, second, his argument for "exclusive rights to" one's natural endowment.

Gauthier presents the case of Eve who has been (sporadically?) cultivating a segment of common land. Eve

> proposes to take a certain area of the island for her exclusive use, so that she (and her family) may benefit by maximizing its productivity. She seeks an exclusive right to a certain portion of the island [215].

Gauthier's asks two questions: (1) Does Eve's acquisition of exclusive use of X better her condition through the worsening of the condition of others? (2) Would the annulment of Eve's exclusive use of X advance some other party's situation through a worsening of Eve's condition? Since, according to Gauthier, Eve's acquisition of the exclusive use does not worsen the condition of others, *and* the annulment of that exclusive possession would worsen Eve's (and possibly that of others) circumstances, Eve's "exclusive right to" X is confirmed.

We turn, then, to the reasoning behind Gauthier's answers to questions (1) and (2). No extensive challenge will be launched against the negative answer to (1). Yet some problems deserve mention. Gauthier's claim that Eve's exclusive use of this parcel of land does not worsen the situation of others appeals to the general and immense benefits of the privatization of land. It may well be—*I* certainly like to believe—that these improvements are such that everyone benefits (relative to . . . ?) from a *system* of private ownership in land. Nevertheless, this is different from claiming that everyone benefits or, at least, is not made worse off, by each particular instance of private appropriation. All those who are affected quite indirectly, via greater economic productivity, etc., may be benefited. But what of Freda who would have appropriated precisely this parcel of land had Eve not? Gauthier, at least, has to argue that Freda's complaint against Eve, namely, that she (Freda) is wrongly precluded from appropriating *this* parcel, cannot be legitimate. He might do so by pointing out that, were Freda's complaint to be assuaged by endorsing Freda's acquisition of the parcel, others, including Eve, would be in the position to make a complaint fully comparable to Freda's current one.

More significant challenges can be directed against Gauthier's affirmative answer to question (2), that is, against his assertion that interference with Eve's claimed exclusive right would violate the proviso. Gauthier points out that there are two forms of annulment to be considered. The land acquired by Eve may nonconsensually be returned to common use, or it may be seized as the exclusive possession of another.

In the first case, the argument for the proviso being violated can focus on the losses to all those individuals who benefit, however modestly and indirectly, from the privatization of this land parcel. Since privatization is productive, its annullment must on net be costly. Its costs must fall somewhere, and its net costliness precludes even compensation for those individuals who were poised to gain indirectly through privatization. So it seems as though seizure of the parcel to return it to the commons does violate the proviso.[23] But would Freda's seizure of the parcel for her own private control also violate the proviso?

In this second case, the land remains privately held. Thus, there are no indirect costs from collectivization, and the argument must focus entirely on the putative direct worsening of Eve's situation. Gauthier's key claim here is that

> [t]he person seizing the right is bettering himself by worsening Eve's

---

23. The proviso, however, is *not* violated if the worsening is merely "incidental" to the gains for some that are achieved through recommunalization. And the worsening does seem merely to be incidental here because those who gain from recommunalization do not gain *by way of* worsening the situation of the indirect beneficiaries of Eve's private ownership. See Gauthier [210–12].

situation, and may avoid this only by paying market compensation, negotiating with Eve for the right to the land on mutually acceptable terms. [215]

But what justifies the requirement of market compensation rather than (merely) full compensation? Why believe that to avoid worsening Eve's situation it is necessary for Freda to pay market compensation? One may well endorse Gauthier's claim that "[a] right *to* land or goods is a right not only to the fruits of use, but also to the fruits of exchange" [215]. And one may well allow that a right to the fruits of exchange is a right to the payment that voluntary (but only perfectly competitive?) exchange would bring. Given all this, *if* Eve's claim to the land represents an "exclusive right to" it, she certainly has a right to this market level of payment should the land be taken; her situation will properly count as having been worsened should she not receive market compensation. But, as far as I can see, the only way to arrive at the crucial judgment, that less than market compensation by Freda will leave Eve's situation worsened, is to start with the premise that Eve enjoys an "exclusive right to" that land. This, unfortunately, is precisely what the argument is supposed to demonstrate. If Gauthier's argument succumbs to this problem, the most that he can ascribe to Eve in the way of a right with regard to that parcel is a "right in" it, that is, an entitlement protected by a full compensation liability rule.

Now let us turn to the question of whether Gauthier is correct in thinking that his proviso supports the conclusion that persons have "exclusive rights to" their own powers. The tone and idiom of Gauthier's argument here strongly suggests a desire to establish robust property-rule rights to natural endowments. Gauthier argues, "Each person has an exclusive right to the exercise of his own powers without hindrance from others" and this is because

> [t]he proviso, in prohibiting each from bettering his situation by worsening that of others, but otherwise leaving each free to do as he pleases, not only confirms each in the use of his own powers, but in denying to others the use of those powers, affords to each the *exclusive* use of his own. The proviso thus converts the unlimited liberties of Hobbesian nature into *exclusive* rights and duties: Each person has an *exclusive* right *to* the exercise of his own powers without hindrance from others. [209–10; emphasis added]

Yet, for Gauthier, the base point established by the proviso must be fully captured by a person's claim to the expected utility associated with the anticipated use of his powers. For "the base point for determining how I affect you, in terms of bettering or worsening your situation, is determined by the outcome that you would expect in my absence'' [204]; and that outcome must itself be specified in terms of utility since ''one situation is better for some person than another, if and only if it affords him a greater expected utility'' [203].

What is up for consideration then, within Gauthier's framework, is not prohibiting interferences as such, that is, prohibiting incursions into the respective moral domains of agents. Rather, what is up for consideration is forbidding the worsening of agents' respective situations understood in terms of levels of expected utility. And surely the proviso does favor prohibiting worsening— which means that it favors forbidding interference with a person's use of his own powers *unless* that person is fully compensated for whatever loss of (expected) utility the interference engenders. Any combination of interference and compensation should be permitted which, on net, does not lower the subject's (expected) utility.

Notice how Gauthier's crucial passage on behalf of ''exclusive rights to'' natural endowments envisions a transition directly from the Hobbesian world of unlimited liberties to the Lockean world of property in one's powers. What has happened to, why is there no consideration of, the intermediate moral universe of entitlements protected by liability rules? Certainly it is plausible for Gauthier to maintain that, in bettering one's situation through the use of others' powers which ''interfere[s] with their own exercise of their powers, one worsens their situation by that interaction'' [209]. But, since it is the worsening, not the interference itself, which is the focus of the negative judgment, that judgment can be forestalled without foregoing the interference. One need only fully compensate those with whom one interferes. A requirement for full compensation for those whose powers are taken *fully* embodies the proviso's strictures.

This is precisely what we should expect. The proviso that is supposed to generate and define each person's rights with respect to his own powers is the same proviso that generates and defines each person's rights with respect to the fruits of his own labor.

It ''prohibits worsening but does not require bettering another's position, in bettering one's own.'' And, what Gauthier says in connection with the application of the proviso to the fruits of one's labor applies as well to its application to one's powers themselves, namely:

> If the benefit I receive is no less, in terms of my utilities, than what I expected from my labour [or from my possession of my powers] in the absence of intervention, then my situation has not been worsened. [211]

Hence, the proviso yields only an entitlement in one's powers that is protected by a liability rule. And that liability rule is a rule mandating only full compensation upon the seizure of one's powers.

And that is all that poor Wilt has, namely, a "right in" his basketball playing powers. Wilt and Wayne each lack the crucial element of having a right to their powers, namely, a right against having them seized, a right against being conscripted into National Basketball (or Hockey) Service. This is the element that Gauthier insists is present in the superstar's moral situation as a mark of his right to his powers. "Wayne Gretzky has the right to his unique hockey skills; *he may use them as he pleases*" [273]. But as long as the fans are (or "society" is) prepared to pay Wilt (or Wayne) enough to compensate him fully for playing, Wilt (or Wayne) has an offer that he cannot refuse—an offer it is permissible to enforce upon him.

Let us suppose, however, that somehow the proviso does get us to the conclusion that Wilt has an entitlement to his basketball powers that is protected by a market compensation liability rule. Still, in neither theory nor in practice, could Wilt be said to have a right to use his natural endowment "as he pleases." In theory, Wilt's claim would merely be a claim against on net ending up below a certain utility level—the level he would arrive at were he freely to sell his services (in a perfectly competitive market). A market compensation liability rule would provide Wilt with no principled claim against interference by anyone who was prepared to thrust market compensation upon him while conscripting his services. Increasing the stringency of the liability rule that defines Wilt's entitlement of his talents makes it more costly for others to conscript Wilt permissibly, but it cannot confer upon Wilt what all of us, including Gauthier, normally mean by "an exclusive right to the exercise of his own powers without hindrance from others."

What entitlements defined by liability rules leave out is the dimension of choice. They leave out the dimension of having moral authority over a certain domain within which the rightholder may "do as he pleases." The seizure of the object of the entitlement defined by a property rule does not only move the agent down along some *value* dimension, for example, utility, but also denies the agent her *rightful choice* over the disposition of the seized item. This loss of choice survives compensating movement back up the value dimension. This element of sanctified choice, authority, or jurisdiction is what makes entitlements protected by property rules more robust (everything else being equal) than those defined by liability rules.

Nevertheless, might not an entitlement over one's natural endowment, which is defined by a market compensation liability rule, assure one, in practice, the free exercise of one's powers? The argument that it would, in practice, provide this protection goes as follows:

> In a "just society" duly devoted to purging itself of factor rent, Wilt will know that the most he can receive on net for playing is no-rent market compensation. Therefore, if offered that level of payment, Wilt will, by hypothesis always accept. He will always *choose* to provide his basketball services for that perfectly competitive market compensation. Hence, no occasion for *forcing* Wilt to accept the no-rent market compensation offer will ever arise.

However, this argument ignores the fact that Wilt will sometimes have reason to reject the offer made to him by a society that is credibly committed to no greater than no-rent market compensation. For, on occasion, such rejections will lead that society to revise upward its assessment of what would minimally motivate Wilt to play were it known to him that no higher payment were possible. The society will raise its assessment when it finds it reasonable, as it sometimes must, to interpret Wilt's rejection of the offered contract, or his refusal to show up in training camp, as good evidence that the payment first offered is in fact less than what would provide Wilt with no-rent market compensation.

Since "society" sometimes will revise its proposed no-rent compensation in response to Wilt's demands for higher payment and his slowdowns or strikes, Wilt has reason to engage in these bargaining maneuvers even if he is convinced that society will never pay him more than it (finally) determines to be his no-rent market compensation. Wilt will know that if he continues to insist ever more vigorously that only some greater payment will induce him to drag his aging bones out on the court, or to insist on the profound costs to him of leaving his beachfront home merely for the sake of practice, he may well convince "society" of the inaccuracy of its current assessment. However, this reasonable willingness of society to revise upward its estimate of no-rent market compensation threatens to unravel the entire no-rent policy. For the rent-seeking Wilts of the world will simply recast their unconscionable demands for gains from trade into claims about the enormous, yet intangible, opportunity costs to them of providing their services to society.

A society that is committed to a no-rent policy will, then, have to couple its willingness to revise upward its estimates of no-rent market compensations with a stern message to would-be rent seekers.

> *We* will determine what would minimally motivate you to play ball were you to know that no greater payment was possible. In reaching this deter-

mination we shall give due weight to indications we have from you regarding the strength and ordering of your preferences. But at some point we will complete our deliberations (which ought not to be confused with negotiations with you) and settle upon a no-rent market compensation. Due to our reasonable willingness to revise payments upward, at that point, you may not *know* that the offer is final, that no greater payment is possible. So, at that point, you may have reason to continue to refuse our offer. But make no mistake about it. At that point, the offer will be final. *You will play for that compensation.* You will play "voluntarily" or you will be required to play albeit with no-rent market compensation. Take your choice—such as it is.

Only by making such an announcement can the society sufficiently dampen the hopes of would-be rent seekers so that its proposals for no-rent market compensation will generally motivate acceptance. A credible, demonstrated, willingness to seize services, albeit with payment of the socially determined no-rent market compensation, is then essential in practice to sustain the no-rent policy.[24]

Would such a no-nonsense no-rent policy—one that would embody direct forced labor—violate persons' rights to their natural talents and powers? It will not violate any rights which can be generated from Gauthier's Proviso. For while such a policy will deprive agents of *choice* about the disposition of their own talents and powers, by hypothesis it will not leave agents with less utility than is due them. If rights over one's natural endowments do not include this dimension of choice, that is, of moral authority over the disposal of those endowments, then rights over one's natural endowments are entirely consistent with the confiscation of rents on those endowments and even the implementation of this confiscation through forced deployment of one's talents and powers. But this is hardly a consistency that will cheer Gauthier, interested as he

24. Recall the language of Calabresi and Melamed in characterizing the position of an entitlement holder under a liability rule:

> Whenever someone may destroy the initial endowment if he is willing to pay an objectively determined value for it, an entitlement is protected by a liability rule. This [socially determined] value may be what it is thought the original holder of the entitlement would have sold it for [or what he would have sold it for in a perfectly competitive market]. But the holder's complaint that he would have demanded more [or would have gotten more even in perfectly competitive exchange] *will not avail him once the objectively determined value is set.* [P. 1092; emphasis added]

Perhaps an entitlement protected by an *actual* (i.e., not perfectly competitive) market compensation liability rule would provide the rightholder with more practical protection. But to move toward such a rule one would have to reject the regulative status of the perfect competitive and, hence, the antirent program.

is to affirm robust rights to one's natural endowments that stand in sharp contrast with Rawls's designation of natural talents as collective assets.[25]

The fact that Gauthier's position fails to achieve this contrast can be seen in the similarity between (1) Gauthier's contention that the only legitimate return to an agent for the socially desirable exercise of his talents is a return that exceeds the cost of his supplying that talent by just enough to bring it to market; and (2) Rawls's contention that "[t]he premiums earned by scarce natural talents . . . are to cover the costs of training and to encourage the efforts of learning, as well as to direct ability to where it best furthers the common interest."[26] The fact that Gauthier and Rawls invoke different principles, namely, minimax relative concession and the difference principle, for governing the division of the "social surplus" which society recaptures from the predatory claws of the talented, does not amount to a philosophical difference with regard to the rights of individuals over their own natural endowments.

If Gauthier had more fundamentally distanced himself from Rawls, that is, if he had vindicated people's possession of robust rights over their respective talents, and if he had not succumbed to the misleading perfect competition model, nothing would stand in the way of his endorsement of rights to economic rents and, hence, to pure profits.

25. See especially pp. 245–54.
26. John Rawls, *A Theory of Justice* (Cambridge, Mass.: Harvard University Press, 1971), p. 311. See also pp. 101–2.

6

The Cultural Justification of Unearned Income: An Economic Model of Merit Goods Based on Aristotelian Ideas of Akrasia and Distributive Justice

Robert D. Cooter and James Gordley

> The chief objection to the most popular of all welfare precepts—equality of incomes—is not that it has no rigorously defensible foundations; the chief objection is that, even so far as tenable, it is completely uninteresting by comparison with the question of its effects upon cultural and economic evolution.
>
> Joseph A. Schumpeter, *History of Economic Analysis* (1954, p. 1073)

Profit is usually justified by how it is earned. Thus the other papers in this volume discuss what entrepreneurs do, how they contribute to production, what they deserve, and the fairness of bargains. This paper, in contrast, justifies profits by how they are spent. Some activities are of greater cultural value than others. Disproportionate profits can be justified by disproportionate expenditure on valuable activities. Rehabilitating the cultural case for unearned income, which has lately fallen out of favor, is the object of this paper.

"Pure rent" refers to income obtained by owning something, not by doing anything. Pure rent exists only as a construct, because all forms of ownership require some minimal level of effort, risk taking, and management. Pure rent, however, is closely approximated by land rents from an inherited agricultural estate, or dividends from a portfolio of securities that the owner did not earn and does not manage. Since pure rent is unearned, its justification must be based upon how it is spent. Passive endowments sustain universities, foundations, and other institutions whose purpose is primarily cultural. The justification of the entitlement of these institutions to unearned profits must rest on the value of the activities in which they engage.

For many centuries, economic rent was defended philosophically by drawing on Aristotelian ideas about cultural excellence. When these ideas lost favor, the cultural case for inequality fell into disrepute. We argue that these Aristotelian ideas fell from favor for reasons that have little to do with their merits. They must be resurrected in some form if we are to make sense of cultural values and explain the role of universities or foundations.

The idea of cultural excellence survives in economic theory through the vestigial concept of merit goods, which we explain and criticize. To make sense of merit goods, we model "akrasia," which occurs when a less worthwhile activity is chosen in preference to one the decision maker knows is more worthwhile. We conclude that although democracies are rightly suspicious of arguments for inequality, merit goods have their place even in a democracy.

LIBERAL AND ILLIBERAL ACTIVITIES

We begin by sketching general features of the Aristotelian conception of property that we will defend. Aristotle believed that some human activities are more worthwhile than others. Consequently, he could analyze the value of consumption, or, as he put it, the value of having external things, by asking about the value of the activities that these things make possible.[1] Aristotle divided activities into two broad groups according to whether their value is intrinsic or instrumental. "Liberal" activities are worth doing for their own sake, independent of any further end to be achieved. Examples are athletics, poetry, and philosophy. Other activities are worthwhile as means to intrinsically valuable activities. These "illiberal" activities are engaged in only for the sake of their effects.[2] Examples are bricklaying and medicine, which would vanish if some technological advance permitted us to have houses and health without these trades, just as the cooper, fletcher, blacksmith, and wainwright have vanished.

In one sense, the illiberal activities are the most fundamental. Without food, shelter, and clothing there could be no liberal activities or, indeed, any human life. Illiberal activities are necessary and useful. In another sense the liberal activities are the most fundamental because they are worthwhile in themselves. Just as the instrument is inferior to the purpose it serves, so the illiberal activities are inferior to those which are "liberal or noble," according to Aristotle.[3]

Moreover, Aristotle held that political arrangements should reflect the superiority of liberal activities, because "political society exists for the sake of noble actions, and not of mere companionship."[4] In particular, property arrangements should reflect the fact that having things permits or facilitates doing things that are intrinsically good. Since any activity is best performed by people with talent and dedication, those with the greatest capacity and dedication for

1. Aristotle, *Politics* 7.1.1323a–23b, 7.13.1332a; *Nicomachean Ethics* 1.5.1096A.
2. Ibid., 8.2.1337b, 8.3.1338a–38b.
3. Ibid., 8.3.1338a.
4. Ibid., 3.9.1281a, 7.1.1323a–24a, 7.8.1328a.

liberal activities have a legitimate claim to the resources these activities require. Therefore, disparities in the value of actions ultimately justify disparities in wealth and power.

REJECTION OF THE CULTURAL CASE FOR INEQUALITY

We think these ideas are worth taking seriously, and we will be exploring their implications in this chapter. We acknowledge that to many people today they may seem strange or wrong. It will be helpful to consider in advance why people think so.

The most obvious reason is that, as citizens of a democracy, we must be cautious toward claims that some people have a greater capacity and desire to engage in worthwhile activities than others. Cultural elites endanger democracy in much the same way as powerful central government. Too much of it, and there will be no democracy. True as that may be, however, we should ask ourselves whether some people have more capacity and dedication to worthwhile activities than others. If they do, then current attempts to ground political theory on the denial of this fact endanger democracy by building a falsehood into its foundation.

Aristotle warned of this danger:

> In democracies of the more extreme type there has arisen a false idea of freedom which is contradictory to the true interests of the state. For two principles are characteristic of democracy, the government of the majority and freedom. Men think that what is just is equal; and that equality is the supremacy of the popular will; and that freedom means doing what a man likes. In such democracies every one lives as he pleases, or in the words of Euripides, "according to his fancy."[5]

This false idea of freedom endangers democracy, according to Aristotle, by confusing the actions in which "democrats delight" with those by which "democracy is made possible."[6] Democrats may delight in saying that freedom is doing what one likes, but democracy may be better preserved when citizens are educated as far as possible to do what is genuinely worthwhile. Democracy may be better preserved when its citizens appreciate the contribution that elites can make within a democracy. In any case, one can love democracy without believing that freedom only means doing what one likes.

A second reason why Aristotle's ideas inspire distrust is because European ruling elites once invoked them to defend their privileges. Liberal activities

5. Ibid., 5.9.1310a.
6. Ibid., 5.9.1310a.

can only be done, or can best be done, by people possessing independence, education, and the leisure to pursue them. These attributes are conferred by rents from owning valuable property. The upper classes claimed that they were, therefore, entitled to their property. In the novel *War and Peace,* Andre complains to Pierre that his scheme to educate the peasants will give them "my tastes without my income." This quip suggests that the proportion of income spent on culturally superior goods rises with the amount of income, or, in technical terms, merit goods are superior goods. To the extent that this is true, the cultural argument figures in the justification of inequality in general.

In Aristotle's terminology, however, this older European society was oligarchic rather than aristocratic. In both aristocracies and oligarchies, an elite has an unequal share of wealth and power, but membership in the elite is determined on different grounds: in an oligarchy, by birth or wealth; in an aristocracy by ability or merit. Aristocracy is a legitimate form of government, according to Aristotle, but oligarchy is not.[7]

It is perverse to use aristocratic arguments to defend oligarchy, but, as Aristotle himself pointed out, to do so is quite understandable. "The best shall have more" sounds more like a moral principle than "them as has [or had] gets." Also, just as Aristotle warned that democracy could be destroyed by a false idea of freedom, he warned that oligarchy was threatened when "the sons of the ruling class in an oligarchy live in luxury."[8] To keep its power, an oligarchic elite should train its children in moral and intellectual virtues and so make itself respected. In that way the oligarchy becomes something like an aristocracy even though the basis of its power is still wealth or inherited status. Members of the elite families in Europe were expected to possess education, courage, honor, and justice not demanded of others. That is one reason they held power as long as they did.

Nevertheless, there was tension between the demands of the aristocratic principle and the reality of the older European societies that claimed to be based on it. The activities deemed "aristocratic" had to be simultaneously within the capacity of those who happened to be born into elite families and beyond the capacity of those born outside them. The result was the sort of behavior Veblen ascribed to a leisure class. (Veblen 1919, pp. 75–85; Elias 1983, pp. 62–67). Activities were deemed "aristocratic" because they were most easily acquired through training in childhood (such as polished manners and facility in foreign languages) or because they demanded large expenditure of wealth (such as horsemanship, opera, and balls).

7. *Nicomachean Ethics* 5.3.1131a; *Politics* 3.7.1279a–79b, 4.5.1292a–92b, 4.7.1293a–93b.
8. *Politics* 5.9.1310a.

Writers, artists, and other culture heroes were patronized by the elite but never quite belonged to it. Writers said they belonged to a separate society, the "republic of letters." Even so, they had to write slavish introductions dedicating their works to wealthy persons, and they had to mind their manners. When Voltaire did not, and was beaten by the servants of a nobleman he had offended, he discovered that none of his noble friends would help him. Just as we can love democracy without subscribing to what Aristotle called a false idea of freedom, so we can dislike the older oligarchy without rejecting the cultural ideals it used for camouflage.

While the founders of the American republic were not in general Aristotelians, they did not regard all activities as equally wise and virtuous, or believe that virtue and wisdom were equally possessed by all citizens. According to John Adams,

> although there is a moral and political and a natural Equality among Mankind, all being born free and equal, Yet there are other Inequalities which are equally natural. Such as Strength, Activity, Genius, Talents, Virtues, Benevolence.[9]

His great adversary, Thomas Jefferson, agreed. In a letter he wrote to Adams toward the end of his life, he said,

> I agree with you that there is a natural aristocracy among men. The grounds of this are virtue and talents. . . . May we not even say that that form of government is the best which provides for a pure selection of these natural aristoi into the offices of government?[10]

Their disagreement, according to Jefferson, was that Adams believed that getting such people into office required strengthening the wealthy, whereas Jefferson believed that the people could be trusted to elect the virtuous and talented. It would be surprising if principles that both Jefferson and Adams agreed upon were antithetical to the Republic they founded.

Another and more profound reason for dismissing Aristotle's ideas is that they depend on a metaphysics rejected by modern philosophers. This metaphysics gave him a reference point for comparing the value of different activities. According to Aristotle, every living thing has an "end," which is what it does when its powers and faculties are developed fully and harmoniously. The end of a frog is the way it lives in an environment in which it can develop all the capacities of a frog. Similarly, the end of man is a distinctively human

9. "Literary Notes and Papers," quoted in Howe 1966, p. 137.
10. Letter of October 28, 1813, in Jefferson 1984, pp. 1305–6.

life in which the unique capacities of the species are fully developed and employed. This ultimate end belongs to man because of the kind of creature he is. Like the frog, man does not choose his ultimate end, but unlike the frog, man can recognize it.[11]

The distinctively human capacity that separates us from other creatures is reason.[12] Man can understand his end and choose those actions that contribute to it. Illiberal actions contribute to man's end instrumentally, by making liberal actions possible. Liberal actions are valuable in themselves because they express man's distinctively human capacities. Furthermore, man becomes vicious when he chooses activities, not because they are intrinsically valuable or instrumental to intrinsic value but on the basis of impulses that run contrary to reason and to man's end.

Aristotle believed there is a hierarchy even in liberal activities, the most valuable being expressions of man's distinctively human capacity to know and to direct his action by what he knows. To understand the most fundamental and universal principles concerning the world is the highest form of knowledge. Consequently, Aristotle considered metaphysics, which studies all reality, to be more valuable than sciences which study only particular aspects of it.[13] The highest object that reason can have when it directs action is to procure the greater good for all the citizens. Consequently, Aristotle considered politics to be more valuable than instrumental reason serving private ends.[14] Thus, while Aristotle recognized different ways in which actions can be more or less valuable, the reference point for determining their value was the ultimate end of man.

Modern philosophers reject the idea that man's ultimate end can be discovered by observing what is distinctive about the human species. By that logic, why not say that man's ultimate end is walking erect on two legs? Why not define man as a featherless biped rather than a rational animal? Discrediting the classical metaphysics undermined the confident belief in hierarchical values. Lacking such a reference point, modern philosophers try to discuss value without making any judgments about the merits of engaging in one activity rather than another. As John Locke said,

> The philosophers of old did in vain inquire whether the summum bonum consisted in riches, or bodily delights, or virtue or contemplation; and

11. See *Parts of Animals* 1.1.639b–40b; *Nicomachean Ethics* 1.7.1097b–98b.
12. *Nicomachean Ethics* 1.7.1097b–98a.
13. *Metaphysics* 1.2.982a–82b; *Nicomachean Ethics* 10.7.1177a–77b.
14. See *Politics* 7.14.1332b–33b.

they might have as reasonably disputed whether the best relish were to be
found in apples, plums or nuts.[15]

The result, very often, has been political theories which begin by assuming
no activity is more worthwhile than any other, and end by paying particular
respect to the values of liberty and equality. This approach entails a limited
and negative notion of freedom and equality. For Aristotle, freedom in the
broad sense means the ability to do those things that are worthwhile. Equality
means distribution of goods according to what people need for what they are
to do. A democracy aims for freedom and equality so that each citizen can do
what is worthwhile, not because there is nothing worthwhile to do. The idea
that freedom means doing whatever one pleases was, for Aristotle, the false
concept of freedom that can destroy democracy. For much of modern philosophy and political theory, however, it is the only possible concept of freedom.

There are, indeed, major problems concerning the validity of Aristotelian
metaphysics, problems that we cannot deal with here. Despite these problems,
few people really doubt that some activities are more worthwhile than others.
Few people teach their children that choosing between riches and right conduct,
or between sensual gratification and study, is like choosing between apples
and plums. If modern philosophy cannot explain why some activities are more
worthwhile than others, so much the worse, in our opinion, for modern philosophy. Without committing ourselves to Aristotle's metaphysics, we will go on
believing that some activities are more worthwhile in much the same way we
will go on believing in the existence of the external world whether or not
philosophers can give us a reason for doing so. We can ask ourselves how in
a democracy everyone can have the opportunity to do what is worthwhile, and
what role, if any, elites could play in the process. If we are to ask these
questions, however, we will not only have to break with certain trends in
modern political theory but rethink the foundations of modern welfare economics.

THE FOUNDATIONS OF WELFARE ECONOMICS

The elements of the formal theory of value in contemporary economics are
deceptively simple: a rational person can rank states of the world from bad to
good. The real numbers can be ranked from small to large. Therefore, better
states can be associated with larger numbers. By this association, the problem
of making the best available choice is recast as the problem of finding the
largest attainable number.

15. Locke, *Essay on Human Understanding* 2.21.55, in *Works*, vol. 1, p. 273.

The mathematics of optimization is purely formal because it concerns the satisfaction of preferences, whatever they happen to be. In contrast, a substantive theory of value must say something about the content of preferences, not just their form. In economics there are two intertwined traditions concerning substantive values. First, according to the utilitarian tradition, the value of something is the total pleasure that individuals obtain from it. The pleasures enjoyed by an individual are added to yield his individual utility, maximization of which is his putative objective, and the individual utilities are added to obtain the total utility for society, maximization of which is the putative goal of public policy. Second, according to the market tradition, the value of something is the total amount that individuals are willing to pay for it. The prices people are willing to pay for the goods they enjoy can be added to compute the wealth of the nation, maximization of which is the market economist's goal.

Should value be measured by pleasure or price?[16] The policy issue that divides the two schools in economics is income redistribution. Utilitarians assert that the value of wealth is the pleasure it affords to people. Material needs are felt so keenly that a poor person allegedly obtains more pleasure from an additional dollar spent on necessities than a rich person obtains from an additional dollar spent on luxuries. To illustrate, Pigou thought that a person has a hierarchy of needs that must be fulfilled by working from the bottom up. The baser needs at the bottom are "material," such as food, shelter, and clothing. The nobler needs at the top are immaterial, such as cultural entertainment. The "material welfare school" of economists thought that expenditures to satisfy material needs yield greater pleasure (or alleviate more pain) than equal expenditures to satisfy immaterial needs. For example, the sum of utilities can be increased by transferring a dollar of expenditure from opera tickets for the rich to bread for the poor. This line of reasoning provided a utilitarian foundation for redistributive policies, such as progressive income taxation and socialized medicine.

In contrast, market theorists assert that, since wealth is the final measure of value, economists can say nothing about *its* value. In particular, they can say nothing about the value of wealth to different classes of people. The claim that the poor need bread more than the rich need opera tickets does not belong in economics, according to the market theorists, because it is unscientific. A dollar is worth a dollar, whether it is spent on bread or opera tickets. Public policy should aim to maximize wealth without regard to its use.

16. These arguments are developed at greater length in Cooter and Rappoport (1984).

Formal economic theory assumed its modern character with the marginalist revolution in the second half of the nineteenth century. The crucial step was combining utilitarianism and calculus to produce decision theory (''the calculus of utilities''). This step initiated the elaboration of the mathematical techniques that are central to modern economic theory. Interpretation of the new mathematics diverged over income redistribution. Utilitarianism developed into the material welfare school, which favored government policies to redistribute wealth. Some of its leading figures, including Pigou, were associated with the emerging socialist movements in the early part of the twentieth century.

The material welfare school was almost swept away in Anglo-American economics in the 1930s by market economists. The views of the market economists were organized in a movement often called the ''ordinalist revolution.'' The ordinalists acknowledge that each rational individual has a preference ordering that expresses his private values. Pleasures and satisfactions are allegedly not observable in the way required to compare between persons. Consequently, the ordering of different people cannot be combined together in any compelling way to yield public values. In contrast, market prices are public and wealth is observable. The best public policies are, consequently, those that give the individual the greatest liberty and wealth to satisfy his private preferences.

SUBORDINATION OF MERIT GOODS[17]

Aristotle's belief that democracies can pursue cultural excellence while committed to liberty and equality is expressed concretely in the history of economics. To tell the story, we must return to the disagreement between utilitarian and market economists. These two schools are joined in a lively debate over income distribution that provokes sharp barbs and yields valuable insights from time to time. The joining of debate is facilitated by agreement upon common assumptions requiring no discussion. One common assumption is that the value of pleasure or wealth is determined by its quantity, not its causes or uses. Consequently, no activities are intrinsically more valuable than others.

For example, Jeremy Bentham, the first systematic utilitarian, held that the satisfaction or pleasure or utility that people get through their choices is equally valuable regardless of the activity that produces it. Thus the belief that the pleasure of poetry is more valuable than the pleasure of dominoes is viewed by Benthamites as a mistake in understanding the metric, rather like thinking

17. This section draws upon Cooter (1990), which appears in a symposium on merit goods. Also see the other articles in the symposium.

that a pound of gold weighs more than a pound of clay. Indeed, the elaboration of Bentham's theory led to the conclusion that base goods are more important for economic policy than noble goods, because a dollar spent to satisfy material needs yields more pleasure than a dollar spent to satisfy noble desires.

Notice that utility theorists and market theorists agree that value attaches exclusively to individuals, either in the form of pleasures they enjoy or prices they are willing to pay. Thus the value of an institution or organization is merely the aggregation of its value to affected individuals. Bentham expressed the point succinctly: "The interest of the community then is, what?—the sum of the interests of the several members who compose it" (Bentham 1948, p. 3). An alternative assumption is that some values cannot be reduced to pleasures of individuals or the prices they are willing to pay. Standards for value distinct from individual preferences are needed to make sense of the Aristotelian ideas of cultural excellence, liberal activities, and hierarchies of goods.

When modern public finance began to emerge in the 1940s and 1950s, much effort was devoted to drawing the proper boundary between the public and private sectors. A seminal thinker about this problem was Richard Musgrave.[18] Musgrave distinguished the public and private sectors in part on the basis of the distinction between public goods, such as military security, and private goods, such as apples. One person's consumption of a private good reduces the quantity available to others. Furthermore, the legal institution of private property enables one person to exclude others from consuming his private goods. In contrast, one person's enjoyment of a public good does not diminish another's ("nonrivalry"), and excluding some people from enjoying the good is difficult or impossible ("nonexclusion"). Government must determine the supply of public goods, according to Musgrave, because the market will undersupply them. In contrast, the market should determine the supply of private goods, because it can do so more efficiently than the government, although Musgrave allows that government may redistribute private goods for the sake of equality.

Musgrave noticed that the public-private distinction seemed to leave out an important class of goods that governments often supply, such as cultural events and liberal education. He described these as "merit goods," because they are valued by a cultural tradition that transcends individual preferences. Thus Musgrave opened a crack for excellence to slip into the debate over equality and liberty.

Merit goods require modification of the mathematical model at the core of

18. A symposium on Musgrave's ideas is in the edited volume by Brennan and Walsh (1990). For a complete bibliography of Musgrave's writings on this topic, see ibid., p. 252.

the economic theory of value, which provides insight into their character. The allocation of goods in the economy is represented by a vector $X = (X_1, X_2, \ldots, X_m)$. The degree to which the preferences of the ith individual are satisfied is indicated by the variable U_i, which is a function of the allocation of goods: $U_i = U_i(X)$. The preference satisfaction of all individuals $1, 2, \ldots, n$ in society is represented by all the utility functions denoted $(U_1, U_2, \ldots, U_n)$. According to conventional economic theory, a social ordering W is a function of the satisfaction of individual preferences: $W = W(U_1, U_2, \ldots, U_n)$. W is strictly individualistic in this formulation because its value depends exclusively on the level of individual satisfaction. According to the conventional conception, social choices should maximize a measure of value W that is reducible to individual values.

To represent irreducible social values, the social welfare function W must be modified so that it does not depend exclusively upon the satisfaction of individual preferences. If some goods have merit (or demerit) that is not merely due to their capacity to satisfy individual preferences, social welfare can be approximated better if these goods enter the social welfare function directly. Denote these goods $X_k \ldots X_m$. The revised social welfare function is rewritten in the form $W = W(U_1, U_2, \ldots, U_n; X_k \ldots X_m)$. Thus the satisfaction of individual preferences $U_1, U_2, \ldots, U_n$ receives weight, but merit goods $X_k \ldots X_m$ receive weight in their own right. The revised social welfare function W depends upon irreducible social values because it does not depend exclusively on individual values. By maximizing revised W, social decisions are guided by a weighted combination of individual and social values.

The next step is to apply calculus to derive the conditions for an optimal allocation of merit goods. According to these conditions, a private good or an ordinary public good should be supplied until the price people are willing to pay for it equals its cost of production. In contrast, the supply of a merit good must be increased beyond this point in order to reflect its irreducible social value. At the optimum, the cost of merit goods equals the sum of their irreducible social value and the amount people are willing to pay for them (Cooter 1990).

To illustrate the use of this formulation, consider an example from Mill (1950). Pleasures, in Mill's opinion, differ according to their quality. Thus poetry affords a higher quality of pleasure than pushpin (a mindless bar room game, the "pacman" of nineteenth-century England). Even if poetry yields the same quantity of pleasure to one person as pushpin yields to another, the former should receive more weight in the social calculus than the latter. For Mill, poetry is a merit good whose value exceeds some peoples' actual preferences for it. The implication, according to the mathematical formulation, is that resources should be allocated to producing poetry in excess of market demand. In fact, the production of poetry in most countries enjoys subsidies from a variety of public and private sources, especially through free education, whereas no one subsidizes pushpin.

The mathematics in effect defines merit goods by the fact that their value to society exceeds their value to individuals. Their intrinsic value tilts the optimal allocation of resources in their favor and calls for a subsidy. The subsidy is a wedge between the cost of a good and the amount people are willing to pay for it.

A wedge between cost and willingness to pay is not unusual in conventional economics, but merit is not the conventional cause. Rather, the conventional cause is the consumer's ignorance about the good's qualities, or the presence of externalities like pollution. These sources of market failure offer no challenge to individual values because the optimal size of the wedge can be computed in such circumstances by the standard techniques of cost benefit analysis. In contrast, the size of the appropriate wedge for merit goods cannot be computed by cost benefit techniques.

A MODEL OF AKRASIA[19]

The preceding formulation captures the idea that the intrinsic value of goods can exceed the amount people are willing to pay for them. Unfortunately, the formulation does not suggest how intrinsic value is determined. Is intrinsic value completely independent of individual preferences? If so, how can it express itself in observable behavior? Or does intrinsic value depend upon the preferences of privileged persons, such as the philosopher-king, the cultural elite, or the National Endowment for the Humanities?

To answer such questions, we will develop a formalization which is more adequate to the tradition of Aristotle. We will begin by considering a problem that arises when a person perceives that one activity is more worthwhile than another. The problem is that the person may be drawn to the less valuable activity in spite of his knowledge of its character. "Akrasia" is Aristotle's term for acting on impulse by choosing an activity that the decision maker knows to be less worthwhile than an available alternative.

The problem of akrasia is not one with which contemporary economic

---

19. This section draws explicitly upon Cooter (1991), and implicitly upon Schelling (1984a, 1984b, 1978, 1986), Elster (1979), Thaler and Shefrin (1981), and Simon (1990). The underlying problem of consistent decision over time draws upon Strotz (1956), Goldman (1980), von Weizsacker (1971), and Becker (1988).

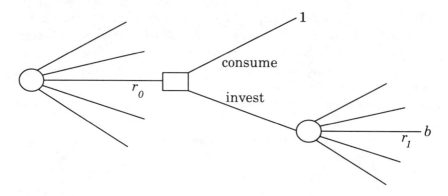

FIGURE 1: Decision tree.

theory finds it easy to deal. Decision makers in economic theory possess preferences and information. Rationality consists in making decisions that maximize
the expected satisfaction from available opportunities. This simple model of
decision making does not encompass conflicting motives. It has no scope for
tension between one desire and another. It offers no account of how or why a
person might vacillate between alternatives when deciding what to do, or regret
what he did.

We will try to formalize "akrasia" and apply our model to the problem of
choosing liberal actions. The simplest form of akrasia concerns the control of
impulses, such as the urge to overeat or drink to excess. Balancing immediate
impulses against future considerations is modeled in economics by time discounting. We model akrasia as time discounting and then extent the model to
cultural values.

The conflict between immediate impulse and future interests is reduced to
its simplest elements in the decision tree in figure 1. The decision-maker's
preferences toward futurity are probabilistic, depending upon mood and circumstances. At the first branching of the tree, the actor draws a subjective
discount rate, denoted r_0, from a probability distribution, denoted $p(r)$. At the
second branching, the decision maker chooses between consuming one unit or
investing it. After the decision to consume or invest is made, the decision
maker once again draws a discount rate r from the probability distribution
$p(r)$. Finally, the investment yields benefits b at the terminus of the decision
tree.

Figure 1 poses a dilemma because it is not clear what discount rate should be used when deciding whether to consume or invest. Economists beginning with Strotz have investigated the problem of consistency in preferences over time. General solutions have been proposed for problems involving "multiple selves." A simple representation seems best for our purposes, even though mathematical elaboration will, no doubt, reveal its implicit limitations.

One possibility is to act on impulse. An impulsive decision maker would compare the value of consumption to the present value of investment, which is computed using the discount rate r_0. Another possibility is to act on considered preferences. A prudent decision maker would compare the value of consumption to the possible future values of investment, which are computed using the possible discount rates r_1. The difference between the two ways of deciding will be characterized formally.

First we explain the calculation of an impulsive decision maker. The value of consumption equals 1 in figure 1. The present value of investment at the moment of choice in figure 1 is computed by using the actual discount rate r_0 that was drawn at the first branching of the tree:

$$PV(r_0) = b/r_0.$$

The amount by which the dollar value of consumption exceeds the present value of investment measures the strength of the impulse to consume, denoted M:

$$M(r_0) = 1 - PV(r_0).$$

An impulsive decision maker would follow this rule:

$$M(r_0) > 0 \quad <=> \quad \text{consume}$$
$$M(r_0) < 0 \quad <=> \quad \text{invest.}$$

Now we consider the calculation by a prudent decision maker who acts upon considered preferences. A prudent decision maker compares the value of consumption to the present value of investment as discounted at each of the possible rates r_1. To arrive at a single number for the present value of investment, the possible rates must be weighted and combined. A good way to proceed is to weight each discount rate r_1 by its probability. Proceeding in this way, we arrive at the following formulation for the expected present value of investment:

$$E[PV(r)] = \int p(r)PV(r)\,dr$$
$$= \int p(r)\,b/r\,dr.$$

The difference between the expected present value of investing and the dollar value of consuming measures the expected regret from consuming, denoted *ER:*

$$ER = E(PV) - 1.$$

A perfectly prudent decision maker would follow this rule:

$ER < 0$ $<=>$ consume
$ER > 0$ $<=>$ invest.

This rule instructs the decision maker to consume only if its value exceeds the expected present value of investing.

As explained, the decision maker may act on immediate preferences r_0, or the distribution of future preferences $p(r)$. The first decision rule gives all the weight to immediate impulse, and the second decision rule gives all the weight to considered preferences. Most decision makers give some weight to each. A little more formalization will allow us to characterize the weighting that a decision maker gives impulse satisfaction and expected regret.

Let the decision-maker's weighting of impulse and regret be represented by a decision function *U:*

$$U = U[M(r_0),ER].$$

Think of U as an ordinal preference function that is increasing in impulse satisfaction M and decreasing in expected regret ER. If the former is strong relative to the latter, the decision maker in figure 1 will consume. Otherwise he will invest.

For simplicity's sake, normalize U so that impulse prevails over deliberation for positive values, and vice versa for negative values:

$U > 0$ $<=>$ consume
$U < 0$ $<=>$ invest.

This decision rule is depicted in figure 2. The indifference curve $0 = U$ bisects the space into areas of consumption and investment. To interpret the graph, consider starting from any point on $0 = U$, such as (M_0,ER_0), and moving in various directions. A move to the northwest represents an increase in impulse satisfaction and a decrease in regret, so U increases. A move to the southeast represents less impulse satisfaction and more regret, so U decreases. A move up the indifference curve $0 = U$ represents an increase in impulse satisfaction and an offsetting increase in expected regret, so immediate behavior does not change.

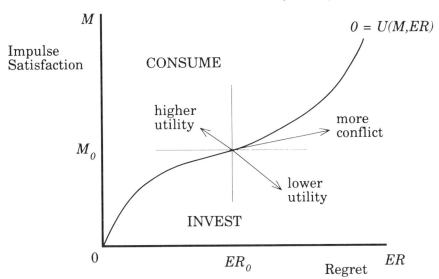

FIGURE 2: Weighting impulse and regret.

For each decision maker, there will be a tipping value of r_0, denoted r^*, which is defined by

$$0 = U[M(r^*),ER].$$

A particular decision maker with preference U will thus follow his impulse when he draws a discount rate r_0 such that $r_0 > r^*$, and he will follow his considered preferences when he draws a discount rate r_0 such that $r_0 < r^*$.

$r_0 > r^*$ $<=>$ consumes
$r_0 < r^*$ $<=>$ invests.

The tipping point r^* divides the probability distribution $p(r)$ into zones of consumption and investment, as illustrated in figure 3.

The value of r^* for a particular decision maker measures his strength of will. The higher is the value of r^*, the stronger is the will of the decision maker. When the decision maker's will is strong, the zone of consumption in figure 3 is small and the zone of investment is large.

Economics has long entertained the possibility of "preferences over preferences" (Lancaster 1958; Harsanyi 1955). We have in effect extended these models to include conflict between preferences. The model just presented departs from conventional economics by permitting the decision maker to recognize conflicting motives and to weigh them against each other. For example,

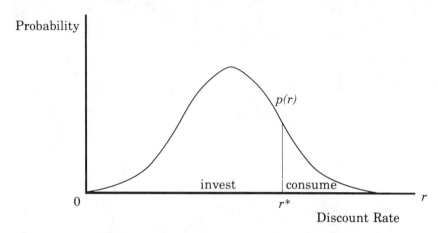

FIGURE 3. Probability of investment and consumption.

the decision maker may say to himself, "I feel like watching television, but it would be better to read a book." To make matters simple, we described his conflicting preferences as operating at distinct moments in time. He can recognize now that his current preferences may not be those he will have in the future. He can read the book tonight because he thinks he may regret having watched television instead.

ORGANIZING FOR EXCELLENCE

We have developed a model of akrasia in which an individual decision maker weighs his immediate impulse and his considered judgment. Our next task is to proceed from individual choice to collective choice and connect akrasia to theories of property and distribution. We will consider why cultural activities might be supported by political decisions, such as government subsidies, tax deductions for donations to the arts or the appreciated value of donated artworks, or laws like the California Art Preservation Act of 1980 that restrict the removal or destruction of artworks. We will argue that private donations to cultural activities, which provide subsidies for merit goods by decentralized, voluntary means, are less problematic in a democracy than state subsidies.

According to the Aristotelian tradition, the dominant principles of resource allocation in a democracy must be equality and liberty, but these principles will be diluted and modified in practice. Modification is required, first, because of their internal conflict due to the fact that freedom in the economic sphere naturally generates inequality. Second, preserving incentives for savings, investment, and risk-taking require unequal wealth. If resources were distributed equally, the incentive to work and invest would be lost, and everyone would become poorer.[20]

The concern of this chapter, however, is with a third reason for modifying democratic principles: the intrinsic superiority of some activities over others, which requires channeling resources to merit goods. Cultural excellence requires the subsidy of liberal activities by private donors or the state. To isolate this issue, we assume away most questions of incentives and focus upon pure rent. By definition, pure rent is income obtained purely from owning property. Our problem is to characterize mechanisms for allocating pure rents to achieve cultural excellence.

COLLECTIVE CHOICE BY IDENTICAL PEOPLE

We begin by considering the simple case in which everyone is alike. We assume that they have equal capacities for liberal and nonliberal activities and equal propensities to akrasia. There are no elites. In terms of the formal model, we are assuming that everyone has the same decision function U, so that r^* is the same for everyone. Furthermore, everyone is assumed to draw from the same probability distribution $p(r)$, so that everyone's expected consumption and investment is the same.

Under these assumptions, everyone would have an equal capacity to choose, and the individual himself would best know the circumstances under which he is acting. Consequently, democracy's principles of equality and liberty commend providing everyone with the means to pursue liberal activities and allowing everyone the liberty to choose his activities for himself. In such a society, there would still be reasons for deviating from the principles of liberty and equality on occasion. Some of these reasons have to do with the amount of economic resources necessary to carry on different activities. The theoretical mathematician needs a pencil, the violinist needs a violin, and the physicist needs a particle accelerator, so the resources that they receive cannot be equal.[21] The principles guiding this unequal division would need to be worked out.

Even under these assumptions, however, there is another reason for deviating from the central principles of a democracy, one that figures prominently in this article. People may wish to tilt the scales, or alter market prices, in favor of liberal activities. One way is by personal commitment. For example, the decision maker may decide not to buy a television, so that he cannot

20. See *Politics* 2.5.1263a–63b, 5.8.1309a.
21. See ibid., 3.12.1282b–83a.

succumb to the temptation to watch it. Or a person may wish to donate to the theater, so that tickets will be cheaper for everyone.

Personal commitments can be made without collective choice. Suppose, however, that some kinds of commitments can only be made collectively. For example, suppose that a town is considering whether to make cable television available to households. The town might exclude cable television altogether, or it might exclude culturally worthless programming. Similarly, it takes a collective decision to preserve the natural beauty of the California coastline or to create the artistic beauty of a renaissance Italian city. Choice is forced into the public domain in such cases because of increasing returns to scale, as in the case of cable television, or public merit goods, as in the case of the California coastline or the renaissance city. The technical consequences of increasing returns to scale and public goods have been extensively analyzed in microeconomics, and the political aspects of public sector behavior have been extensively analyzed in collective choice theory. Instead of recapitulating familiar theories, we turn to novel considerations raised by our model of akrasia.

The model of akrasia suggests that even a rational person occasionally experiences powerful impulses that can lead to future regret. Given this fact, the rational person provides in advance against occasions when dangerous impulses are strong. The classical example is Ulysses tying himself to the mast in order to resist the sirens' song. Game theorists describe such devises as "commitments." Collective choice can be a rational commitment on the part of individuals not to succumb to their worst impulses, as we will explain.

Suppose that most people prefer more worthwhile activities most of the time. In formal terms, the density of the probability function $p(r)$ in the region below r^* exceeds the density above r^*. Under that assumption, the conduct of the more worthwhile activities will win a majority in a vote. Taking choice away from individuals and relegating it to majority rule in these circumstances is a form of commitment to excellence. This kind of rationale could be given for the decision to subsidize education or theater. Everyone might want subsidies to overcome the impulses to scrimp on their children's education or to stay home and watch television.

This justification for collective action is premised upon the proposition that the average preferences of people are similar to their considered judgments. Collective choice in democratic assemblies is made by a process intended to produce considered judgment, such as public debate and the requirement of concurrence in two houses of the legislature. As Aristotle said, the many, of whom each individual is but an ordinary person, when they meet together may very likely be better than the few good, if regarded not individually but collectively, just as a feast to which many contribute is better than a dinner provided out of a single purse.[22]

This argument for collective choice has not been captured previously in formal economic theory. It is, however, similar to the well-known result that majority choices are superior to individual judgments when everyone agrees on the evaluative standards and everyone receives information with a random error term.

COLLECTIVE CHOICE BY DIFFERENT KINDS OF PEOPLE

The preceding argument assumed that everyone is like everyone else, including being susceptible to the same impulses. As long as this is true, everyone's considered judgment is the same, so collective choice will be unanimous and state subsidies involve no coercion of dissenters. Under these circumstances, state subsidies of worthwhile activities are a form of personal commitment.

A more difficult and realistic case is one in which peoples' considered judgments are different. In technical terms, we are assuming that people have different decision functions U, so they have different tipping points r^*. Under these assumptions, collective commitment differs from personal commitment. With personal commitment, a person's better self coerces his worse self. With collective commitment to merit goods and a heterogeneous population, some people's better selves coerce their own worse selves and other people.

People who insist that their cultural values are better than others' must advance such claims with great caution in a pluralistic democracy. To help us think about this difficult problem, let us imagine a society consisting of three classes. One class is a cultural elite, composed of people who have a superior capacity to engage in liberal activities. The second class is an economic elite, who have greater wealth and income-earning ability. We will assume that membership in these two groups does not overlap greatly, and that the two together comprise a minority of the population. Finally, the third class is the majority of citizens who are not distinguished by wealth or culture, but whose numbers gives them control over democratic politics. The three classes of people are the best, the rich, and the many. That was much the way Artistotle

22. Ibid., 3.11.1281a–1281b.

saw the world, or, for that matter, the way Jefferson described it in his letter to Adams.

One can describe the relationship among these three classes by drawing on the model of akrasia. People always tend to think that the activities that they like, do best, and best understand are the most important. The average citizen is likely to think that the most important activities are those familiar to him, activities which are within the reach of everybody. The rich are likely to think that the most important activities are those requiring personal wealth. Thus, as we have seen, the oligarches of earlier European society prized activities that require either a great deal of money or an upperclass education in one's early years. Similarly, those who spend their lives engaged in liberal activities will think them the most important.

In deciding what is worthwhile, three classes of people draw their preferences from three different distributions. The preferences anyone draws can diverge from the truly desirable, but members of the three groups are not equally likely to diverge, or to diverge in the same direction. To the extent that the best are true aristoi, the mean of the distribution from which they draw is closest to the truly desirable. The distribution from which the rich draw will deviate from the truly desirable in the direction of those activities that cost money. That of the majority will deviate in the direction of those activities familiar to everyone.

It is possible for each group to recognize its own proclivity to deviate and to correct its behavior accordingly. This possibility is suggested by Voltaire's report that the English gave Isaac Newton the funeral procession of a king, even though neither the poor who watched nor the rich who participated understood much about his discoveries. For the majority or the rich to choose to provide the correct support for liberal activities depends on its ability to recognize a bias in its own preferences. The disagreement between Jefferson and Adams concerns which group was most likely to make the correct political choices. Jefferson did not claim that virtue and wisdom coincide with the views of the majority, or Adams that they coincide with the views of the rich. Their disagreement concerned whether the majority or the rich were more likely to respect virtue and knowledge that they did not fully share.

Rather than trying to resolve this disagreement, we will consider some insights that our analysis offers into the institutional mechanisms by which cultural activities can best be supported. The majority, when it supports cultural activities, has two alternatives: to make voluntary contributions, or to enact public subsidies. Our analysis should make us aware of some perils of the latter alternative. Recall that the argument for state subsidies of cultural activities rested upon a personal commitment by citizens to excellence. A modern democracy provides many private means of personal commitment to excellence besides the state. Using state power to enforce such a commitment coerces minorities in a pluralistic democracy, whereas the private means are not coercive. The citizens of a pluralistic democracy should regard skeptically anyone who wants to enlist state power to extract support for cultural activities, not because all activities are equally worthwhile but because the state should maintain substantial neutrality toward alternative visions of worthwhile activities.

This skepticism should assume a characteristic form inspired by the economic framework for justifying public policy. Proponents of collective commitment should have the burden of proving a "market failure" that obstructs personal commitment. For example, such a demonstration might begin by proving the existence of increasing returns to the scale of commitment. Or the demonstration might proceed by proving that a certain class of merit goods also have the character of public goods.

It seems likely that many of the public subsidies for the arts cannot be defended on grounds of increasing returns to scale or the public character of merit goods. For example, poetry reading and symphonic music probably lack these characteristics. Consequently, there must be a presumption that these merit goods should be subsidized largely from private donations, in order to avoid coercion and corruption of purpose that plagues collective action.

After demonstrating a market failure, the next step in justifying collective action is to demonstrate that the incentive structure of the institutional form for implementing collective choice will serve excellence rather than merely transferring income to politically favored groups. In a democracy, the beneficiaries of public subsidies inevitably organize themselves as interest groups to maximize transfer payments. This is true of all three classes (rich, majority, aristoi), as evidenced by industrial subsidies, social security payments, or cultural subsidies. Collective provision of merit goods must be organized to avoid an incentive structure that rewards wasteful expenditures by the beneficiaries to increase their level of subsidy.

We have argued in favor of individual donations over taxes as a means of supporting cultural activities. Individual donors can support cultural activities in two distinctly different ways. One possibility is to contribute to current expenditures on particular activities. Another possibility is to create passive endowments for institutions such as universities and foundations. Our analysis shows that there is one great advantage to the latter alternative. Unlike hereditary elites, passively endowed organizations can have an internal structure designed to promote excellence over many generations. Consequently, the foundation for excellence in a democracy should be the endowment of private institutions dedicated to cultural activities.

CONCLUSION

The modern case for economic equality rests upon the belief that equal is fair. Opposed to it is the belief that exchange should be free and free exchange is efficient. Thus the modern debate about redistribution turns upon the ideals of equality, liberty, and efficiency. The ancient debate, however, focused more on cultural values. The best should have more, according to the ancient argument, for the sake of cultural excellence. We have tried to rethink the cultural argument for unearned income in order to situate it in a democratic society.

Cultural excellence exerts a continuing influence in a democracy, as evidenced by some current data on cultural subsidies in the United States. In 1987, 8% of American households contributed to charities in the category "arts, culture, and humanities," and 15% contributed to educational charities.[23] Furthermore, the endowment of institutions of higher education in the United States exceeded $50 billion in 1985–86.[24] Turning to the public sector, the National Foundation of Arts and Humanities had appropriations of $140 million in 1988.[25] The National Science Foundation had appropriations for research and related activities of $1,453 million in the same year.

The justification and critique of these expenditures must rely upon the cultural defense of unearned income. This defense requires a framework which recognizes that some activities are more worthwhile than others and acknowledges that organized interests drive democratic politics. We have tried to expand economic theory to provide such a framework by combining Aristotle's concept of akrasia with collective choice theory.

Our model of akrasia suggests how cultural excellence should be furthered in a democracy. First, personal commitment should be preferred to collective commitment. Personal commitment might take the form of donations and voluntary support for cultural organizations, as opposed to public subsidies from taxes. Unlike hereditary elites, passively endowed organizations can arrange their internal structure to promote excellence, and their success in doing so

23. United States, *Statistical Abstract* (1990b), table 619, p. 372.
24. Ibid., table 292, p. 315.
25. United States. 1990a. *Budget of the United States Fiscal Year 1990*, pp. 9–177.

will determine the extent to which they flourish in the competition for voluntary contributions.

Second, collective provision might be required in some circumstances. Proponents of collective provision of merit goods should have the burden of proving a ''market failure,'' which obstructs personal commitment or gives a public character to the merit goods in question. Having demonstrated a market failure, proponents should go to the next step of demonstrating that the incentive structure for implementing collective choice will serve excellence rather than transferring income to politically favored groups.

REFERENCES

Aristotle. 1941. Citations to Aristotle's *Metaphysics, Nicomachean Ethics, Politics,* and *Parts of Animals* are in a form found in any standard edition. Quotations are from *The Basic Works of Aristotle,* ed. Richard McKean. New York: Random House.

Becker, Gary S., and Kevin Murphy. ''A Theory of Rational Addiction.'' *Journal of Political Economy* 96 (1988): 675–700.

Bentham, Jeremy. 1948. *An Introduction to the Principles of Morals and Legislation.* New York: Hafner Publishing Co.

Brennan, Geoffrey, and Cliff Walsh, eds. 1990. *Rationality, Individualism, and Public Policy.* Canberra: Centre for Research on Federal Financial Relations, Australian National University.

Cooter, Robert D. 1990. ''Merit Goods: Some Thoughts on the Unthinkable,'' in *Rationality, Individualism, and Public Policy,* ed. Brennan and Walsh (see above).

Cooter, Robert D. 1991. ''Lapses, Conflict, and Akrasia in Torts and Crimes: Towards an Economic Theory of the Will.'' *International Review of Law and Economics* 11:149–164.

Cooter, Robert D., and Peter Rappoport. 1984. ''Were the Ordinalists Wrong about Welfare Economics?'' *Journal of Economic Literature* 22:507; reprinted in *Pioneers in Economics Section IV,* ed. Mark Blaug (Aldershot, England; Brookfield, Vt.: Edward Elgar Publishing Limited, in press). Comment by I. M. D. Little and reply by Cooter and Rappaport, *Journal of Economic Literature* 23 (1985): 1186, 1189.

Elias, Norbert. 1983. *The Court Society.* Trans. E. Japhcott. New York: Pantheon Books.

Ellickson, Robert C. 1989. ''Bringing Culture and Human Frailty to Rational Actors: A Critique of Classical Law-and-Economics.'' *Chicago-Kent Law Review* 65:23–55.

Elster, Jon. 1979. *Ulysses and the Sirens: Studies in Rationality and Irrationality.* Cambridge: Cambridge University Press.

Feld, Scott L., and Bernard Grofman. 1990. "Collectivities as Actors: Consistency of Collective Choices." *Rationality and Society* 2:429–48.

Frank, Robert. 1988. *Passions within Reason: The Strategic Role of the Emotions.* New York: Norton.

Goldman, Steven M. 1980. "Consistent Plans." *Revue of Economic Studies* 47: 533–37.

Harsanyi, J. C. 1953. "Cardinal Utility in Welfare Economics and in the Theory of Risk Taking." *Journal of Political Economy* 61:309–21.

———. 1955. "Cardinal Welfare, Individualistic Ethics, and Interpersonal Comparisons of Utility." *Journal of Political Economy* 63.

Heimer, Carol A. 1988. "Social Structure, Psychology, and the Estimation of Risk." *Annual Review of Sociology* 14:491–519.

Howe, John R., Jr. 1966. *The Changing Political Thought of John Adams.* Princeton: Princeton University Press.

Huang, Peter, and Ho-Mou Wu. 1992. "Emotional Responses in Litigation." *International Review of Law and Economics* 12:31–44.

Jefferson, Thomas. 1984. *Writings.* New York: Library of America.

Lancaster, K. 1958. "Welfare Propositions in Terms of Consistency and Extended Choice." *Economic Journal* 68.

Locke, John. 1823. *Essay on Human Understanding.* In *The Works of John Locke.* London.

Mill, John Stuart. 1950. Introd. A. D. Lindsay. "Utility." In *Utilitarianism, Liberty and Representative Government.* New York: E. P. Dutton, Everyman's Library.

Plato. 1937. *The Republic.* In *The Dialogs of Plato,* trans. B. Jowett. New York: Random House.

Pigou, A. C. 1932. *The Economics of Welfare.* London: Macmillan; New York: St. Martins's Press.

Rorty, Amelie. 1980. "Akrasia and Pleasure: Nicomachean Ethics Book 7." *Essays on Aristotle's Ethics.* Berkeley: University of California Press.

Schelling, Thomas. 1978. "Egonomics, or the Art of Self-Management." *68 American Economic Review Papers and Proceedings* 68:290–94.

———. 1984a. *Choice and Consequence.* Cambridge, Mass.: Harvard University Press.

———. 1984b. "Self-Command in Practice, in Policy, and in a Theory of Rational Choice." *74 American Economic Review* 74:1–11.

———. 1986. "Against Backsliding." Pp. 233–38 in *Development, Democracy, and the Art of Trespassing,* ed. Alejandro Foxley, Michael S. McPherson, and Guillermo O'Donnell. Notre Dame: University of Notre Dame Press.

Scott, Elizabeth. 1990. "Rational Decisionmaking about Marriage and Divorce." *Virginia Law Review* 76:9–94.

Simon, Julian L. 1990. "The Theory of Binding Commitments Simplified and Extended, with Generalization to Interpersonal Allocation.'' *Rationality and Society* 2:255–86.

Strotz, R. H. 1956. ''Myopia and Inconsistency in Dynamic Utility Maximization.'' *Revue of Economic Studies* 23.

Thaler, Richard H., and H. M. Shefrin. 1981. ''An Economic Theory of Self-Control.'' *89 Journal of Political Economy* 89:392–406.

Tobin, James. 1970. ''On Limiting the Domain of Inequality.'' *Journal of Law and Economics* 13:263–77.

United States. 1990a. *Budget of the United States Fiscal Year 1990.* Washington, D.C.: Government Printing Office.

———. 1990b. *Statistical Abstract of the United States, 1990.* Washington, D.C.: Government Printing Office.

Veblen, Thorstein. 1919. *The Theory of the Leisure Class.* New York: B. W. Huebach.

von Weizsacker, Carl. 1971. ''Notes on Endogenous Changes of Tastes,'' *Journal of Economic Theory* 3:345–72.

Winston, Gordon C. 1980. ''Addiction and Backsliding: A Theory of Compulsive Consumption.'' 1 Journal of Economic Behavior and Organization 1:295–324.

Contributors

Robert D. Cooter
School of Law
University of California, Berkeley
Berkeley, CA 94720

Robin Cowan
Department of Economics
University of Western Ontario
London, Ontario N6A 5C2
Canada

James Gordley
School of Law
University of California, Berkeley
Berkeley, CA 94720

Peter J. Hammond
Department of Economics
Stanford University
Stanford, CA 94305

Israel M. Kirzner
Department of Economics
New York University
New York, NY 10003

Eric Mack
Department of Philosophy
Tulane University
New Orleans, LA 70118

Jan Narveson
Department of Philosophy
University of Waterloo
Waterloo, Ontario N2L 3G1
Canada

Mario J. Rizzo
Department of Economics
New York University
New York, NY 10003

Index

accidental profits, 16
acquisition, 11–12
action theory, 15
Adams, John, 154
advantage, 77–78, 125
adverse selection, 103
aggregate production efficiency, 93, 104–7
Akerlof, G., 103
akrasia, 161–66, 168, 170, 172
Allais, M., 110
abitrage theory, 37–38, 41, 44–46
aristocracies, 153
Aristotelian philosophy, 150–56
Arrow, K., 100, 110
asymmetric information, 88, 113
   incentive constraints and, 94–95, 102–3,
      108

Bauer, P. T., 14
beauty contest, 51–53, 62–64, 85
Bentham, J., 158–59
Bergstrom, T., 97
Blackorby, C., 9

capital suppliers, 81–84, 93
charity, 73, 172. *See also* cultural excellence; welfare economics
choice models, 167–72
   akrasia, 161–66, 168, 170, 172
Cicero, 88, 113–14
Clark, J. B., 27–28, 30, 34
collective choice models, 167–72
commitment to cultural excellence, 167–72
commodity taxes, 105, 114
complete markets, 109–10
confiscation of property, 7
confiscation of rents, 19, 126, 129, 133–36
consequentialist ethics, 5, 6–9
consumer judgment, 84–85
consumer sovereignty, 89
consumption expenditures, 114–15
contingent commodities, 108
contracts, 109
convergence to equilibrium, 111
cooperation, 58, 126n
cooperative surplus, 136–39

Cooter, R., 19, 150–73
cost of production theories of value, 137–39
creation, 15–17
creativity, and entrepreneurial profit, 41,
   44–47. *See also* discovery
cultural excellence
   Artistotelian ideas, 150–56
   collective choice models, 167–72
   state or private subsidies, 166–72
   See also merit goods

Debreu, G., 108, 110
decision making. *See* choice models
decision theory, 158
democracy
   cultural elites and, 152
   resource allocation principles, 166–67
deontological ethics, 5, 9–14, 56–57
desert, 19, 48
   consumers and, 84–85
   effort and, 51
   entitlement and, 49–54, 60–61, 79–80
   Labor Theory of Value, 80–83
   natural qualities and, 61–65
   of profits, 73–79, 86
   Rawls on, 65–68
   rights and, 49–50, 59
   as value concept, 50, 55, 86
   See also distributive justice
Deserving (Sher), 49
deserving. *See* desert
Diamond, P., 95, 105, 107, 110
dictatorship, Pareto efficiency of, 97
disclosure, 10
discovery, 15–17, 39–48
   distributive justice and, 46–47
   perfect competition model, 132
disequilibrium, 31–32, 35, 41–42. *See also*
   equilibrium
distributive justice, 90
   confiscation of economic rents, 133–36
   created or discovered gains and, 46–47
   efficiency and, 99–102
   gains from profit redistribution, 114
   liberty and, 116
   markets and, 103–4

179